TRAVELER

A SMALL KEY
OPENS
BIG DOORS

50 YEARS OF AMAZING
PEACE CORPS STORIES

VOLUME THREE: THE HEART OF EURASIA

Edited by

JAY CHEN

Series Editor
JANE ALBRITTON

Travelers' Tales
An Imprint of Solas House, Inc.
Palo Alto

Travelers' Tales and *Solas House* are trademarks of Solas House, Inc. 853 Alma Street, Palo Alto, California 94301. www.travelerstales.com

Cover Design: Chris Richardson
Interior Layout: Howie Severson
Production Director: Susan Brady

Library of Congress Cataloging-in-Publication Data

A small key opens big doors : 50 years of amazing Peace Corps stories / edited by Jay Chen.

    p. cm. -- (The heart of Eurasia ; v. 3)
  ISBN 978-1-60952-003-8 (pbk.)
 1. Peace Corps (U.S.)--History. I. Chen, Jay.
 HC60.5.S57 2011
 361.6--dc23

                    2011026698

First Edition
Printed in the United States
10 9 8 7 6 5 4 3 2 1

*To the Volunteers in Eurasia who understood
their presence and struggled to serve
and to the locals that let them.*

Table of Contents

Part One
ON OUR WAY...AND BACK AGAIN

Part Two
WHY ARE WE HERE?

Part Three
GETTING THROUGH THE DAYS

Part Five
SUSTAINABLE PEACE

Series Preface

THERE ARE SOME BABY IDEAS THAT SEEM TO FLY IN BY STORK, without incubation between conception and birth. These magical bundles smile and say: "Want me?" And well before the head can weigh the merits of taking in the unsummoned arrival, the heart leaps forward and answers, "Yes!"

The idea for Peace Corps @ 50—the anniversary media project for which this series of books is the centerpiece—arrived on my mental doorstep in just this way in 2007. Four books of stories, divided by regions of the world, written by the Peace Corps Volunteers who have lived and worked there. There was time to solicit the stories, launch the website, and locate editors for each book. By 2011, the 50th anniversary of the founding of the Peace Corps, the books would be released.

The website had no sooner gone live when the stories started rolling in. And now, after four years and with a publisher able to see the promise and value of this project, here we are, ready to share more than 200 stories of our encounters with people and places far from home.

In the beginning, I had no idea what to expect from a call for stories. Now, at the other end of this journey, I have read every story, and I know what makes our big collection such a fitting tribute to the Peace Corps experience.

Peace Corps Volunteers write. We write a lot. Most of us need to, because writing is the only chance we have to say things in our native language. Functioning every day in another language takes work, and it isn't just about grammar. It's everything that isn't taught—like when to say what depending on the context, like the intricate system of body language, and like knowing how to shift your tone depending on the company you are in. These struggles and linguistic mishaps can be frustrating and often provoke laughter, even if people are forgiving and appreciate the effort. It takes a long time to earn a sense of belonging.

And so in our quiet moments—when we slip into a private space away from the worlds where we are guests—we write. And in these moments where we treat ourselves to our own language, thoughts flow freely. We once wrote only journals and letters; today we also text, email, and blog.

Writing helps us work through the frustrations of everyday living in cultures where—at first—we do not know the rules or understand the values. In our own language we write out our loneliness, our fury, our joy, and our revelations. Every volunteer who has ever served writes as a personal exercise in coming to terms with an awakening ignorance. And then we write our way through it, making our new worlds part of ourselves in our own language, in our own words.

The stories in these books are the best contribution we can make to the permanent record of Peace Corps on the occasion of its 50th anniversary. And because a Volunteer's attempt to explain the experience has always contained the hope that folks at home will "get it," these stories are also a gift to anyone eager and curious to learn what we learned about living in places that always exceeded what we imagined them to be.

It has been an honor to receive and read these stories. Taken together, they provide a kaleidoscopic view of world cultures—beautiful and strange—that shift and rattle when held up to the light.

I would like to acknowledge personally the more than 200 Return Volunteers who contributed to these four volumes. Without their voices, this project could not have been possible. Additionally, editors Pat and Bernie Alter, Aaron Barlow, and Jay Chen have been tireless in shepherding their stories through the publishing process and in helping me make my way through some vexing terrain along the way. Special thanks to John Coyne whose introduction sets the stage for each volume. Thanks also to Dennis Cordell for his early work on the project.

There are two people critical to the success of this project who were never Peace Corps volunteers, but who instantly grasped the significance of the project: Chris Richardson and Susan Brady.

Chris and his PushIQ team, created a visually lush, technically elegant website that was up and ready to invite contributors to join the project and to herald both the project and the anniversary itself. He took on the creative challenge of designing four distinct covers for the four volumes in this set. His work first invited our contributors and now invites our readers.

Susan Brady brought it all home. It is one thing to collect, edit, and admire four books' worth of stories; it is another to get them organized, to the typesetter, the printer, and the team of marketers on time and looking good. Susan's good sense, extensive publishing experience, and belief in the worthiness of this project sealed the publishing deal with Travelers' Tales/ Solas House.

Finally, there are the two others, one at each elbow, who kept me upright when the making of books made me weary. My mother—intrepid traveler and keeper of stories—died four months after the project launched, but she has been kind enough to hang around to see me through. My partner, cultural anthropologist Kate Browne, never let me forget that if Americans are ever going to have an honored place in this world, we need to have some clue about how the rest of it works. "So get with it," they said. "The 50th anniversary happens only once."

—JANE ALBRITTON
FORT COLLINS, COLORADO

✳
✳ ✳

Thirty Days That Built the Peace Corps

JOHN COYNE

In 1961 John F. Kennedy took two risky and conflicting initiatives in the Third World. One was to send 500 additional military advisers into South Vietnam. The other was to send 500 young Americans to teach in the schools and work in the fields of eight developing countries. These were Peace Corps Volunteers. By 1963 there would be 7,000 of them in forty-four countries.

—*Garard T. Rice,* The Bold Experiment: JFK's Peace Corps

KENNEDY'S SECOND INITIATIVE INSPIRED, AND CONTINUES TO inspire, hope and understanding among Americans and the rest of the world. In a very real sense, the Peace Corps is Kennedy's most affirmative and enduring legacy that belongs to a particularly American yearning: the search for a new frontier.

Two key people in Congress, Henry Reuss (D-Wisconsin) and Hubert Humphrey (D-Minnesota), both proposed the idea of the Peace Corps in the late 1950s.

In January of 1960, Reuss introduced the first Peace Corps-type legislation. It sought a study of "the advisability and practicability to the establishment of a Point Four Youth Corps," which would send young Americans willing to serve their country in public and private technical assistance missions in far-off countries, and at a soldier's pay.

The government contract was won by Maurice (Maury) L. Albertson of Colorado State University who with one extraordinary assistant, Pauline Birky-Kreutzer, did the early groundwork for Congress on the whole idea of young Americans going overseas, not to win wars, but help build societies.

In June of 1960, Hubert Humphrey introduced in the Senate a bill to send "young men to assist the peoples of the underdeveloped areas of the world to combat poverty, disease, illiteracy, and hunger."

Also in 1960, several other people were expressing support for such a concept: General James Gavin; Chester Bowles, former governor of Connecticut, and later ambassador to India; William Douglas, associate justice of the Supreme Count; James Reston of *The New York Times;* Milton Shapp, from Philadelphia; Walt Rostow of MIT; and Senator Jacob Javits of New York, who urged Republican presidential candidate Richard Nixon to adopt the idea. Nixon refused. He saw the Peace Corps as just another form of "draft evasion."

What Nixon could not have foreseen was that a "day of destiny" waited for the world on October 14, 1960. On the steps of the Student Union at the University of Michigan, in the darkness of the night, the Peace Corps became more than a dream. Ten thousand students waited for presidential candidate Kennedy until 2 A.M., and they chanted his name as he climbed those steps.

Kennedy launched into an extemporaneous address. He challenged them, asking how many would be prepared to give years of their lives working in Asia, Africa, and Latin America?

The audience went wild. (I know this, because at the time I was a new graduate student over in Kalamazoo. I was working part-time as a news reporter for WKLZ and had gone to cover the event.)

Six days before the 1960 election, on November 2nd, Kennedy gave a speech at the Cow Palace in San Francisco. He pointed out that 70 percent of all new Foreign Service officers had no foreign language skills whatsoever; only three of the forty-four Americans in the embassy in Belgrade spoke Yugoslavian; not a single American in New Delhi could speak Indian dialects, and only two of the nine ambassadors in the Middle East spoke Arabic. Kennedy also pointed out that there were only twenty-six black officers in the entire Foreign Service corps, less than 1 percent.

Kennedy's confidence in proposing a "peace corps" at the end of his campaign was bolstered by news that students in the Big Ten universities and other colleges throughout Michigan had circulated a petition urging the founding of such an organization. The idea had caught fire in something like spontaneous combustion.

The day after his inauguration, President Kennedy telephoned his brother-in-law Sargent Shriver and asked him to form a presidential task force to report how the Peace Corps should be organized and then to organize it. When he heard from Kennedy, Shriver immediately called Harris Wofford.

At the time, Shriver was 44; Wofford was 34. Initially, the Task Force consisted solely of the two men, sitting in a suite of two rooms that they had rented at the Mayflower Hotel in Washington, D.C. They spent most of their time making calls to personal friends they thought might be helpful.

One name led to another: Gordon Boyce, president of the Experiment in International Living; Albert Sims of the Institute of International Education; Adam Yarmolinsky, a foundation executive; Father Theodore Hesburgh, president of the University of Notre Dame; George Carter, a campaign worker on civil rights issues and former member of the American Society for African Culture; Louis Martin, a newspaper editor; Franklin Williams, an organizer of the campaign for black voter registration, and a student of Africa; and Maury Albertson, out at Colorado State University.

Unbeknownst to Shriver and Wofford, two officials in the Far Eastern division of the International Cooperation Administration (ICA) were working on their own Peace Corps plan. Warren Wiggins, who was the deputy director of Far Eastern operations in ICA, was still in his thirties but had already helped administer the Marshall Plan in Western Europe. He was totally dissatisfied with the manner in which American overseas programs were run; he called them "golden ghettos." With Wiggins was Bill Josephson, just 26, and a lawyer at ICA.

They started developing an idea that would be limited to sending young Americans overseas to teach English. But as they worked on it, their vision broadened. The paper detailing their recommendations was titled "A Towering Task." They sent copies to Wofford, Richard Goodwin at the White House, and to Shriver, who thought it was brilliant and immediately sent a telegram to Wiggins inviting him to attend the Task Force meeting the next morning. It was Wiggins who advocated initiating the Peace Corps with "several thousand Americans participating in the first twelve to eighteen months." A slow and cautious beginning was not an option.

Three times in February, Kennedy would telephone Shriver to ask about progress on the Peace Corps. The final draft of the report was created with Charles Nelson sitting in one room writing basic copy, Josephson sitting in another room rewriting it, Wofford sitting in yet another room doing the final rewrite, and Wiggins running back and forth carrying pieces of paper.

Shriver held the position that Peace—not Development, it might be noted—was the overriding purpose, and the process of promoting it was necessarily complex. So the Peace Corps should learn to live with complexity that could not be summed up in a single proposition. Finally, the Task Force agreed on three.

- Goal One: It can contribute to the development of critical countries and regions.
- Goal Two: It can promote international cooperation and goodwill toward this country.
- Goal Three: It can also contribute to the education of America and to more intelligent American participation in the world.

On the morning of Friday, February 24, 1961, Shriver delivered the report—the Peace Corps Magna Carta—to Kennedy and told him: "If you decide to go ahead, we can be in business Monday morning."

It had taken Shriver, Wofford, Wiggins, Josephson, and the other members of the Mayflower Task Force, less than a month to create what *TIME Magazine* would call that year "the greatest single success the Kennedy administration had produced." On March 1, 1961, President Kennedy issued an Executive Order establishing the Peace Corps.

And today, fifty years later, we are still debating what the Peace Corps is all about. As Sarge Shriver thought all those years ago, "the tension between competing purposes is creative, and it should continue."

Well, it has!

John Coyne, who is considered an authority on the history of the Peace Corps, has written or edited over twenty-five books. In 1987 he started the newsletter RPCV Writers & Readers that is for and about Peace Corps writers. This newsletter, now a website, can be found today at PeaceCorpsWorldwide.org.

Introduction

Eastern Europe and Central Asia are not typically places people think of when they hear about the Peace Corps. The mention of the Peace Corps tends to evoke images of young, bright-eyed Americans working in Third World continents like Africa. Those familiar with the history of the Peace Corps know that it was actually Eastern Europe and Central Asia, then under the flag of the Soviet Union, that drove the creation of the Peace Corps. In the midst of the Cold War in 1960, President Kennedy pointed out that in the Soviet republics were "hundreds of men and women, scientists, physicists, teachers, engineers, doctors, nurses...prepared to spend their lives abroad in the service of world communism." To counter this, the United States needed to train its young men and women, to be "ambassadors of peace," and to "serve the cause of freedom." While the Peace Corps was initially unable to pierce the heart of Eurasia because of the Iron Curtain, the fall of the Soviet Union three decades later saw Volunteers working side by side with locals in newly independent republics that had been considered a threat to global stability just a few years earlier.

Volunteers who come to serve in the region find a peculiar juxtaposition of Soviet civilization built upon the ancient cultural landscape of Turkestan, which once stretched from Siberia in the north to Iran in the south. Dating back as far as the third millennium B.C., Turkestan covered most of the Silk Road, and was the center of cultural diffusion between the East and the West—over time seeing the influence of the Huns, Chinese, Arabs, Turks, Mongols, Tartars, Persians, and finally the Russians. Within this historical landscape, Volunteers across Eastern Europe and Central Asia find people who speak both Russian and their native languages, cookie-cutter concrete Soviet apartment buildings built next to centuries-old mosques, and railway systems lain across the same grasslands where nomadic herders grazed their sheep. Discovering the new and the old in a land once forbidden to Americans, Volunteers find that Eurasia is a land of contradictions and juxtapositions.

Sometimes those juxtapositions follow us back to the United States. As the most recent returned Volunteer of the four editors in this series, the feeling of being an alien in my own country after spending three years abroad in Kazakhstan is still fresh in my memory. With barely a month between my return and the start of law school, I found it impossible to square my former identity as a university English teacher in Kazakhstan with my new identity as a law student in the United States. No longer was I teaching English to 500-plus students and working with fellow faculty members on community projects; instead I found myself spending hours in the library, reading indecipherable legal cases and being thrust into the hyper-competitive madness of a first-year law student's life. Finding other people who understood the experience of working before law school was already difficult, much less working in a developing country. The stress of transition as well as law school and its arbitrary standards of self-worth often caused me to gloss over the value of the experiences I had in Kazakhstan. Was it worth it, I would ask myself, putting myself three years "behind" by electing to volunteer instead of going directly to law school from undergraduate study like so many of my peers?

Going through the stories in this volume and seeing the struggles and triumphs of fifty years' worth of Volunteers from the region was therapeutic for me, and it put much of my work in Kazakhstan in context. I am honored to have had the opportunity to edit these stories and reflect upon them. The theme running through this volume is common to all Peace Corps stories: While we may not have saved the world like many of us thought we would, each of us did our best to make it a better place and found local people who shared those beliefs. What little we accomplished in those two to three years may seem miniscule in our overall impact on the direction of the country, but as I learned through these stories, the value and impact of our work often cannot be understood until several years, sometimes decades later.

Today, I still hear from many of my former students and colleagues, as many have gone on to become successful English teachers in Kazakhstan and translators for international firms. Others received grants to pursue higher education abroad. The earnestness with which my students approached me in my last year, when they asked how they could start a Kazakhstani Peace Corps so that they could also do their part for the world, gave me hope that while I may not have made significant lasting change myself, I have at least planted some seeds for such change. I look forward to hearing what they will go on to accomplish.

We Peace Corps Volunteers came to the heart of Eurasia for various reasons—some for patriotism, some for adventure, some for friendship, some for peace. The stories in this volume by no means claim a full understanding of the people or the cultures in the countries that we served, but they do document the effort spent to understand our roles as American volunteers in lands that experienced more political turmoil in a span of a few years than we would ever see in a lifetime. We came to show that American foreign affairs also came through peaceful means, not just military action. We were Kennedy's "Ambassadors of Peace," and in that effort, we built relationships and bridged cultural divides with those that we once as a nation considered enemies. After two decades of work in the former Soviet Union and five decades Peace Corps work in total, it turns out that we too, are from a land of contradictions and juxtapositions.

—JAY CHEN
SAN FRANCISCO, CALIFORNIA

PART ONE

ON OUR WAY...
AND BACK AGAIN

✦
✱   ✱

September 12th

In the days following the fall of the World Trade Center towers,
Volunteers found that locals often knew more about it than they did.

THIS MORNING BEFORE CLASS STARTS, BOLORMAA ASKS ME IF I
have seen the news on Mongolian National TV. She says
"New York" and points to the words "mafia," "airplane,"
and "dangerous" in the Mongolian-English dictionary that
she always carries. As usual, I can't fully comprehend what
she is talking about. There must have been some report about
the airports in New York or something. I have been living in Bayandelger for only two weeks, and my grasp of the
Mongolian language is greatly lacking in comprehension ability. It seems like she is saying that there is a war in New York
and that no one can leave or go to New York. It doesn't make
any sense to me. From what I understand, she is talking about
a "dangerous airplane war" in New York. She is drawing
rectangles and airplanes on my lesson plan paper and gesturing
wildly with her hands.

I nod and chalk it up to my horrible Mongolian language skills. Why didn't I work harder during the six-week
Mongolian language classes we attended during training? I

3

should have paid more attention. But if something bad had really happened, I would definitely have heard from Peace Corps or from my family, even though I'm not sure exactly how they would contact me. I tell Bolormaa that I will see her later, and then I teach my fifth-grade class how to express likes and dislikes. "I like apples. I don't like oranges."

After teaching, I head back to my *ger*. On the way, Gerlee, one of the *jijurs,* which is like a janitor, at the hotel/bank/ office building/bar stops me in the road and asks me if I have seen the news. She is rambling off in Mongolian. I nod to her, but the only thing that I comprehend is the phrase, "*New York mohai.*" *Mohai* is an ambiguous, slightly overused Mongolian word that means "dirty" or "very bad." If you spill something on your floor, it's *mohai.* If your clothes are wrinkled, they're *mohai.* If someone drinks too much vodka and dies of liver disease, it's *mohai.* If a student talks back to a teacher in school, they're *mohai.* Now this makes more sense. There must have been something on the news talking about all of the garbage and litter on the streets of New York City. I agree with Gerlee that New York is indeed *mohai.*

Back in my *ger,* I eat some bread with jam and wonder what could have been on the news last night. Baatar comes in. I think he is asking about my family in New York. *"Ger bul san oo?"* How is your family? But he is making wild gestures with his hands. He grabs the dictionary off the desk and points to the words, "death" then the flipping of pages, "destruction" and finally "annihilation." In between, he keeps saying the words New York and asking, *"ger bul san oo?"* I understand him saying that the news will be on at 6 P.M. Someone calls him from outside, and he leaves. My mind is swirling with confusion and bewilderment.

I tell myself that the language barrier is making this seem much worse than it is. Litter in the streets or a dangerous airplane war causing death and destruction in New York? It makes no sense to me, and again if something crazy is really going on, I am sure that I will hear something from Peace Corps.

I am still hungry and decide to fry an egg. It's warm today, and I leave my *ger* door open so that I can sit and look at the sheep grazing on the mountainside. I tell myself that I'll put all of this bewilderment out of my mind and stay busy until six when I can watch the news. Some of the men in the village are helping Baatar build a *haasha,* a fence, around my *ger*. It will keep wind, cows, dogs and horses from going bump against my *ger* in the dead of the night. But I will miss the open views of the steppe all around me.

I hear the men chattering away in Mongolian and laughing. I hear dogs barking in the distance and children in front of the school laughing. My egg is frying. Then I hear Batuya shouting, one of the men runs into my *ger* and pulls me outside by the arm. Everyone is shouting. Batuya points to the small wooden house across the road that serves as the village's post office. Hanging outside the post office door wearing a bright purple *deel* is Tuya, the post office lady. She is waving frantically to me. I have a phone call, my first phone call in Bayandelger.

My knees are turning to jelly as I am walking. Should I be running? What is happening? A phone call. Will I get to the phone only to be told that there really is death and destruction in New York City? Did something happen to someone in my family?

Inside the tiny, one-room post office Tuya ushers me into a little yellow phone booth in the corner. It looks like a closet with a small glass window on the front. The phone inside is off-white, and it has no dial or buttons. I can see Tuya nodding to me and saying something through the glass window. My hand is shaking as I pick up the phone. I can only hear static. Then I hear Tuya's voice clearly and some clicking sounds and I wait. Finally I faintly begin to hear the voice of Enketuya, one of the administrative officers at the Peace Corps office in Ulaanbaatar.

She sounds like she is yelling, but I can barely hear her. She asks me if I have heard about the "incidents" in New York City and in Washington, D.C. I don't know what to say. She says that she is going to read a bulletin from the State Department. I hear static. Someone outside is trying to start an old motorcycle. "Access to New York City and Washington, D.C. is restricted." Someone is hammering something. "...bridges and tunnels are shut down...Pentagon...Americans abroad should keep a low profile."

I ask Enketuya to tell me what happened. She says that she can't hear me. She asks me if I have heard from my family in New York. I am screaming, but Enketuya says that she cannot hear me, but that she will contact my family and call me back. She said something else, asked a question I think, but the phone line is dead. Scared and baffled I stand in the little yellow phone booth clutching the buttonless, dialess phone.

The post office lady is saying something to me. She is asking me what is going on and what happened, but I cannot answer her. I have no answers.

Back toward my *haasha*, it seems like the whole village is standing in front of my *ger*. They want to know what the phone call was about. Everyone is in my *ger*, and I step inside and sit on the bed. Someone has turned off the wok and set the egg on a plate. Someone says that they saw the news last night and that it was *"mohai."* Someone else points to "terrible" in the dictionary. My head is in a fog. I don't know what is going on. What could cause all of this? And now something is going on in Washington, D.C., too? Is what's happening affecting my family?

I try to stay calm by walking. I want to stay close to the post office for Enketuya to call me back. And until 6 P.M. when the news comes on again. Some of my students run up to me and tell me that I have a phone call at the post office.

Inside the phone booth the connection this time is a little better. Enketuya tells me that she has a message from my mother, "...family is fine including Aunt Meryl who works.... Please don't worry. We are fine." Enketuya says that she has many other calls to make and hangs up the phone before I can ask her to explain what is going on. I have only one current thought about my family being O.K.: I am so relieved. But on the way back to my *ger* another thought starts to creep up on me. Aunt Meryl? Why Aunt Meryl and not the dozens of other family members that live in New York? I have so much family in New York.

In and out people come to my *ger* to ask about my family and about New York. At least now I can say *"Minnie ger bul san."* My family is O.K. They drink tea and eat candy and talk about what they saw on the news or heard on the radio. They point to the words, "bandits," "airplane" and "death" in the dictionary.

Bolormaa comes to my *ger* to tell me that I should come to her house by five to watch the news and to make croutons. Last week she came to my *ger*, and I had a bowl of Campbell's ABC soup with some croutons that I shared with her. She had never had croutons before and wants to know how to make them.

Since she speaks a little bit of English, I try again to ask her what happened in New York. She takes out paper and a dictionary. She draws rectangles and airplanes again. She is saying something about buildings. Are the rectangles buildings? It sounds like something blew up. I point to the word "bomb" in my English-Mongolian dictionary. Bolormaa shakes her head no and points to the word "airplane" in her Mongolian-English dictionary. It makes no sense to me, an airplane crashed in New York or in Washington and caused so much damage that Peace Corps needs to call me and tell me to keep a low profile? An airplane crash affected my family in Queens, Aunt Meryl in Brooklyn, and the Pentagon in Washington, D.C.?

At 4:40 P.M. I walk to Bolormaa's. She lives in a small blue-and-white concrete house with three rooms and a small kitchen. I have bought some leftover stale bread for the croutons. She has an old black-and-white TV with the kind of staticky reception that one gets in a tiny village. While we make croutons and mutton soup, Bolormaa's husband tries to adjust the TV antenna.

At 6 P.M. the nightly Mongolian national newscast comes on, and the first thing the newscaster says is about New York. I can only understand the words "New York" being said. He is talking so fast. Then on Bolormaa's fuzzy, black-and-white TV, I see New York City. It looks like downtown. There's smoke everywhere. People are screaming and running. Some of them look like they are covered in blood. People are running away from the smoke. I am almost waiting for Godzilla to step out of the smoke. Then I see the World Trade Center, those two beautiful, silvery gray, shiny towers, but they look like they might be on fire, but I really can't tell because the Mongolian news is cutting back and forth so much.

Then I could have almost sworn that they showed an airplane crashing into the North Tower and going right through the South Tower, but the TV is so fuzzy. Bolormaa's husband is messing with the antenna and Bolormaa turns up the volume. Is this a movie? They must be talking about a movie. I'm not even watching the news. I'm watching a movie. Something is wrong. I know that something is very wrong because through the fuzzy black and white snow on Bolormaa's TV, I think that

I am seeing the twin towers crumble and fall down, disappearing into a cloud of smoke. Faintly underneath the Mongolian newsman's voice I think I hear Bernard Shaw say, "destroyed by a large-scale terrorist attack."

I don't know where I am or what is happening. Am I in Mongolia, making croutons and watching the Twin Towers crumble and fall down? Bolormaa is writing the number 200,000 and saying the word "people" and pointing to the word "death" in her dictionary. Bolormaa's husband is shaking his head and asking me questions, but I can't understand. I have only two clear thoughts, the clarity of my mother's message about my Aunt Meryl, my only relative who works at Solomon, Smith & Barney located at 7 World Trade Center and the urgent need to get to Ulaanbaatar.

This same day my grandmother is in her apartment in Brooklyn, sitting in her reclining chair dictating a letter to the home attendant who comes every day to wash and feed her.

9-12-01

Hello, Dara,

How are you? I received your letter, and photograph, they are lovely. I am happy that you are enjoying your stay and you are coping very well.

We had a terrorist attack on our country, we lost the World Trade Center and a lot of lives. It was a terrible thing to see. I saw it on TV. It was very nice for you to call to see how we were. It is like the book I used to read to you, *It Could Be Worse.*

I love you and God will take care of all of us. Stay well.

Love,
Granny

Dara Ross was the first African-American Peace Corps Volunteer to serve in Mongolia, M-12, from 2001-03. She is now an English teacher at the Brooklyn International High School, living in Harlem with her adorable husband Tim who served in the Peace Corps in El Salvador.

DIANA J. LAVIOLETTE

*

Peace Corps Expectations

*How a girl from the Midwest came to love eating
white cheese and olives for breakfast.*

As a teenager, I listened to President Kennedy's speech inviting us to ask ourselves what we could do for our country. I was young and inexperienced, but he inspired me and caused me to hold on to a dream that I would some day serve my country. After college and two years of high school teaching in Kansas City, I knew what I wanted to do: join the Peace Corps and carry American values and talent to remote corners of the world. The fact that I had limited talent or international understanding mattered little at the time.

On my application, I asked for a Spanish-speaking country because I had taken Spanish (forget that I barely passed) in college. When I ultimately was accepted and assigned, I read the name of the country with some alarm, for I did not know where Turkey was. The more I learned, the more apprehensive I became. Turkey was in the Middle East, and what I knew about that area of the world at the time was all about war and political upheaval. No one I knew spoke Turkish or knew anything about Turkey. Most of my friends would smirk and go "Gobble, Gobble" when I spoke about it.

Nonetheless, I packed my bags and traveled to New Mexico for orientation and language training, which only caused my fear and feelings of inadequacy to worsen. Once in Turkey, the cultural shock was significant. Who knew about such things as Eastern toilets; eating olives and white cheese for breakfast; vendors wanting to sell you flying carpets; bottles of lemon-smelling fluids poured over your hands; men who stalked you, calling out a sum they would pay for one of those promiscuous American women (an attitude only confirmed by American movies); taxi drivers that paid no attention to stop signs; a city that seemed to jump out of the Arabian Nights stories I heard as a child; all sights and smells that completely overwhelmed. There were some sleepless nights when I concluded that "educating the Turkish citizenry to a better way of life" was not in my future.

Tenacity is one of my sometimes-dubious attributes, and I was flattered that the office staff felt my teaching experience would be helpful in certain schools. At that time so many Peace Corps Volunteers were just out of college, or dodging the draft. The school they assigned me to was in Istanbul, where many spoke English, and where life would be, or so I imagined, more normal. In truth, I began this journey with all the wrong ideas and ideals. Thankfully, I listened and learned and, in the process, became aware of the beauty, the history, the people. I fell deeply in love with it all.

Before departing for Ankara, the capital, in 1969, my father, who loved to tease, told me that knowing the trouble I normally caused, Turkey would soon send us all home. In a fashion, that is exactly what happened. The Turkish government did not exile us, but an administrative decision was made for the Peace Corps to voluntarily leave Turkey—forever—because of the growing threat of anti-Americanism. Although, the anger was more appropriately directed at the U.S. military, a significant presence in Turkey at the time, it was the Peace Corps that was more vulnerable.

By the time of our departure in the summer of 1970, I was well aware of the fact that one's expectations seldom jive with reality. There were Turkish teachers who could not find jobs because American PCVs, free to the government, were holding positions otherwise available to them. It is also true that many of the Volunteers, including myself, were not properly trained for dealing with the multiple issues in complex, multicultural situations. As teachers, we Volunteers allowed for a lot of freedom in a classroom, a type of buddy system, whereas Turkish teachers demanded structure and strict enforcement of rules. This different approach caused great frustration and anger with the Turkish faculty, and, of course, the students put the foreign teachers on a pedestal, which undermined the attempts by resident faculty to keep order. It was also difficult at times for us to keep order within our own classes, and when I sent a student to the principal one time, I was horrified when the student later returned with a black eye.

All that being said, I would not trade what I gained from the experience for anything. As a country, Turkey, benefitted little from my presence, but my life and who I was then changed significantly. My comfort level had been shaken, and I emerged a much different and (I like to think) better person, with many new friends and a greater understanding of life beyond my small space. I now love *beyaz peynir* (white cheese) and olives for breakfast. Istanbul, where I lived for those many months, is the most fascinating, most enticing city in the world. I have the greatest respect for the Turks, their history, their religion, their willingness to take a stranger into their home and lives.

Turkey, its people, its artifacts, its cities and villages are an intricate part of who I am today. In that sense, my dream and Kennedy's challenge came true, for I have long been in service: as a prison teacher, prosecutor, judge, and civic leader. I married a Peace Corps Volunteer who had served in Libya, and largely because of the Peace Corps, we are better, more informed citizens, conscious of the differences in the world, and of the many reasons for mutual respect of our diverse heritages.

Riding on a ferry across the Bosporus in the early morning, with that incredible skyline in front of me, drinking hot Turkish tea (not that apple stuff they have now for the tourists) is one memory I will hold forever. But there are many others. I am eternally grateful to Turkey and to the United States for making it possible for a girl from a small town in the Midwest to see the world, and to thereby gain insight otherwise never obtained.

Diana J. (Ziegler) LaViolette served in Turkey, T-17, from 1969-70. Diana was born and raised in Indiana, growing up in one small town after another. She graduated with a BA in liberal arts from Texas Christian University in 1967, teaching at Independence High School in Kansas City for two years before leaving for Turkey. Upon returning to United States, Diana first worked as a caseworker for a welfare office in Indiana, and then taught for approximately ten years before entering law school, graduating from Indiana University School of Law in 1981. Diana worked as a deputy prosecutor for several years before running for Circuit Court Judge. Now retired from full-time work as a judge, Diana serves as a Senior (not old) Judge, covering conflict cases and vacations for sitting jurists. Diana is married to John LaViolette, and they are the parents of two children, Alan and Jean.

JULIA WELLER PFITZER

Two Years of Days

*There are just some experiences you can't describe to
those back home—like the taste of the wine made from
grapes you pressed yourself in a faraway land.*

PEACE CORPS CAME TO MOLDOVA IN 1993, ONLY TWO YEARS
after the fall of the Soviet Union. Since those first eight
Volunteers arrived, more have been invited by Moldovan officials each year. We served as English and health teachers and
worked with farmers and non-governmental organizations that
work for development projects.

I came to Moldova a month after graduating from college.
I had my teaching license and time. I was ready to trade the
Hoosier comfort I grew up in for something unknown. I knew
that the term was two years.

When the forty-eight Moldova Group 8's first arrived in
country from our staging site in Chicago, Peace Corps had
given us policy and health and safety trainings. They'd also
thought to give us dictionaries and an hour or so of language
training before loading us on buses and delivering us to one of
four sites where we'd train in earnest for the next two months
before moving to our permanent sites. After twenty-four hours

in Moldova, I still only knew two words of Romanian. *Hello* and *thank you. Bună ziuă şi mulţumesc.*

My summer host family came to the village school to pick me up, and we walked back to their house with lots of smiles and nods. After they'd helped me put my bags in my room, we went back to the kitchen for tea, still with smiles and nods. Suddenly my host mother stood up and started gesturing over her hair, her underarms, her face, feet and privates. *"Vreau să te spăl?"*

She went through the dance several times before she gave up, grabbed my hand, and led me out the back of the house, past the rabbits, the pigs and into a separate room at the back of the chicken coop. She filled a basin with hot water that had been heating on an outdoor fireplace, showed me where to put my clothes and proceeded to help me bathe in two buckets of water. That day third day in Moldova, I learned my third word. *Baie.* Bath.

By the time I left her home at the end of the summer, I was still being bathed, but I could speak well enough to buy tomatoes in the market and tease my younger host sister with her long blond ponytail that matched mine. They didn't tell me until I came to say goodbye at the end of my two years that I'd been mispronouncing her name. The way I pronounced *Veorica* had become her nickname that the whole village had accepted; this is what brings tears to my eyes.

Peace Corps staff—half Moldovan and half American—sends its Volunteers into the cities and into the villages. They try to learn who we are during our first eleven weeks there. Then when they think they know us, they assign us a permanent site. They try to send us where they think we will fit best. My host mother at my permanent site never offered to bathe me, but she cared for me over the two years I lived with her just the same, practicing Romanian with me until I could even discuss politics.

We lived in a tiny village down a ragged dirt road at the southeastern tip of Moldova out of the general political fray. My village was bordered on three sides by Ukraine. At times I could see the armed guards on the hill at the back of the village. I did not walk that way on my own. Rather, I would wander the dirt streets that made up the heart of the village. I would marvel at the intricate metal gates that separated each of the houses on their long narrow swatches of land. Most days I walked I would be drawn into one of these gates by a student or a family friend for a taste of fresh baked bread or newly killed pork. And I would go home flushed with wine rather than by the exercise I had sought.

While I lived and breathed Moldova, there were many days when it became too much, and I made lists of what I would leave my host family and the shorter list of what I would need to pack for my trip home to America. I could not imagine then how strongly I would miss the smells and tastes of my village. I did not know then that now, in America, there are days that I make lists of what I would bring home to Moldova. As Gibran's *Prophet* says, "Nor is it a thought I leave behind me, but a heart made sweet with hunger and with thirst."

I did hunger and thirst while in Moldova, and many days wanted to turn back. But now my throat clenches when I think about the glasses of wine we'd drink on Sunday: red wine full of the layers of pride and crushed grapes and old barrels and rich earth and the satisfaction of having helped with the pressing. We'd pass a single tumbler around the circle of guests until the bottle was empty.

The only time I saw my Moldovan host father drunk, really drunk, was in the basement cellar of our home. He'd just arrived home from a neighbor's when my friends arrived on the bus from the capitol. He had to show them his pride and joy, which was in the cellar. He managed to make it down the steep steps and duck his heavy head to miss the low entry before it opened to our left. Then he reached up and held on to the string of the naked light bulb for balance with his lock of white hair—normally neatly combed—hanging down over his ear and his glasses slipping down his very Russian nose. He stood there for a minute swaying with the light bulb until his grey eyes adjusted to the basement dimness.

This was in early fall, so the basement was full of glowing jars of compote and the ripe dusty smell of pickles and sauerkraut. Along the north wall sat the milk jugs full of pickled green tomatoes covered only with plates, each weighted down with a large rock. I wasn't fond of the flavor and disliked being sent to retrieve them from the foul (to my nose) slippery juice they soaked in. The far wall was lined with stacks of crates of potatoes, apples, carrots, cabbages, and the large beets. The beets were mostly food for the pig (who I called Bombur because I was sure he dreamt of better morsels).

The long west wall was lined with two ceiling-high shelves filled with jars of canned red tomatoes (these I liked to pop out of their cool salty skins and smear on bread) and countless varieties of compote and preserves, canned salads and meats. These held the vitamins and flavors we would need to lighten the darkness of winter. On the bottom shelves were the heavy jars of lard that sat unused for two years because the Peace Corps medical staff had told my host mother that Americans didn't eat lard anymore.

But it was what stood between the two shelves that interested my host father on this day. His champagne maker was a large tank of CO_2 and an implement he'd rigged up himself to pump it into bottles of his homemade wine stored in wooden or plastic kegs on the south wall. He wanted to show it off to my American friends who had followed us carefully down the stairs and now stood in a circle watching Vania fill a tumbler full of deep red wine. As he passed it and filled it for each of us, he swayed just a little bit, holding on to the bulb for balance.

We cheered each other loudly in Romanian (*Hai noroc*!) while I passed a basket of bread, and he passed the wine until finally, without warning, he'd had enough and led us back up the stairs and into the light of the autumn afternoon.

When he and my host mother went to bed at dusk, my friends and I drunkenly fried potatoes and washed them down with more wine.

It has taken time to be able to tell stories about Moldova. It had been a full body and mind experience that the first summer I was home I couldn't talk about it. "How was Moldova?" "Fine." "What was the Peace Corps like?" "Good."

I often think that it is no wonder that I felt conflict while I was there. Conflict, sometimes violent, over borders, languages, culture, rule, water rights, even the history of the word Moldova have marked the Moldovans as a people. The country is one of the poorest in Europe, corruption is rampant, access to schooling is inequitable and its quality questionable, imports far outnumber exports and increased reliance on assistance appears inevitable.

Even how they spoke about time seemed in conflict with what I knew. When you speak of a period of days, such as a week, or a month or a year you include the phrase that literally translates for "of days."

"How long are you here?"

"Two years."

"You are here for two years of days?"

This phrase stretched out time into measurable, tangible, increments. While I was there, thinking of the years of days ahead of me was often too much. I was used to my English speaking ways of grouping time into weeks, months, or years without much consideration for the days that made them up. Now I think of how lucky I was to have those two years of days.

Maybe I am starting to get far enough out that my years of days can join themselves into stories made of words instead of the long low yell I so often wanted to make while I was there. I can feel the rickety springs of the *rutiera* minibuses seats crowded with anxious villagers heading to town to sell their wares. I can feel the chair in my summer bedroom where I would read for hours to get away from the poverty and hard work. I can feel my husband's hands on my waist the first time we danced at the disco. I can remember the taste of the Snickers Molly and I would eat for breakfast when we met in the capital. I can smell the iron my *Tata* used so meticulously on my clothes. I can hear the laughter of my friends while we danced for no reason at all. I can see the depths of the abandoned missile silo. I can see the disillusionment of the faces of our young charges when we arrived in Chelyabinsk, Russia, after four days and nights traveling on a bus. I can hear the chalk scratch the painted metal sheet used as a chalkboard in my classroom. I am still struggling to pull each word out; but soon, I think, I could give you a story for each of my two years of days.

Julia Weller Pfitzer served as an English teacher in Caplani, Republic of Moldova, M-8, from 2000-02. She worked with local and regional teachers on lesson planning and curriculum development, as well as youth programs such as Debate Club and Odyssey of the Mind. Since her return to the United States she has lived and taught in Washington D.C., Indiana and Colorado. She currently lives in Colorado and is raising two daughters along with her husband Chad (M-9).

CRISTINA T. O'KEEFFE

A Carrot Cake in
a Revolution

*Some were for Yushchenko. Some were for
Yanukovich. Cristina was for cake.*

SEVERAL YEARS HAVE GONE BY. I WAS IN UKRAINE FOR TWO-and-a-half years, and I am now home. But with each autumn chill comes the memories of what it was like to be there, how out of place I felt in that tumultuous climate. I don't mean weather, but revolution. The famous "Orange Revolution" took place during my time in Ukraine. Looking back on it now, the outcome of the revolution is probably not what many people dreamt about when they suffered the cold to protest, living in tent cities in the Ukrainian capital of Kyiv for several months. That time was undeniably electric. A current of emotion had swept through cities, towns, and villages. I was definitely charged, listening at work to stories and opinions as best I could as a non-native speaker. But I was torn as well. In the middle of this revolution was the American Thanksgiving holiday, and I desperately wanted to celebrate. So, this is how I ended up transporting a carrot cake through Ukrainian streets during the height of the Orange Revolution.

21

The cake I carried was brown with a white top. I'll say that up front. I was not running around with a big orange torte. My carrot cake in no way had any political affiliations. It was an unbiased cake. Those of you who know carrot cake well, know that it is neither truly orange, colors of the "opposition," nor is it blue and white, colors of the party controlling Ukraine at that time.

But the cake was still a problem. I mean, Ukraine was having a revolution, and there I was, cake in hand, making my way to the tram. That's American nerve for you: celebrating an American-only holiday in the middle of someone else's revolution. But it was Thanksgiving. To give it up would admit defeat, and as a Peace Corps Volunteer, every small psychological battle won is a major accomplishment. The show would go on. And so would the revolution.

No one could believe that the opposition would last that long in Independence Square. But if the non-believers lived here and saw people waiting in line to buy train tickets, making transactions at a bank, or picking up a package at a post office, they would understand the endurance of Ukrainian citizens. And that doesn't even count the types of hardships the average person endured during communism. Even those of us with an understanding of Ukrainian stamina were impressed. Would the demonstrations, protests, and blockades yield results? Surprisingly, they did.

The first result was the international media attention. As a PCV in Ukraine, the biggest complaint I had about friends and family back home was that they kept calling my country of service Russia. No matter how hard I tried, I somehow ended up in Russia, or worse yet, the Soviet Union. I mean, USSR? C'mon people. Work with me. A now-RPCV told me about a friend on the New York City subway who heard the name Ukraine and asked, "Is that upstate?" A comment like that manages to insult Ukrainians and upstate New Yorkers simultaneously. But sometimes you just have to let it go.

So all it took was a major revolution to bring the Ukrainian nation into the spotlight. Covers of magazines featured stories about the "Orange Revolution." Back in America, friends were hearing news updates about Ukraine on Top 40 radio stations and the local evening news. PCVs and RPCVs everywhere were hailing the miracle that people would now recognize Ukraine. Pointing it out on the map? Well, that was a separate promotional campaign.

The bigger story was the domestic media attention. Television stations that had followed the government mandates about what to broadcast, switched positions right on the air saying they would no longer toe the party line and now supported the opposition's efforts. Following months of news stories investigating the alleged murders of outspoken journalists, the action of those journalists who made public pronouncements was like a mini-revolution itself as efforts at unbiased reporting filled the airwaves.

The second result of the mass demonstrations in Kyiv was the rallying of Ukrainian people. There was the physical rallying: physical movement to the capital to show support, the bringing of food and clothing to demonstrators by local Kyiv citizens, and the strikes happening throughout the country. But there was the mental rallying as well.

Ukrainian people were plagued with outside perceptions about their nation, the most major being the supposed cultural divide between the east and west, the Ukrainian and Russian speakers, and the values of the old and the young. There were many convenient juxtapositions for the purposes of news stories, but in the end, those differences were not what we observed. In Kyiv, Russian and Ukrainian speakers were gathering without qualms. Old and young stood together. If the extremes existed, Ukrainians were able to put aside those differences for the purposes of standing united. To we foreigners, that type of mentality was impressive.

Equally impressive were the efforts of some organizations and schools to use the election as a catalyst to improve East-West relations. Round tables, dialogues, discussions and celebrations were organized to address the divide in the cultural identity and find areas of common ground. This type of cooperation was less shocking for outsiders who spent two weeks watching massive crowds stand in Independence Square or in local town squares throughout Ukraine and not disintegrate into violent mobs. The politeness, respect and courtesy shown on television were only reiterated by witnesses who spent time in Kyiv and testified themselves that this was true.

Why do I tell you all of this? I tell you this only to make you understand how possible it was to carry a carrot cake through the streets of L'viv and onto a crowded tram in the middle of a revolution. It was the spirit of the time. People were motivated, enthusiastic, but not aggressive or angry. A cake could be carefully carried through the crowd, down the street and onto the tram. People on the tram could make way, and the cake could be safely transported to the site of our celebration. Yes, in the middle of a revolution.

But I also tell you this because the cake not only could be, but also had to be. In the midst of the demonstrations and political upheaval, in the midst of the enthusiasm, the disappointment, the opposing opinions, an American living in Ukraine for two years had to be grateful. The political process, however scandalous, however rocky, however tentative, was taking place all around us. From freedom of speech to legal actions, the Ukrainian people were making motions in court and appealing those motions. They were protesting and counter-protesting. In each heart, there was hope for a different outcome. Some for Yushchenko. Some for Yanukovich. And some of us for carrot cake on Thanksgiving Day.

Cristina T. O'Keeffe served as an Economic Development Volunteer along with her husband Thomas in Ukraine, Group 24, from 2003-05. At the L'viv Youth Employment Center, she developed the self-sustaining Youth Leadership Program. She also founded the L'viv Youth Hostelling Association to bring the first youth hostel to L'viv, and authored the survival tourism guide Personal Guide to L'viv *as a fundraising enterprise. She taught seminars on marketing, public relations, creative writing, and leadership at local schools and universities. Upon her return to the U.S., Cristina worked as a communication consultant for an international software firm. Today, her company LookOut Communications, provides marketing writing services to small businesses. She lives in Stewart Manor, New York, with her husband and two daughters and welcomes visitors to her website www.lookoutcommunications.com.*

BARBARA BRYAN

✦

After Thirty-Seven Years

*Even after being away for thirty-seven years, returning to the
country you served in seems like returning back home.*

A HUM, THEN A ROAR, AND THE MOTORBIKE JUMPS FORWARD. I
cling tightly to Fatih's waist and chance a sideways glance at
the boats dancing about in the sunshine. Fatih calls out land-
marks, but between the unfamiliar helmet and the traffic noise,
all is a muddle. I stop trying to understand, and focus on the
palm trees, white buildings, and distant mountain views. How
in the world have I, a sixty-year-old bespeckled grandmother,
come to be taking my first motorcycle ride ever in Marmaris,
Turkey?

To answer that question, we must go back to 1966. I
was one of many recent college graduates who, thrilling to
President Kennedy's call for service, found a way into the
Peace Corps, for travel, adventure, personal growth and the
chance to make a difference in the world. I was teaching
English as a foreign language in Eskisehir, Turkey. I've always
been grateful that I was able to serve in Turkey, a land of
abundant hospitality and fascinating history, architecture, and
culture. But I had wondered, over the years, whether it was

only I who had gained from those two years. Did the students get anything out of my efforts?

My Peace Corps roommate Donna Chmara and I were in the sixth largest city in Turkey, teaching at Eskisehir Maarif Koleji, a middle and high school with students aged eleven to eighteen. Our school was one of seven in the country designed to develop a core of fluent English speakers. The program began with a preparatory year during which students studied English twenty-five hours a week. After that year, all their math and science courses were taught in English. In our first year, there were three preparatory classes. Donna, Susan (a Peace Corps teacher in her second year), and I were the English teachers for these three classes, so these eleven- and twelve-year olds had unusual exposure to young American women teachers.

In our second year, the school moved to a new building and expanded: there were more Peace Corps teachers, and there were five preparatory classes. I was a far better teacher in my second year, but the most vivid memories from those long-ago times are from the old building with its coal-fired stoves, the little shop where the children could buy treats, the communal hot lunches at long tables, and the overworked janitor whose job included serving tea in the teachers' room. Most of all, I remember the children, some remarkably fluent in English after only one year, some struggling; some clearly well-off, others from villages where enormous sacrifices had been made to send them to this school; some very naughty, some who could be counted on to help you out if things got really out of hand.

In 1968, I said goodbye to students, Peace Corps, and Turkey, and began a new life in New York City, the perfect antidote to the Anatolian plateau. Sadly, I failed to answer the letters that I received from a few of those students. But memories of Turkey were warm and compelling. In July 1996, Donna and I fulfilled a dream when we visited Eskisehir with our husbands. We were impressed at the school's further expansion, we met two Turkish teachers of English and enjoyed shop talk with them, and we were honored by the school's principal and a vice mayor of the city. But it was summer vacation, and so, to our disappointment, we couldn't observe any classes, and we were able to find only three former students, from classes that we had not taught.

Fast forward to 2004. An email arrives from the webmaster of the "Friends of Turkey" list serve. A former student, Metin, has emailed the site, inquiring about "lost" Peace Corps teachers. Am I willing for this forty-eight-year-old gentleman to be given my email address? You bet! I even remember him! This is the beginning of a rush of memories, reintroductions, and invitations. Donna and I become members of the class's Yahoo group. We learn that in April 2005, our school, now renamed Eskisehir Anadolu Lisesi, will celebrate its fiftieth anniversary.

To the amazement of our students, Donna and I decide to spend two weeks in Turkey to attend this event and meet as many of our former students as we can. Among them are architects, doctors, scientists, professors, military officers, business people. There's a dentist, a jazz guitarist, and, yes, several English teachers! Although a few have not used their English and are reluctant to speak it, most can make themselves understood, and many are totally fluent. Some tell us that knowing English changed their lives. Touchingly, others say that the kindness and interest that their Peace Corps teachers showed them opened up new possibilities to them. We revisit the old school and re-enact an English lesson. On a visit to the "new" school, a student interviews us, in English, for the school newspaper. At parties of our preparatory classes, cameras flash and people push forward to greet us. There is singing, dancing, sharing pictures from old times, and much laughter. There are tears over classmates who have died.

Metin and Nevin, a married couple who were our students, are our hosts and fellow adventurers during our entire trip. They drive us from the Black Sea to the Mediterranean (in Turkish, its name is "White Sea"), with the Eskisehir reunion in between. We share many adventures and much laughter. When curious onlookers ask us who we are and how we happen to be together, their mouths drop open in amazement as we retell the story of students finding long-lost teachers, and how we have formed new bonds as friends. Now we are in Marmaris to visit our student Fatih, who promised that if we came back to Turkey, he would give us a motorbike tour.

A pro after an hour on the bike, I relax my grip and lean back nonchalantly as Fatih glides to a halt in front of the outdoor café where Nevin, Metin, and Donna are cheering, laughing, and taking pictures. We "toss a few beers" together. Finally, the proprietor, overcome by curiosity, comes over to ask what's happening. "You found them, and they came all that way, after thirty-seven years? All I can say is bravo to you all!" He reminisces about some Peace Corps teachers he had as a student in Marmaris all those years ago, and in Turkish, he murmurs, "They gave a lot."

Since the 2005 reunion, we have seen Ibrahim, Cihat, Cemil, Metin, Nevin, and Onder on their visits to the United States, and we're making plans to see our microbiologist student, Gulsen, at an upcoming conference. We've even met some of the next generation, the children of our students. We never imagined those two years would still bring us such joy forty years later. I no longer wonder about who—teacher or students—gained more from those years. We have all benefitted, and continue to do so; we have become life-long classmates in a global learning community.

Barbara Bryan taught English in Eskisehir, Turkey, T-13, from 1966-68. Most of her post-Peace Corps career has been as a manager in nonprofit organizations, culminating in eighteen years as president of a membership association of philanthropic organizations. Now retired, she and her husband, Will Freeman, savor the joys of urban life—lots of museums and music—along with camping, hiking, travelling, and spending time with their two grandchildren.

JOHN P. DEEVER

Back in the USSR

Sometimes leaving a country is just as hard as getting there.

In June, during a scorcher of a week, Misha stopped by my dorm while I was packing. Books, clothes, photographs, and souvenirs were strewn all over the place. It was almost 90 degrees outside, and sweat dripped from my forehead as I separated clothes into piles.

"How are you going to get all this stuff home?" he asked, eyeing my Ohio State t-shirt.

"I'm not," I said, tossing him the shirt.

"*Klass!*" he said, holding it up against himself and tossing back his hair.

Returning from a trip to the United States had been hard, but I finished the school year. My special after-school English club went so well that we produced a class newspaper, Xeroxed it, and sold it throughout the school in the last week of May. Against my wishes, the kids named the paper "Mr. John and his Johnovtsi." Saying goodbye to my Johnovtsi, and especially to my fifth graders, the kids I had watched grow up in my class for two years, made me glad I had returned, and somewhat unbelieving that this time, I would not do so.

"What about all this other stuff?" Misha asked.

"The typewriter, cassette player, and books go to School 23, kitchen things to my teacher friends...let's see, neckties..."

"For me," Misha said, grinning. In packing for Peace Corps I took ten nice silk ties and had used all of them. My three favorites I kept for job interviews in America. The rest were his. While I spent the afternoon stuffing my backpack full, Misha tried on ties and admired himself in my mirror.

"Look at this," I said, pulling a box from the closet. From inside the box, I removed a piece of paper with instructions, printed in tiny Russian. Misha came over and asked what it was for.

"First thing I ever bought here," I told him. "It's a brand new lamp, never been used."

The July week I arrived in Zhitomir in 1993—before I could communicate at all—all I could think about was finding the word for *writing desk* and a lamp to go with it. When the dormitory superintendent had tried to tell me about a television set that I didn't want, I had set off on my very first spree alone, gung-ho to prowl the town and practice my reconnaissance shopping. In a store full of junk, I found the tulip-shaped lamp with a curved neck and a round base. I spent ten bucks on it. Only when I returned to the dorm did I realize that it was a wall lamp, hopelessly unbalanced, and would never sit on a desk. It turned out to be impossible to hang as well, and there was no place to plug it in. It reminded me of how confused I had been at first, how eager to prove myself and unaware of how foolish I must have looked in school, in town, and in people's homes. Wandering around like a zombie, I had been taken in, reassured, even pampered.

The useless lamp, which had stayed in my closet unused for the whole two years, brought back that time so vividly I thought for a moment I might cry. Those two years were over now, and when I moved out of the dorm, that lamp would stay and I would leave. Maybe the super would discover it and figure out how to hook it up in his office.

Misha returned to the mirror, intent on carefully adjusting and readjusting the tight triangular knot in one of his new ties. "By the way," he said offhandedly, "did you take a shower this week?"

"Umm, no," I said, not sure what he was suggesting. "Why?"

"Just thought you'd be happy about the hot water coming on."

I yelped like a wounded dog and shoved past him and into the bathroom. Turning the squeaky tap as fast as I could sent cinnamon-colored muck into the sink. The thick gush turned from brown to clear, and in seconds steamy water raced around a sink basin that had known only cold for what, a year now? No, *over* a year. Way back in October I had given up hoping for hot water. I had quit touching the left tap through two long winters of cold, dark evenings in this apartment, my nights filled with dreams of a luxurious bath. Hot, clean running water flowed copiously: in July. It was a sick joke.

"It's the middle of summer!" I shouted. "What do we need hot water for now?" In horror, I realized that my words echoed exactly those with which the super had answered my complaints about cold showers one hot August week so long ago when I had moved in.

"Oh, I don't know," Misha said, still more interested in his tie. "I think the Institute got some bonus credit or state subsidy or something. The girls downstairs have been lined up taking showers for days."

"Days?" I screeched. "You mean I had hot water and didn't know?" I put my hand under the faucet, and though it nearly scalded me, I held it there a long time. Hot, very hot, running water.

"Don't feel bad," Misha said. "Rumor has it that it will go off any day now. Maybe tomorrow."

For the rest of the week I could hardly keep from laughing.

My experience of Ukrainians as pleasant, thoughtful, and long-suffering had permeated me until by the time I departed, I trusted everyone. But after so many months of acculturating myself to ignore Ukraine's hostile, bureaucratic xenophobia, I had grown complacent, believing that any difficulty thrown before me I could overcome. I was practically a native. Only on my very last day in Ukraine did I realize how far such a perspective was from the truth. That was the day I almost found my way into a Ukrainian jail.

On the Fourth of July weekend, my girlfriend Lisa and I and a few other Volunteers met in the western Ukrainian city of Lutsk before beginning our summer backpacking tour around Eastern Europe. Giddy with summer's long days, yet still saddened by the freshness of painful goodbyes, we boarded a train for Poland. We would be in Lublin that night, and later that week in Krakow, the most beautiful city in Eastern Europe. Our spirits were high.

The Soviet Union, to thwart invasion by train, built its railroads according to a gauge a few centimeters wider than rails in the rest of Europe. Thus, every train leaving or entering former Soviet countries has to wait several hours while each car is lifted into the air and a new set of wheels attached. Because I had crossed this same border several times, I was confident and relaxed, even melancholy, wondering if I were really ready to leave. Still, the border crossing's high level of security and the preponderance of armed guards always set me on edge. I was eager to be away.

Traveling with Lisa and me were Kate, Carlos, and Steve. Three of us were carrying Peace Corps "cash-in-lieu" reimbursements for the flight home we had chosen not to take, opting instead for an end-of-service jaunt. Thus I had over $1,000 cash in the security wallet attached to my belt. In 1995, it was illegal to take more than $500 out of Ukraine unless it could be explained (and documented) where the rest of the money had come from. During our Peace Corps close-of-service conference, we had been unofficially advised to declare less than $500, hide the rest, and not worry. We had made our money legally, and so I filled out my customs declarations and wrote in "$300."

The train reached the border, the cranes appeared, and the wheel exchange process that took place dozens of times a day began. The passport checker moved down the car collecting passports. Next arrived the customs official, a woman with big hair streaked half blond, half brown, like a weave gone bad. Like many Ukrainian women, she wore heavy makeup, especially a lot of something purplish around the eyes. After collecting our declarations she eyed the five of us skeptically.

"Do you speak Russian?"

"A little," we answered modestly.

We left our coupe for the cabin-checker to search. He worked his way along each wall panel, tapping lightly and listening for the hollow sound he expected to hear. Then he unscrewed the ceiling vent and climbed up to look around. Not infrequently, people tried to escape the country by opening the ceiling panel in the bathrooms and hiding in the tiny spaces above the train cars. As he shoved his flashlight into every dark nook and cranny of our cabin, we joked in the corridor about how good it felt to leave such bureaucratic hassles and suspicion behind.

The same big-haired customs woman, who slightly resembled a thinner Tammy Faye Bakker, returned. She asked us as a group if we were all sure we had declared everything. We nodded, and said, "*Da.*" Slowly she examined every face and then settled her glare on mine.

"Everyone in the corridor except you," she said. "You'll be first."

Alone in the cabin, she sat on the bench across from me. I began to feel itchy, like something was wrong. "Pull out your bag," she said. I had nothing but clothes, cassettes, books, a few souvenirs, but who could know what might be selected as evidence of criminal misbehavior. Border guards were known for confiscating anything, without explanation.

Before going through my bag, though, she asked me once more. "Are you certain you have declared everything here?" I remembered my camera, which you were supposed to declare. I guessed I could use stupidity to bluff out of that one. Anyway, it was too late to change my mind now. I'd already said yes once.

Another customs official then entered the cabin and sat directly beside me. Now I began to feel nervous. My friends were just outside in the corridor, but I felt as if they were hundreds of miles ahead of me and I was still stuck in the cabin, stuck in the train, trapped in Ukraine. My heart started pounding and my face must have betrayed my fear. The following moments seemed to happen slowly, and I remember each glance, each gesture perfectly even now, as if a movie of it were etched onto my brain forever.

"O.K.," she said. "Let's see the money."

I was screwed. I was screwed and I knew it. I realized my mistake and felt suddenly that I was about to throw up in the compartment.

When I pulled out my wallet my hands were shaking. I showed her the single $100 bill I was carrying, the only one I expected to spend in Poland. The only one I'd kept out separate. I had to produce two more.

For a split-second I thought I of extending the lie. I could say that the other two hundreds were in my backpack, stashed away. But she would then tell me to show them to her. Right there, attached to my belt, was all the rest of my money, money which I expected to spend traveling around Europe the whole summer: ten crisp one-hundred-dollar bills.

Even then, my consciousness resisted visualizing the consequences of what was about to happen. Without thinking, I gambled that perhaps she was intensely stupid. So I pulled out my belt wallet, still attached by its leather strap to my belt loop. It was jammed tight with paper. From a visible wad, I peeled off two one-hundred-dollar bills and showed them to her.

I still hate to remember how clumsily I lie under pressure, how incredible was my lame attempt at deception. The customs man next to me saw the bills as easily as if I had waved them under his nose. The gamble failed: Tammy Faye was by no means stupid.

"Give me this *portmanchik*," she said. Her stoolie, who didn't want her to get all the glory, quickly burst out: "He's got more there, a whole lot." He was fairly drooling with delight. She opened the belt wallet, pulled out my stack, and flipped through, counting my thousand dollars in cash. They exchanged looks of half amazement, half smug righteousness. Tammy Faye said, "*Bolshe shtuke*," gangster-style street slang for "over a thousand." He gave a low whistle and scurried away. And I, gazing longingly at those bills, kissed my summer of travel goodbye.

She turned to me now, mainly angry, and shouted, "How are you going to explain this?" I was surprised to feel an aggrieved but relieved shock of having nothing more to hide. The lie discovered, I could relax a little. But it was about to get worse.

"You understand," she began, "that by lying to us on this form, you've just broken Ukrainian law." She paused, as if for effect. I hoped my friends in the hall were listening. "I asked you if you had anything else and you said 'no.' Now we find this money. Which we must assume you made illegally." I was about to interrupt before she finished, "You have big problems, and they're just beginning."

The flunky returned with another man. "That's him, Sasha," he said.

Sasha had blond hair and a squashed, sneering nose on his ugly face that made Tammy Faye and her boy look kind in comparison. He sat down as if tired and removed his police-style hat, resting it in his lap. As Tammy Faye got up to leave the compartment, taking with her the $1,000 in cash, formerly mine, now folded inside my false declaration. Sasha idly played with the black shiny brim of his hat. It was his turn to interrogate me.

He grimaced at me, his eyes in a squint, and began asking questions in a soft, low voice meant to sound threatening.

"Do you know what you've done?" I hated his arrogant leer immediately and couldn't answer.

"Why did you write only $300?"

"We were told we could only declare this much," I said.

"*Who* told you?" Unfortunately the phrasing I'd used in Russian translated not so much "we were told," as "they told us."

For some stupid reason I told the truth: "Friends," I said.

He snorted. "Friends? Which friends?"

I needed to backtrack and start thinking straight. "Our organization paid us this money for our flight home and told us we could take it out of the country," I said. This was sort of true. I was feeling defensive, like my every word was being chased. "I've visited Poland many times and never had problems before."

"And every time you lied on the declaration, right?"

"No, no..." I stuttered, and almost said, "Only this time."

"And all of your friends are doing the same right now, correct?"

Now instead of just wrecking myself I was dragging in Lisa, Kate, Carlos, and Steve. The best answer in Russian I could come up with was, "I only answer for myself." But they really weren't guilty of anything and now I had implied that they were. I was digging the hole deeper with every word.

"Don't worry," Sasha said, reassuringly. Then his eyes narrowed further. He sneered, "We know everything." He said this with one Russian word: "*Znayem.*" We know.

In a real movie, I thought, this would be ridiculous dialogue: forced, fake, overdramatic. I was a player in Sasha's idea of grand theatre, a prospect almost more sickening than the fact that my plight was real. Inside me I felt an irrational surge and almost leaped across the cabin to break his nose. Suddenly his tone of voice lightened.

"Where are you from in the United States?" he asked.

I was so surprised at the apparent switch—and eager to return to a saner standard of conversation—that I answered back cheerfully.

"Ohio!" I said. "Do you know it?"

"I know," he answered ever so softly, narrowing his eyes to thin slits. "You won't be seeing Ohio for a long, long time."

So much for my long-awaited travel in Eastern and Western Europe. In fact, so much for ending my Peace Corps service in Ukraine on a good note. For the past two years I'd suffered regular bureaucratic hassles, pointless questioning by police, and the officially systematized barriers to any accomplishment that characterize getting around the former Soviet Union. Trying to leave, once and for all, I was going to conclude with a bad aftertaste. Now I had been caught dead to rights lying on the customs form, breaking the law. It looked like I would wind up my Peace Corps service with a little stint in jail, out a thousand dollars in an instant.

I stood in the train car corridor staring out the window at the dingy border post. Maybe I could get someone from the

Peace Corps in Kiev to talk me out of jail. Before leaving Kiev I had turned in my green card, my alien identification that noted our organization's ties with the American embassy. Now Steve was being interrogated by Sasha, and I overheard him attempt to explain that we were all "volunteers," that we had come to "help" the Ukrainian people. At that Sasha laughed nastily.

Tammy Faye called me back in, saying, "Take all your things and come with me." Lisa looked me in the eyes and without hesitation said, "I'm coming with you."

She quickly arranged with Kate to meet at the central bazaar in Krakow at one P.M. on Saturday—two days from now. At the time, the promise seemed awfully optimistic as far as I was concerned. Kate, Carlos, and Steve wished us luck. We got off the westbound train.

Lisa and I stood on the platform in bright July sunlight, with our luggage piled around us. I had no idea even what the name of the nearest town might be. We waited for our next orders from the Ukrainian customs officials.

Tammy Faye said I needed a bank document to prove the money was mine. Without this permission, I couldn't cross the border. She explained that normally in this procedure I would be arrested, a "protocol" (or charges) would be drawn up, and my money would be confiscated. The word "protocol" heightened my anxiety, as I remembered its frequent use in Solzhenitsyn's *Gulag Archipelago*, which I'd recently read. But the way she had said the word "normally" gave me hope. I asked about the money.

Tammy Faye shouted to the passport checker, who came over to where we stood on the platform. He handed Lisa and me our passports, smiling in the most pleasant, everyday way. Tammy Faye then checked the time of the Kharkov train, one track over from ours and heading the opposite direction, back east into Ukraine. Suddenly, with jubilation I sensed that Tammy Faye was improvising. Maybe she didn't relish the idea of locking me up and didn't want her post to attract unnecessary attention or scrutiny for something minor.

She told me to leave my things on the platform and to follow her. We went into the customs building through a special back door for officials only. There she counted out the $1,000 into my hand, one hundred at a time. Then she told me to count it myself, which I did quickly, my hands now shaking with joy instead of panic. "Let's go," she said abruptly. "Your train is leaving."

My understanding of my fate had reversed; it looked like Lisa and I would get to leave, money and all. While Lisa still waited on the platform with our backpacks, I followed Tammy Faye to the Kharkov train, where she found the conductor. "Of course," he agreed. "I'll make up the ticket to Kiev right away." Still following her like a lost puppy, back toward the platform I crunched across the gravel spread between tracks. My confidence rose again.

"Because you are 'volunteers,'" she said haughtily, "we are not going to show you the inside of a Ukrainian prison. You will go back to Kiev. There you will open a new account at a Ukrainian bank and deposit your dollars. Then you may withdraw them with a receipt."

"Can't I just call my office?" If she was going to let me off, why should I have to ride all the way back to Kiev, an overnight fifteen-hour train ride east in the direction I had just come. "They can fax me a copy of the receipt for this money."

"A fax is no good," she said. "It must have actual signatures."

"Can't I call them from here?"

"There are no telephones."

"You have no telephones at all?" For an international border crossing this seemed impossible even in Ukraine.

"Not long-distance telephones," she said, then turning sour. "And not for you."

With my money back safely in my pocket, my panic had evolved into indignant anger. As Lisa and I took our bags across the tracks to the Kiev train, I explained Tammy Faye's orders, which sounded ridiculous when repeated in English. We threw our bags into the empty cabin and slumped into our seats. Another woman had the next-door cabin to herself, and it was full of boxes she was carrying in from Poland. She was doing business and had no doubt paid some bribe to be carrying that amount of goods in a train car by herself. That added to my growing fury and instead of being grateful to be newly acquitted and safe from a border-post prison, I sulked and stewed.

Always the clear-headed one, Lisa thought a moment and said, "Look, we could get off at the next stop. We can call Peace Corps from there. They'll send us some documents or a statement by train tonight. In the morning we'll cross the border." That sounded good; much better than going all the way back to Kiev certainly. I felt immediately cheered up.

The conductor came in with the tickets, a scissored scrap of paper from an old outdated pad of tickets. Across the cut-up slips he had scrawled in ballpoint "Kiev. Three million kupons." An unreadable purple mark had been stamped across the writing.

"We're only going to Kovel," I told him.

"But I've already made up the tickets for Kiev!"

"We go to Kovel," I said firmly. I was sick of being pushed around, and his little impromptu hand-scissoring and scribbling seemed irrelevant to my situation. He started to shout.

"And who'll pay for these?"

"I don't know!" I shouted back, crossing my arms. "Not me."

He stormed off. Lisa pursed her lips at me to say "you ought to settle down a bit." I felt victoriously triumphant for a moment. Until the conductor returned with Tammy Faye.

"What's this about not paying?" she began yelling. "I *know* you have enough money."

"We'll get off in Kovel and telephone."

"You'll pay for these tickets to Kiev! Three million kupons! Or twenty dollars." We no longer even laughed at the sad, ludicrous exchange rate.

"No. I won't," I said, using exactly the petulant phrase and tone of voice of my students when they refused to complete an assignment in class.

"You want to be arrested again?" she screamed. "You'll pay right now and stop acting like a child! Or you'll get off this train, too, and have real problems. Hurry up, the train is leaving!"

Even Lisa lost her temper. "Please," she said to Tammy Faye. "There's no need to shout."

"I have no kupons," I told the conductor, "because it's illegal to take them out of the country, right?"

"You have dollars."

"But no small bills," I said. Sarcastically I said, "Do you have eighty dollars change?" From his front pocket, he instantly pulled out a wad of dollars bigger than mine. He slapped three twenties and two tens on the table, saying, "Count it."

I forked over one of my troublesome hundreds and took the change. As Tammy Faye got off the train she fired back her parting shot: "You act like this after we made an exception for you."

"Exception?!" I shouted back, though she was gone. In English I said, to no one at all, "I don't even want my money any more. I just want out of this country!"

Kate and Carlos and Steve continued west into Poland; Lisa and I headed back toward Kiev, through the Ukrainian countryside to which I'd spent the whole morning sadly waving farewell. Now it roared past in the wrong direction as our train churned on. Back to what, just three years earlier, was the USSR. All the struggles of living in Ukraine, all the petty griefs I had suffered and long since forgiven, rushed back into my memory in a torrent. My mood turned foul and black.

In two hours we reached Kovel, where Lisa and I got off the train and began looking for luggage lockers, telephones, and trains to L'viv. Hoping to reuse our tickets, we asked the train station manager to stamp "Ostanovka" on our tickets, which might theoretically enable us to reboard a different train. Sorting out all our stupid documents, I was trying to come up with a plan, when Lisa had a brilliant idea.

"Let's see if there's a bus from here to Chelm."

Now that was thinking creatively—using Ukie cunning, I might even say. Stuck in the mindset of attempting to jump through official hoops as I was told, I hadn't realized we were still only about fifty miles from Poland.

The bus station turned out to be next door, its cashier accepted ten dollars and a few kupons for two tickets, and in less than thirty minutes after getting off the train we were on our way back. Nine Ukrainians were aboard, loaded down with cartons of cigarettes to sell in Poland. When one woman asked if I would carry a carton or two over for her (since I was obviously under the safe limit), I shuddered and refused. We neared the border, and a few men (some in uniform, some not) came on board to collect "fees," but we soon arrived at a different international border crossing. Tammy Faye was nowhere in sight.

This time I put my extra Peace Corps money in my shoe, declared an amount equal to that in my wallet, and—most important of all—let Lisa do the talking. The border official looked us up and down and asked us what was in our backpacks. Lisa said, "Not much. Clothes. A tent for camping. Things for cooking." The young man smiled at her ever so slightly, and then lifted his hand in the gentlest gesture, almost like that of a priest delivering a blessing. His dismissive wave said, "Go in peace." And we did.

Back on board after passing customs, we sat quietly. The bus crept along in the traffic at the border crossing. I held my breath as we made our way across a narrow suspension bridge amidst hundreds of semi trucks. Although we would reach Chelm, then Lublin that very night, and would be in Krakow on time to meet Kate and the others later that week, it seemed that for the rest of that afternoon we sat still on that bridge on the border. Nobody was going anywhere.

Now and then our bus inched forward, eventually approaching the halfway point in the middle of the river. When it did, I looked upstream and downstream at two sets of fences, between them very neatly cut grass and the softly flowing creek. Anyone could have swum across it in a matter of seconds, were there not so many men with automatic weapons standing around smoking, watching for something just like that to break up the monotony of their days. Otherwise, I saw nothing but fields, one field really, with a line drawn through it. On one side was Poland—what I thought of rather melodramatically as "freedom"—and on the other Ukraine. However arbitrarily located the line through the terrain looked, it was very real. Crossing it in either direction meant something very complicated. Something even now I cannot quite piece together. After two years, I had almost grown to believe I was part Ukrainian. But here I was wondering why I had moved to Ukraine for two years in the first place.

"Look," said Lisa. "I see Polish uniforms."

She was pointing out the window, up ahead on the bridge, toward something I couldn't see. Instead of trying to look out, I turned to look at her. The laugh lines around her eyes crinkled, and I found her hand, which felt warm and smooth.

John P. Deever served as a TEFL Volunteer in Ukraine, Group 1, from 1993-95. He married Lisa, and they live with their two children in Ohio.

BRIAN FASSETT

The Dead Pig

Brian discovers the Bulgarian meaning of "pigging out."

I WAS GOING TO CALL THIS PIECE, "HOW PIGS CAUSED THE DEMISE of the Ottoman Empire," but I decided that the story I wanted to tell wasn't really about the Ottoman Empire or its inevitable demise, though a few Bulgarians I know might beg to differ. This story is about the necessary, and maybe even religious, demise of not just one, but thousands of pigs every fall in Bulgaria.

Bulgarians have an almost religious connection with pigs. Many believe that it is the pig that kept their culture alive during the 500 years of Turkish domination. The Ottoman occupation of Bulgaria was ruthless. Soldiers would terrorize the local people, trying to break their spirit. They came into towns, killed the men, raped all the women, and took the children, or at least the boys, to brainwash them and turn them into warriors. Years later, they would send those grown-up boys back to their hometowns with explicit instructions to kill their parents or grandparents or siblings. When the Turks were busy raping and pillaging, as if that wasn't enough insult and injury, they also made it a practice to leave the Bulgarians with nothing to eat. They would burn their crops and their granaries. They would kill livestock, or take it to feed the hungry troops. But the one thing that the Turks would never touch, as devout Muslims, were the pigs. Since pork, as a food is impure, they left the pigs behind. In doing so, they allowed the Bulgarian culture to survive.

It felt like we took more than a few steps back in time our first autumn in Bulgaria when we went to the village to visit this age-old tradition of killing a pig, and in that act, revisiting the demise of the Ottoman Empire, paying homage to the animal that would feed the family for the entire winter. My wife Kate and I became witness to a medieval experience that could be described as nothing less than a complete cultural difference. We were invited over for *na gosti* (literally to be guests) for the big annual *koleda* (pig killing) at Tanya's house in the village. This was a big deal, as Tanya had promised Kate she would do her nails, we were going to eat lots of Bulgarian food, and we were going to witness a fundamentally important annual event. We were invited for the killing at 9 A.M. sharp, but opted for a delayed arrival of 10 A.M. to reap the benefit of their hard work without having to witness the animal's death sentence.

Walking through their front gate, I felt like we walked back in time several hundred years. The surroundings were modern, relatively speaking, by Bulgarian standards, but we were in the middle of what was immediately apparent as a very important and timeless ritual. It was obvious that the men and the women had their separate roles, in this place where gender defines a lot more than which bathroom you use and who cleans up after dinner. The men, about seven of them—cousins, uncles, grandfathers, brothers, and sons—were hard at work hovering over the dead pig, each with his own task. Only one man used the torch, and only one man wielded the ax. Another did nothing but the skinning. The women were also hard at work, three generations of this small family, all going in different directions, playing their own part. All the actions were centered on the fact that the family had come together that day to kill, eat, and preserve that pig.

When we laid our eyes on the 300-pound beast, it stopped us in our tracks. It had already been killed, was lying very unnaturally on its back on the cold cement with its thick skin yellowing with death. The passing of time was stiffening its legs with *rigor mortis*, stretching them skyward. The men looked big and strong compared to the women, but didn't compare in size with the dead animal at their feet. They were wrestling it around to gain access to both its tail and ears so they could be removed first. These parts were quickly thrown on the hot charcoal grill to serve as sustenance for the rest of the day's activities. As they walked from side to side, their black rubber boots sloshed through the bloody water at their feet. Noticing that, it made me realize the ground all around us was red with pig blood; even I was standing in it. But not even the blood that had spilled out onto the ground went to waste. The family's matriarch, Baba Tana, took a broom and dustpan and swept up that bloody water and poured it into the potted plants next to the front door of the house.

So, there we were, staring at this naked 300-pound beast. Its glassy eyes had rolled back in its head, as it was lifted onto a raised wooden platform. Six or seven Bulgarian men were huddling around it, all offering suggestions about what to do next, and who should be the one to do it. They were like a bunch of high school football players preparing for their next big move. But not without taking a break to have some *rakiya*, the local plum brandy that seems to be the crown jewel lubricant of all important social functions in this country. With some grunting and grumbling, and a swig or two of red wine to dilute the *rakiya*, things started to happen very quickly.

After the ears and tail disappeared to the grill, the next task at hand was burning all the hair off of this big lifeless blob so they could gain access to (and eat) the skin, and everything that lay beneath it. That immediately filled the air with a thick white smoke, and the unmistakable smell of burning hair and flesh. That smell, once it gets into your nostrils, gets burned into your olfactory library, never to be forgotten. You can almost taste it, and it sits heavy on your clothes until they get scrubbed clean. If anyone has taken a propane torch to pig hair, you know that it doesn't just burn off quickly and easily. It takes a few passes to get that wiry, course white hair burned down to the skin. But, in doing so, the skin got charred black from the flame that is big enough and hot enough to be used to burn the fields in spring.

The women were working the grill, cooking up the ears and tail, once they had been chopped into little pieces. The women were also answering to the demands of the men, though they were both equally busy, scooping up the last of the coagulating blood off the ground right outside the kitchen door where all of this was taking place. They were preparing the work area, the knives, and the jars that would eventually hold the meat, fat, and bones for storage through the winter and into the next year.

As the obvious foreigners, and self-appointed guests of honor, we took a little break to enjoy a "typical" breakfast on this day of pig killing. This was an important day, and although Kate and I had both, unknowingly, already eaten breakfast once today, we would have to be polite and eat again. We were served bowls of room temperature chicken and rice soup that quickly told our taste buds that the main ingredients were vinegar and salt. The soup was a unique enough flavor that it was to our advantage to have a drink to wash it down. We needed a chaser. And, as in every Bulgarian social event, there was more than enough of everything. Some fresh, room-temperature orange soda came first, and then we were served coffee and tea, since it was breakfast after all.

If the temperature and taste of vinegar wasn't enough to encourage Kate to revive her vegetarian eating habits, finding the neck, gizzard and a foot of an old laying hen in her bowl of soup quickly made her decide that I got to finish her portion. We had been invited over specifically for this meal, so Kate wasn't about to let us leave without cleaning up our plates. So, on top of my two servings of less than appetizing "chicken" soup, we were offered some traditional *banitsa*—my favorite Bulgarian breakfast food—a filo dough, egg, and cheese pastry. A torturous thing. My favorite food gets served after I had just finished choking down two bowls of vinegar chicken neck soup, which washed down the grilled pig tail that was served before we even set foot in the house. This was the saving grace of the meal. But you can't just have vinegar chicken soup, orange cola, coffee and *banitsa* on the day the family kills a pig, you have to have some cabbage salad with it too.

I proceeded to stuff myself with the cabbage salad and *banitsa* that had been prepared just for us, all the while telling myself the *banitsa* would be my saving grace, diluting the undoubtedly adverse effect that soup would soon have on my digestive system. We later learned that there is a defined order for this particular breakfast, which, of course we didn't follow. The soup is first, with the orange soda and cabbage salad, then on to the *banitsa*. All of this is supposed to be washed down with coffee or tea. But where does the grilled pig ear fit in? Maybe it didn't count because we had eaten that outside, standing next to and staring at the animal whose ears had just been cut off.

About the time we realized that we could not do any more justice to the "breakfast" that had been served to us, we made our way back outside to check the progress on dispatching the dead pig. The large torch that had been singeing the hair and blackening the skin was actually cooking the skin just enough to loosen it on the fat layer between the skin and the muscle so it could be more easily peeled off. It was almost like peeling an over-ripe peach. But unlike the peach skin, the pigskin was not thrown away. The pig had been propped up on boards, so it was off the ground, with its feet straight up in the air, legs stiff. The smoke and smell of burning flesh still assaulted our noses and burned our eyes; it was apparent something significant was about to happen.

Of course, when you have a dead hairless pig lying on its back on a board with its feet in the air, there are three obvious next steps. One, carve a deep cross into the chest of the pig between the front legs, and fill it with salt. Two, start peeling away the warm, slippery skin in big patches, starting in the pits of the front legs and the flank, all the while eating the first pieces dipped in that salt. Three, cut the legs off at the knee so the pigs feet can be saved for flavoring a soup or some other dish. As the exposed skin was peeled off, it was dipped in the salty cross, rubbed over the gelatinous liquid pooling in the exposed knees, and eaten with great relish.

Watching the way each of the men took turns cutting off that perfect piece of skin, smashing it into the salt laden cross, smearing it across the knee bones, and eating it, I decided just made sense that I should also have some pig skin and *rakiya* to finish off my "second" breakfast of the day. And, if that wasn't enough to eat, the ears and tail were ready almost immediately after. These parts had been singed so there was no hair, but everything else was completely intact: skin, fat, cartilage, and a little bit of tailbone. The breakfast of champions. No meat, just skin, fat, and cartilage.

Not to let the party die, there was still a whole pig to dismember, so they brought out a few knives, a hammer, a hatchet, and an ax and went to work, all the while eating salty pig skin and pieces of the ears and tail. With the tools ready and food in their stomachs, the next task at hand was getting the body cavity opened and then getting the head dismantled. With seven sets of skillful hands, the work went quickly. One man set to work skinning the parts of the head that were accessible in preparation for chopping it off with a hatchet. A few other men were busy disemboweling the quickly cooling carcass. There was a large metal tub brought in close so all of the organs could be transferred into it without touching the ground. At the same time, the head—now completely skinned—was first split in half and then taken completely off the animal with three or four very strong and skillful whacks with the hatchet, which looked like it could have been 500 years old.

Having participated in butchering many animals myself, I was particularly interested in the care and attention that were going into the entrails. At home, these were the first things to be discarded, but not here. The kidneys were immediately pulled from the jumbled mess of guts and fat. They were split and sent to the grill for cooking. Next was the liver; after that the bright green, teardrop-shaped gallbladder was skillfully removed. Then the heart was split and sent to the grill, which by this time was full with all the other parts. The only part that was immediately discarded was the gallbladder. The lungs were the next things to be pulled from the mix, carefully separated from everything else and laid into a metal bucket with a lid. The stomach was tied off at both ends and the additional fat that was clinging to it was pulled off, but not discarded. Finally, the intestines were checked over meticulously. By the time all of this was done, there was nothing left in the big metal pan. Though I wasn't able to get an explanation as to what would happen to everything, it was obvious that there would be virtually no waste.

While one set of hands was working through the entrails, piece by piece, others began cleaning the body cavity and cutting off all the fat and meat that was not closely connected to bone. These parts went to a small stump where another man set to work carefully separating all the meat and fat, though I am not sure why as we had equal portions of each in our lunch two hours later. By this time, I had eaten my fill of grilled ear and tail, and Kate had watched as much as she could stomach of the process. After all, she didn't want to spoil her appetite for lunch.

It was such an interesting thing seeing these men, squatting down close to the dead pig, talking excitedly, drinking *rakiya* and dissecting the animal with one hand while eating with the other. There was no second thought given to switching hands from time to time, which I saw more than a couple of them do. Though they each had their own roles, and distinct characteristics, they were all also one. They were all big, brash Bulgarians; each wearing his faded blue communist work clothes. There was more than sixty years age difference between the youngest and the oldest, but their ages didn't differentiate them any more than their actions did.

They were all wearing the same clothes, they were all focused on the same task, and it forced me to think back to a time in their history when this was an act of survival instead of an act of tradition. A time when saving every part of the animal was a necessity so they could feed themselves and their families, so they wouldn't starve to death at the hands of the Turks. These men were so close to their ancestors, and it seemed like they were doing it for them, sitting on their haunches, arguing about what part to dismember next, and starting to eat the animal on the spot. They did all of this not because they were hungry or might lose the food to predators, but because it was the way they had always done it. This one dead pig would undoubtedly become food for the whole winter, and would keep the traditions and rituals (that might seem out of place on a cement patio in the middle of the village) alive for another year.

Back inside we went, to continue with our *na gosti*, literally a time to come and visit. *Na gosti* has a start time, but never an ending time, being an age-old cultural tradition where a clock is completely irrelevant. Time, relative to a *na gosti*, is defined by either daylight or darkness and always revolves around food and conversation. And though we had eaten breakfast twice already that day, it was time for our lunch. We began to see more plates of food coming toward us, mocking our full stomachs and our inability to say, "no thank you." These were heavy with the spoils of the dead pig: chunks of liver, heart, kidney, and meat were being served just two hours after our last meal. These delicacies were meant to be eaten slowly, while enjoying a conversation, some *rakiya* of course, and some music blaring from the TV that was always on in the background.

The short break between meals gave our hostess enough time to smoke a few cigarettes and prepare the table for an afternoon of sitting and talking. Since we had been in country less than four months, we reviewed some Bulgarian vocabulary so as to not sound less intelligent than that pig out in front of the house. And, though it wasn't a regular routine of hers, Kate had just enough time to get her fingernails painted by a friend who had made a special trip to do just that.

I allowed myself to get lost in thought, as my language ability wasn't comparable to Kate's, and I wanted to reflect on all that we had just observed. I was wondering what stage of dissection the pig was in, and where all the bones would go. Could the gallbladder really be the only thing that didn't get used? How many quart jars would it take to can 300 pounds worth of pig meat? And how long would you have to cook all of that before it could be canned? Were they going to make soap with the rendered fat like I knew some of the neighbors did? My pig curiosity far outweighed the uneasiness that came from new foods and overfull feeling I had in my stomach. It was also an excuse to get up and move around a little bit before we might be hit with another course of food.

Less than two hours had passed and the pig was gone, the grill was off, and the patio was all cleaned up. The only parts left visible were the two hams hanging from meat hooks off of the grape trellis and a few other random straps of meat. The innards, which were now outards, were spread around in various buckets being soaked in a salt brine solution. The rest of the meat had been boned out and was inside an outbuilding lying on the board in various sized chunks. The fat and bones were nowhere to be found, and the family (men and women still separated) had taken a break to have their lunch, too. The women sat at a small round table on the patio where they had spent all morning cleaning, and the men at a long table in what appeared to be an old restaurant next door. They were enjoying more meat, and of course, *rakiya*, so they were all smiles, something that is not common here unless someone has just told a joke or they are in the company of close family and friends.

Our third meal of the day was served: some of the fresh pork, which had been cooked with pickled cabbage, and big chunks of fat. We got to sample the prime spoils of the day's work. And, it was good.

Brian Fasset served in Bulgaria, B-16, from 2004-06 as a Community and Organizational Development Volunteer. He and his wife Kate served together in Plovdiv, the second largest city in Bulgaria. There, he worked with Land Source of Income Foundation, an NGO that provides microcredit loans to Roma (Gypsy) farmers, as well as teaching English. Brian's favorite English word he learned in Bulgaria is "draggle." Brian and Kate finished their service as Technical Trainers for the B-20 Volunteers. Back in the U.S., Brian spent three years in microfinance in Portland, Oregon, before becoming a staff development specialist at a local credit union.

REGINA LANDOR

✶

Returning to Macedonia

The power of the Peace Corps experience is that even if a service ends unexpectedly early, it leaves a permanent mark on the Volunteer's life.

I WAS THIRTY-FIVE YEARS OLD WHEN I JOINED THE PEACE CORPS. I was recently divorced and broken-hearted. After the break-up with a man I loved but who, sadly, did not want to have children, I did not know what I wanted to do with my life. My sister said "Peace Corps," and I knew right away that was my ticket. I was a teacher and I loved to travel. I filled out an online application and nine months later, I was in Washington, D.C., staging to go to Macedonia. We had barely settled into our seats when our staging guy said to us, "Look around you. Some of you may end up getting married." I scanned the room. I don't think so. There was no one in this room I was going to marry. Besides, marriage was far from my mind. Right now all I wanted was to volunteer and do my job.

I was, however, open to friendships, and that is exactly what happened with this group of people: we bonded uniquely over the next few months and over a series of circumstances that would change our lives forever. Most of us did fall in love. I certainly did in the end. I fell in love with Macedonia.

I fell in love with my host family, who welcomed me as one of their own. These were hard-working people who took care of me for three months, who helped me learn the language, who laughed with me at a wedding as I gaped in amazement at the head of a pig that was jubilantly offered to the bride and groom. I fell in love with the welcoming culture where it was customary to spend hours and hours sitting in a living room drinking coffee and visiting with neighbors. I fell in love with the gorgeous countryside, where grapes grow abundantly and where it's so rural that cars share the road with horses and carts carrying loads of hay. I fell in love with the contrasts of the environment where sheep's eyeballs in a jar sat in a window next to an ice cream shop; or where huge slabs of animal carcasses would line the window of a butcher shop next to a clothing store; or where my friend's host mother came home from her job in a jewelry store and before changing her clothes, cut the head off a chicken for their dinner. Everything was so new and different. I felt alive with excitement at having experiences that were so vastly different from anything I had ever known.

I knew before joining Peace Corps I was taking a risk signing up to live with a family for three months, strangers on the other side of the world. You just don't know what you'll end up with. When my family and I met, however, I felt like I ended up with a family I must have known in a past life. I felt like I was coming home. When I walked into their living room for the first time, I was presented with a little glass dish with something on it that I was expected to eat. I had no idea what it was. The son took the dish, and ate it himself, broadly pantomiming "delicious." I had some, too. And it was delicious. I later learned that *smokvie*, or sweetened figs, are presented to guests of honor. And later still I got to watch my host mother make *smokvie* in her kitchen, stirring an enormous pot of figs from their own garden on their wood-burning stove. People live close to the land, and I loved that, too.

In the evenings, I did my homework sitting at the table in the kitchen by the wood-burning stove. Never without my dictionary, I used the Macedonian I was learning as best I could to communicate with the family. They encouraged me. And we laughed a lot, sitting around that table, the dad swigging back his *rakija*, a homemade brandy, and everyone asking me questions about my life in America. Their house was so quiet at night; it was on a little hill at the end of a long drive. Occasionally, I'd hear horses' hoofs and a cart going by in the street. In the mornings, a rooster woke us up.

We were studying Macedonian so intensely, four or five hours a day, so we would be prepared to go off on our own to our sites where we all had jobs and where villages all over the country were expecting us. Toward the end of our three months of training, the teachers—whom we also grew to love for their utter devotion to helping us learn Macedonian—held a ceremony where we were told just where in the country we were being sent. No one knew where they were going, and we were jittery with excitement, waiting to be told. Finally the moment arrived. We were in a large field outside our training building. The hills of Kavadarci were in the distance. It was a gorgeous, warm summer afternoon. We stood in a line in front of our teachers. An enormous map of Macedonia was spread out on the ground behind them. As they called out our names, they handed us one word written on a piece of paper: the name of the town where we were going. There were shouts of excitement. I jumped up and down, and then went to stand on my spot on the map. Gradually, others stood near me, so I could see which friends I would be living near. I was going to be living in the north, in a village called Delchavo, by the Bulgarian border. I had been there on a visit a month back. It was a perfect spot. It was in the mountains. The small group of Volunteers I had gone with had a unique weekend there: we serendipitously saw a wedding in a small church; afterward, the priest invited us all inside to his private quarters for coffee. So, that's where I was going; I was thrilled. The teachers popped open a bottle of champagne in celebration.

I told my host family where I was going. It was about three hours by bus from them. I had grown particularly close to my host sister, Frosina, and her husband, Goran, during my stay. Frosina and Goran lived with their little girl and Goran's mother in a separate apartment, about a thirty-minute walk from the house I lived in with her mother, father, and brother. Frosina and I bonded. She wrote poetry, had a wonderful sense of humor, deep humility, and a deep soul. We understood each other and really grew to love each other. She told me at one point that I was the sister that she'd always wanted. She had a friend in Delchavo, the town I was moving to, and she gave me her number. That would be a good connection. I planned on coming back to Kavadarci in the fall to make roasted red peppers with my host family. The family was so used to taking care of me; they wondered how I would survive in an apartment on my own. I wondered, too. I joked with them that I needed them to come with me to continue taking care of me. Who was going to iron my clothes? Me?!

One week before we were sent to our sites, fighting between ethnic Albanians and Macedonians drastically increased. Devastating things were occurring in the country. It looked like a war was imminent. It also looked like there was a possibility that Peace Corps would have to pull out. Yes, we would. We were leaving. We were shocked. We were too stunned to speak when our Country Director gave us the news. We were angry. We were going to break promises. We felt a sense of shame. I told my host sister, and we cried and cried. Our group was numb. Then, unbelievably, a decision was made to keep Peace Corps in the country. Volunteers going to the south, where the fighting was the worst, would be found another site. So, we were staying after all. Before leaving my host family's home, my host mother made my favorite dessert one last time: *taloomba*, a puffed pastry soaked in sweet syrup. I quietly watched her every move as she showed me exactly how to do it. I took notes. Then, the next day my host brother drove me to the bus station with my luggage, and I was on a bus heading north, my new home for the next two years.

I had been at my site for one week, meeting my neighbors, meeting my new colleagues whom I would teach with, buying food at the outdoor markets, using my Macedonian, and actually taking care of myself. (No ironing, but definitely cooking.) I loved my new apartment with its view from the balcony of hills and red rooftops. I was practicing what one of our Peace Corps trainers told us to do: Sometimes it's more important to *be* than to *do*. I was *being* in my community, getting a feel for it, going on walks, and making connections with strangers. It all felt so right.

The phone call came at the end of my first week. One of my language teachers called to tell me the bad news: we were being evacuated. She started to cry on the phone. She told me that of all the sites that she worked on matching for the Volunteers, she thought that mine was the most perfect match. I quietly accepted this devastating news. I was too numb to cry anymore. I had been on such a roller coaster of emotions; I went into auto-pilot and started packing. The next afternoon, I said goodbye to Macedonia.

When I called my host mother on the phone in the middle of a plaza in a city in Bulgaria where we had been evacuated, the first thing she said to me was, "Are you eating?" I knew that that conversation was the last time I would be able to speak with her in her language. I was going to Romania in a few days. The Macedonian I had studied so hard to learn would simply fade away.

I boarded a plane in Sofia. I was with another American woman who, like me, was also determined to stay in the Peace Corps. A new training program had just begun in Romania. They needed teachers, and we were available. She and I practically clung to each other on that plane ride, so much did we feel that our world had just turned upside down. The ground beneath our feet had just disappeared.

And there we were a few hours later, plopped down in another country, meeting new Americans who'd already been in Ploiesti for a few weeks, who all knew each other. We were walking down a broad boulevard on a tour of our new city. No more Macedonia. Our group that we had become so close with: gone. My family whom I grew to love: gone. We were such fish out of water, staring wide-eyed at this strange environment, hearing a new language, and trying to feel normal. In the middle of our tour, my friend who was with me, and I stopped, looked at each other, hugged, and burst into tears. We were on sensory and cultural overload.

Eventually we adjusted and got a grip. Two other Americans from our Macedonia group joined us a few days later. Amongst this new Romanian Peace Corps group, the four of us became known as "The Macedonians."

A few weeks later, I met Billy Woodward, another Volunteer. He came to Ploiesti to teach the new Volunteers "coping strategies" once at site. He made a roomful of people laugh when he described getting his backpack stolen at an internet café while simultaneously reading a "Dear John" letter from his now ex-girlfriend. He was still in Ploiesti the following day, hanging around the training site, building up the courage to ask me out on a date. I did go out on a date with him and after our first kiss the first thing he said to me was, "Thank God there was a war in Macedonia." I guess it was fate. My topsy-turvy world was finally starting to make sense. One year later, Billy and I got married. A year after that, we had our first child, a boy we named Ethan.

My host family from Macedonia was never far from my mind. We did keep in touch, but I wondered under what unusual circumstances I would ever possibly see them again. I was living in Peoria, Illinois, raising my children (a second son, Gabriel, came along) and nowhere near that little village in the hills, so far away. Eight years passed, and then the universe took over and started working in its mysterious ways. Billy was hired by USAID and got posted to Belgrade, Serbia, which put us a mere five hours from the Macedonian border.

A few weeks after we arrived, I took Billy and my children to a place I once called home, however brief that time was. The village of Vatasha, Macedonia, in my mind was another lifetime ago. In some ways, I think I believed that in return-ing, nothing would be the same. Goran's mother would no longer be alive. My host family would surely have a shower installed by now. The village would of course have hot water all day. I found out I was wrong on all counts. Nothing seemed to have changed. Time stood still for me and allowed me to walk in the front door of my host family's home and smell the same smells, see the same pictures hanging on the walls, the same old-world furniture, the same welcoming, open arms, the same laughter, the same humor and kind faces, the same hard-working people who know how to embrace life, despite what little they have.

Of course I cried when my host mother and father embraced me. I walked into their front door and there they were, just as before, smiling at me as if to say, "You've finally come home."

I expected my host family to greet me with open arms, but I did not consider the neighbors, who also remembered me. Billy and I walked past the old lady with the goats, wearing traditional clothing: a skirt, a headscarf, and an apron. When she saw me her face lit up. She came out from behind her wooden fence, heartily took Billy's hand in hers and gave me a big hug. I could not believe she remembered me.

The family owns a small vineyard. Each evening we were there, they came home on their tractor with crates and crates of grapes to be pressed into a huge vat. A family member came over in the evening to help with the winemaking. When he came into the garage where the pressing was happening, he gave a great big shout of greeting when he saw me. I was shocked that this man also remembered me. Other neighbors also greeted me warmly, surprised at seeing me walk by their front door. All I could think of were my Peace Corps buddies. If they could be here, then they would also see that our brief encounter with this tiny corner of the world had not been in vain. I am remembered, but surely they are, too, and I believe that I was embraced so warmly by these neighbors because they knew our intentions, which were to do good for their country. So I like to think that those embraces were for all of us and that we did leave our mark, however small, and that the mark was one of goodwill.

On our first morning there I took Billy and our boys for a walk along the river that runs by the little road I lived on. It was an absolutely gorgeous fall morning: the smell of firewood burning was in the air; I think the same horse was drinking from the river; and the same ducks and chickens were running around. This was the river that a small group of us helped clean up. Apparently, no one has thought of doing that in a long time: plastic bottles and all sorts of trash again line the riverbank. The Roma homes were where they were before, further on down the river. We passed the homes where my friends had lived. We walked by the building where we sat in a cold room and were taught Macedonian by Betty, one of the kindest teachers I've ever had.

In the evening, Billy and I planned to go out with Frosina and Goran, my host sister and her husband. We walked the thirty minutes to their house, and my feet just showed me the way. I remembered how to get there and arrived at their front door. Goran's mother was there—alive, but with fewer teeth—blessing me and kissing my forehead.

We drove to a few sites around Vatasha. We went to an ancient Roman settlement and when we pulled up to the café and gift shop (which weren't there before) Billy had his own personal feeling of pride: a USAID plaque was on the building stating that funds from USAID had been used in constructing the café and shop. The same was true of a park we went to: another USAID sign.

Something really beautiful happened that weekend. I saw again that what I received from my Macedonian host family was so genuine and real, and it wasn't fleeting. It lasted, that mutual love and respect and friendship lasted over time and over continents.

Regina Landor started out her Peace Corps service in Macedonia. Three months into training there, her group, Mac-6, was evacuated. One week later, she started up with a new group in Romania, RO-12, and served from 2001-02, teaching English to 5th-8th graders. There were blessings in her leaving beloved Macedonia: she met her husband, another PC Volunteer, in Romania. They continue to travel with the Foreign Service and currently live in Belgrade, Serbia, with their two boys, Ethan and Gabriel.

RICHARD SCHWARTZ

Images of Turkey

You can leave Turkey, but it never really leaves you.

THE IMAGE IS INDELIBLE. IT'S LASTED OVER FORTY YEARS.

Here I am standing on the outskirts of this small Anatolian market town in north central Turkey, 1966. I'm in a field of dirt, mottled occasionally with patches of grass, a few boulders, and lots of rocks. The sun is just reaching high in the sky, and it's a very clear and cool day.

Next to me a group of schoolboys are laughing and playing soccer with a tin can. They're in their school uniforms, including a school cap, which looks like the kind commercial pilots wear. The kids beckon me to play, but I'm too chicken. If the game involved using my hands or arms, I'd join them. Some of them are my students, and it would be a good way to build rapport. But when it comes to soccer, I have two left feet.

To my back is the place I call "home." I live in the basement of a two-story, gray, cinderblock building. I have cold running water, an indoor toilet, "bomb site" of course, a bed, and a kerosene-burning room stove. Altogether it's not too bad a place by local bachelor standards, or my own, and I am quite comfortable there.

Along the path that runs beside where the kids are playing, I spot a donkey approaching from the distant village. It's nothing unusual. Donkeys, ducks, sheep, and horses have all trod by, leaving their respective droppings, the identification of which I've become somewhat expert. As the donkey gets closer, I notice its rider is an elderly man, a grandfather-type of guy, whose legs dangle almost to the ground. He's dressed in traditional peasant garb. His pants are loose fitting, his jacket an old two-buttoned sport coat, and on his head he's wearing an old, black stocking cap. His shoes are black lace-ups, dirtied with mud, and the backs of the heels are forced down so they resemble slippers. His white beard is well trimmed and neat.

While it's the dangling legs that initially draw my attention, it's the image of his face—eyes covered by sunglasses and ears covered by headphones attached to a portable transistor radio—which grabs my imagination.

I don't know what he was listening to, but I've always assumed it was the news. The image is very powerful. Talk about connectivity! In 1966, that man was connected. His communications technology was modern. He knew what a radio was. He knew it came in "wireless" format. He knew it was powered by batteries. He obviously knew how to use it. He may have been the passive recipient we all are when we use radio, but then again the interactive world of the Internet had not yet been born.

The image of that man and his donkey has unspooled itself on a regular basis over the past forty years. It sustained me through graduate school and perhaps motivated me, in the first place, toward my doctorate in anthropology. Old values, new values; technology old and new. The blending of cultures. The diffusion and assimilation of new thoughts and ideas. The rejection of others. The melding of the East and West. He's my personal symbol of complexity and simplicity rolled into one. I still wonder about that old man. What was he actually listening to? What did he think of the changes affecting his life and those of his friends and family? Did he feel powerless to do anything about the inevitable unfolding of events that swirled around him?

There are many other images of Turkey that have stuck with me. Another involves my male "piggishness." I admit it. It is of two women who passed me on the street in Izmir while I was window shopping in one of the finer neighborhoods of the city. Izmir is the third largest city in Turkey and quite modern. As Turkish women often do, they were walking arm in arm. At first I saw them only from the back and noticed that one, quite shapely, was wearing tight-fitting black slacks and a colorful top and heels. The other was covered in an all black *chador*. I could tell little about her clothes, her shape or her age.

I guessed that they were mother and daughter and that, of course, the mother was wearing the chador and the daughter the slacks. When they stopped to window shop, I passed them. What a shock! It was the mother who was the "modern" one and the daughter, whose face was uncovered, who was dressed more traditionally. This image was in 1997, more than thirty years after I stepped foot in Turkey for the first time. And my shock stands to reason given the unpredictable, topsy-turvy and apparently random evolution (some would call it the "devolution") of political, religious, and cultural mores in the country. That struggle seems never to abate.

I've been back to Turkey over a dozen times since leaving the Peace Corps in 1967. I've enjoyed each trip and always learn something new. Of greatest importance to me is that I continue to enhance my relationship with my friend Osman, his immediate and extended family, and a wide variety of people he and his wife have introduced me to. Osman and I are the same age and have children who are close in age as well. He has two boys. I have two girls. Osman hoped, I believe, that we could arrange a marriage between his older son, Okay, and my older daughter Rachel. It didn't work out. They've each married someone else though they met in Turkey in 1999. That was another image. Rachel and Okay, along with Lexy (my younger daughter) and Gungor (Osman's wife), sitting around the table playing a board game. It was pure joy. And while my girls knew only a few words of Turkish, and Okay and his mother a couple words of English, they played for hours like they were old friends. Language may have been an impenetrable barrier prohibiting Rachel and Okay from getting to know each other better, but it certainly didn't stop them from trying nor from having a good time.

I can't wait for my next trip.

Richard Schwartz spent 1965-67 in Anatolian Turkey as a TEFL teacher in Merzifon, a market town near the Black Sea coast. When he returned to the States he earned a M.S. degree and Ph.D. in anthropology at Washington University, St. Louis. From there he spent seven years teaching anthropology at Roanoke College in Salem, Virginia, before beginning his business career in Houston. He's been in Houston for thirty years, is married, has three grown daughters and a granddaughter. Though an accomplished career changer, Richard's love and respect for the people of Turkey, and their history, has been constant. His wife and two of his daughters have accompanied him on various trips to Turkey. He's returned to Turkey many times and maintains a close and warm relationship with his Turkish friends.

Taking Pictures in Central Asia

Some sights simply are not meant be experienced through photos.

I HAD TERRIBLE LUCK WITH CAMERAS DURING MY TWO YEARS with the Peace Corps in Uzbekistan. While wandering through a crowded Bukhara bazaar, my camera, filled with shots of old *madrassahs* and mosques, disappeared from my coat pocket. In the city of Shakrisabz, another camera smacked hard on the ground, sending my traveling companions Nate and Jordan shaking with laughter, and it then refused to work afterward. A few months earlier, I wandered about the busy Quva bazaar with my camcorder to my eye, only to be stopped and interrogated by the *militsya*. No pictures here!

At the time, digital cameras were still a novelty, and I envied the few Volunteers who brought them. They didn't have to bother with photo developing or printing. My pictures that did survive came out faded, the colors a muddy hue, the result of bad processing by Fergana's photo shops. The PCVs with digital cameras didn't have that problem.

"I took two hundred pictures of this trip so far," Jordan boasted during our trip to Shakrisabz, the birthplace of the cruel Tamerlane. Digital cameras made the discretion of selective picture taking obsolete. A roll of camera film had only thrity-six exposures, and I attempted to frame up a postcard perfect image of a colorful *madrassah*, as Jordan snapped a dozen photos of the same sight.

Jordan and I had gone AWOL from the Peace Corps for a weekend, escaping the confines of Peace Corps regulations. To hell with Hassan and the whereabouts policy! We headed out of Tashkent, and I thought *I'm an American taxpayer! Hassan is working for me!* We were bound for Jizzak to pick up Nate, and then to Shakrisabz, and from there not exactly sure of our itinerary. We were simply going.

Tall, with blonde, Aryan features, Jordan had a cynical urbane wit. "Uzbeks are mad!" he would exclaim. Mad as in crazy, he would elaborate, and then rail at the shifty taxi drivers trying to overcharge us.

"I told the Peace Corps recruiter during my interview I wanted to join so I could have time to read Proust. That was the end of the interview. I was in."

Jordan would ask locals to pose for photos, and after they happily obliged, showed them their frozen images in the viewfinder. They stared amazed, having never seen such a camera before.

"No film!" he would explain in Uzbek. The locals looked at him as if at a simpleton, wanting to say, "Maybe you should put some film in your camera!"

The taxi dropped us off at the bus station in Jizzak where we waited for Nate. Growing hungry, we sought out an *oshkhona* for a bowl of rice pilaf. Locals pointed us to a smoking kebab stand across the street. A man in a greasy apron there shook his head—no pilaf here!—and pointed us in the direction from where we just came. "Uzbeks are mad!"

A passenger bus rolled to a stop at the curb, and the doors parted to reveal boyish Nate, smiling and full of his usual enthusiasm. "To hell with Peace Corps regulations!"

We negotiated with another taxi driver to take us further south. The gray ribbon of road snaked through foothills. Soon Nate was eagerly pointing out the pass we were driving through as the very route Alexander and his armies had traveled through millennia before, on their way north to conquer Samarkand. Before I could snap a photo, Jordan had clicked off five.

Until my camera went flying through the air to break on the ground, I was able to capture a few shots of Shakrisabz's main feature, the remains of Tamerlane's fifteenth-century palace, the Ahk Serai. After centuries of conquest and pillage, a pair of tall pillars pointing skyward was all that remained of the fabled palace. The colorfully tiled monoliths, towering over a hundred feet, were still impressive, and attested to what ancient travelers claimed to have been a magnificent palace. We circled the towers, where swallows nested and swooped amongst the moldering bricks. The few photos I snapped show patches of colorful tile work arranged in intricate, hallucinogenic patterns, still adhering to the twin monoliths after so many centuries.

A fifteen-minute walk from the Ahk Serai, Tamerlane's grandson Ulugbek had built the Kok Gumbaz Mosque, surrounded by a complex of *madrassahs*. As we wandered about the buildings in the afternoon sun, I looked up to notice whiskery weeds and tiny brown blemishes in the elaborate, multicolored dome. Tiles from the dome were losing their grip and falling to the ground, only to be discarded by the groundskeepers. Jordan gestured to a trash heap, and then held up an intact multicolored tile. Its simple fleur-de-lis design belied the intricacy of the dome's ornamentation that, to the distant eye, appeared extraordinarily detailed.

Despite the age of the mosque, the tile's antiquity was questionable. Much of the renovation of the nation's mosques and *madrassahs* hadn't occurred until the latter part of the Soviet era. During the dark era of the early, hard-line regime, restrictions on religious expression resulted in the closure of religious centers. Many were converted to stables or into anti-religious museums, the buildings allowed to decay with age.

Following the death of Stalin, renovation ensued. A picture from the early 1960s showed Samarkand's Registan Square absent of its famed turquoise domes, the facades of the *madrassahs* in a sad state of disrepair. Since then, the complex's splendor had been restored. The Soviets realized the opportunity to make money from tourism.

The following day, we were there in Samarkand; the three of us at a café table, sharing a pot of steaming tea, and admiring the view of the famed Registan across the street. Alexander had been to Samarkand in 329 B.C., and declared the city to be the most beautiful he had ever laid eyes on. History, however, had not been kind to Central Asia. Over the centuries, invading armies had repeatedly destroyed the city's charms and splendors. Almost two thousand years after Alexander had set foot there, the city experienced a renaissance under the tyrannical Tamerlane and his heirs.

We strolled about the *madrassahs* of the Registan with its minarets and turquoise domes gleaming in the afternoon sun. The *madrassahs* were typical of Central Asia in that their magnificent facades lured visitors into a less than flattering courtyard interior. Inside its walls, arched chambers opened into bare courtyards. Vendors occupied the alcoves that once housed religious students, selling antique busts of Lenin alongside intricately designed carpets. Many of the ruby-colored rugs had been smuggled from Turkmenistan, adorned with the hallucinogenic patterns identical to those of the tiled mosaics decorating the *madrassahs'* walls.

The Registan was the spiritual center of Uzbekistan. The image of the plaza with its three ornate *madrassahs* adorned the *som* notes and political murals throughout the nation. If

Tamerlane were to come back to life and return to the site, he would recognize nothing. Domed caravansaries and mosques had occupied the site during his life, only to be torn down by his grandson Ulugbek, who inherited his grandfather's ambitious plans. Ulugbek's artisans had built the first of the current three *madrassahs*; the other two were erected in the seventeenth century to complete the current symmetrical layout. The massive square had served as the setting for military parades and public executions under generations of presiding khans. The Bolsheviks used it for political rallies and veil burnings. Today, the site was used as an epic backdrop for televised folk performances.

Jordan wandered off to meet a friend, and Nate and I sought out a taxi to take us to the Bibi Xonum, the grand mosque dedicated to Tamerlane's Mongol wife. On the taxi ride through the city's busy streets, I read from Nate's guidebook of how the emperor had set out to build the most splendorous mosque in all of Islamdom. The entrance had been epic, towering over a hundred feet, dwarfed by even taller sleek minarets pointing toward heaven. Intricately carved marble, inlaid with semi-precious gems, adorned the edifices of the vast complex of chambers. The scope and grandeur were typical of the emperor's excesses.

"Here we are!"

As we stepped onto the curb, I saw that the mosque was only a shell of its former glory. An earthquake a century before had leveled much of the complex, and the restoration that had taken place since was based on the imagination of the restorers. In the fore courtyard squatted a marble platform that once held a sixteen square-foot Koran from the seventh century, the booty of Tamerlane's conquests.

We strolled past the main gate that towered over a hundred feet, the façade replete with intricate blue-and-white tile.

"When I was here a few months ago, a lot of these doorways weren't closed off," Nate said at the sight of boarded-up arched passageways. Seeing no one in sight, my companion quickly removed a spare board, and hoisted himself into a dark interior.

"Are you coming?"

Sneaking through a few bare, forgotten chambers, we climbed to a precipice, and took in the vast complex of the Bibi Xonum. Beyond the stucco walls lay a gray urban horizon. Spindly TV antennas and grim apartment blocks spoiled any illusion of this former Silk Route destination. The sights of the ancient fabled center of the Timurid dynasty had been reduced to small islands within this Sovietized urban sprawl, the second largest city in Uzbekistan. The gems of that ancient era were certainly here, but they required savoring at close range, and not on a wide scale.

On a later trip to western Uzbekistan, I discovered the fabled city of Khiva to be much different from Samarkand. Khiva was the only Silk Route city that I was able to successfully photograph. My pictures reveal a collection of khaki-colored edifices lining the narrow alleys, and populated with prowling tourists and vendors. There were no street-sweeping *kaelins* here, no neighborhood kids playing soccer. Khiva was an open-air museum with state-licensed vendors selling souvenirs to crowds of wandering foreigners. The city's largest *madrassah* had been turned into a state-run hotel.

If Samarkand was a hodgepodge of the glorious old and the ugly urban, and Khiva was an uninhabited museum setting, then the heart of Bukhara's old city contained the best of all the Silk Route cities.

Chris had hired a van and a driver for his family and friends to make the ten-hour trip through the western desert to Bukhara. As miles and miles of desert scrub rolled by, Chris and his brother passed the time devising a plan to purchase the huge statue of Lenin lying in a Nukus junkyard, then transporting it home to the U.S., in the hopes of finding an eccentric millionaire to whom they could sell it. While they chattered, I stared out the van's window at the Amu Daryo River, and beyond it, Turkmenistan. The desert horizon was blurred by dust devils and clouds of windswept sand. An unusual ten-foot tall bump of earth blemished the flat terrain.

"Zoroastrian burial mounds," Chris explained. "They're thousands of years old." A Volunteer described how he had clambered up such a hill only to accidentally unearth a baby's skull.

We reached Bukhara at sunset, feeling a tad queasy after ten hours of bumping along the potholed freeway, desperate to escape the van. The inn we checked into lay in a *mahallah* of narrow alleys near the city's center, the blistered, carved doors of private homes attesting to the age of the neighborhood. We strolled about the city, cameras in hand, in search of a restaurant.

"How much meester? First price, very good!" Vendors called to us from their dank chambers in the moldering caravansery. Chris's mother studied a beautiful silk carpet. A salesman proudly showed off his collection of war carpets, rugs from Afghanistan with depictions not of the customary intricate Turkmen designs, but of tanks and Kalashnikovs. I snapped a photo of Chris and his brother negotiating the price of a stringed *dootar*.

The following afternoon, after wandering about the old city, I said goodbye to my friends as they boarded their van to continue eastward to Samarkand. I had plans to remain behind for a few extra days with Volunteers, and to deliver HIV presentations to local students. Over a plate of pilaf I switched rolls of film, and headed off to retrace my steps in search of photo opportunities.

I snapped photos of the synagogue in the Jewish quarter, where a once thriving Jewish community 800 years old had dwindled, within a decade, to a handful of residents. Through an arched doorway, I leaned back to shoot the Kalon minaret, the "Tower of Death," where subjects who had displeased the khan were taken to the top and tossed to the gawking crowd far below. Later, the minaret was used by Bolshevik soldiers for target practice. My grainy photos show the holes in the tower punched out by cannonballs.

I retreated to an outdoor café, parked myself at a *xontakta* under a mulberry tree, and ordered a bowl of *laghman*. An afternoon of snapping photographs left me content. I had proof of the numerous sites I had visited that I could share with friends and family back home. The ancient carved wooden doors of the Old City, the mosques, the alleys through which Marco Polo must have strolled.

It wasn't until I packed my belongings and rushed to the airport a few days later that I realized my camera was missing. The day before, I remembered feeling its weight in my jacket pocket as I hurried through the bazaar to catch a *marshrutka*. Its presence there had then slipped my mind.

Tom Fleming served as a health instructor, where he focused his efforts on HIV/AIDS prevention, in Uzbekistan from 2003-05. Currently Tom is completing a master's degree in Russian studies at the University of Texas at Austin.

PART TWO

WHY ARE WE HERE?

BRIAN FASSETT

The Other Bulgaria

*Though Volunteers are invited to the countries they serve in,
locals often struggle to understand the Volunteers' purpose.*

GETTING OFF THE BUS IN ISKAR WAS LIKE WALKING INTO A stranger's living room. Bags in hand, we were ready to stay for the weekend, but we hadn't been invited. There was that awkward moment where they were sizing us up, and we were second-guessing our decision. Maybe we should cut our losses and go back. Maybe they would invite us in to sit down. If we moved slowly and talked quietly, maybe they wouldn't notice we were different. It was as if we had flown into town on our very own spaceship. Another Volunteer who had lived there almost six months was with us, but he was still as much of an outsider as we were. It wasn't being American that made us stand out, it was just blatantly obvious that we didn't live or work close to the land. We didn't have dirty fingernails, we didn't have clothes that were faded and worn by sun and work. It was apparent we didn't do manual labor. We were office and apartment dwellers. We stepped off a country bus, five hours from our big city apartment in Plovdiv, and found ourselves in the middle of the "other" Bulgaria, not our Bulgaria, not at all.

Four steps off that bus, and we had been stripped of our big city anonymity. We didn't stick out quite as much in the middle of 400,000 people as we did in the middle of 2,000. There were as many sheep and horses and horse carts in our immediate proximity as there were people. In this place, it was harder to find a car than a donkey cart. In Iskar, everyone has a direct tie to the land, whether by choice or by necessity. The unemployment rate in this other Bulgaria is close to 40 percent, but that doesn't mean almost half the population sits at home wanting something to do. It just means they don't get paid (by someone else) for all their days full of labor. They are working to feed themselves. Their hands are busy trying to keep their modest homes from falling apart as the hundred-year-old mud bricks disintegrate in the elements. They preserve their own food for the winter, sew their own clothes, and fix things when they break. Every person in town is a jack-of-all-trades, but a master of none. They aren't really unemployed. They just aren't employed.

Iskar was the other Bulgaria that we had only tasted for our first three months of training. We remembered the flavor, and the novelty was not gone. Life in the other Bulgaria was the Peace Corps experience that our friends and family in the U.S. imagined we would have. It was the physically difficult and necessity deprived existence that could justify comparison to that "mud hut experience" in Africa: the quintessential Peace Corps life of physical discomfort and mental reward that everyone holds in their imagination. Did it make us any less as Volunteers to be living in a new apartment in what was arguably the nicest city in the country? A city that had been continuously inhabited since Neolithic times, where we took for granted the Greek and Roman ruins that we walked past each day. Besides upending our limited sense of history, it made us second guess our potential impact on a place that had been civilized since before the Bronze Age.

For Matt, the TEFL Volunteer living in Iskar, there wasn't any novelty left in this "typical" Peace Corps placement. As much as we were longing for an assignment like he had, in a town where everyone knew his name—and maybe they knew even more about him than he knew about himself—he wished for our big city luxuries. He worked in the Bulgaria where wireless internet connected his students to the world, but they walked to school on dirt streets, passing herds of sheep, not sure whether the electricity or water would work on any given day. We had multiple movie theaters in town and more restaurants than we could explore in two years of service, but found ourselves wanting to be closer to the chickens and sheep, and the people who produced all of the food they ate. While he wanted a place to spend his extra living allowance, instead of saving it up every month, we were longing for that small town existence where we could afford to save at least a little of our two living allowances.

What else were we wishing upon ourselves? Did we want to be in that fishbowl that we had been warned about so many times during training? We had conveniently avoided that by living in the city. We had just come to visit Matt for the weekend and spend some time celebrating Orthodox Easter (though not with anyone who was Orthodox). Instead, it felt as if we had just opened up our underwear drawer for everyone in this little town to have a look in. Getting off that bus in Iskar was like re-living our first day of training with our host families.

Everyone's mental notes were broadcast loud and clear:

> *Are you someone's relative?*
> *Maybe the friend of a neighbor?*
> *Or are you just lost?*
> *Are you alone? If so, why?*
> *If not, who are you with?*
> *Could you be German or maybe British?*

Are you carrying something interesting?
Is it properly concealed in a plastic shopping bag?
How long are you going to stay?
Do you even speak Bulgarian?
Can you speak at all?
Are you another American?

Could there really be another American that gave up a good job, living near family, home, car, belongings for this? For Bulgaria?

They never said a word, but they asked all of these questions, and more. Luckily, since Matt had been in Iskar almost a year, he was a known entity. He was the anchor for all of those questions, and the answer to a few. His familiarity allowed us a little leeway. It let us slip by with a little less scrutiny, and a little more credibility. Because Plovdiv has so many foreigners, and so many people, no one noticed if we had guests, nor did they notice or care whether those guests spoke Bulgarian, had a third arm, or had horns growing out of their heads.

Matt had two extra mouths to feed, and none of us wanted to run out of food on our three-day sojourn in the wilds of the village. Grocery shopping in Iskar should have been simple enough. We only needed bread, eggs, vegetables, fruit, soda, sugar, toilet paper, cheese, and yogurt. However, to find those things, we ended up going to four different shops—all four shops in town. When we asked for eggs at each place, storeowners looked at us with incredible pity, as if we hadn't already done enough to make ourselves outsiders in this little town. Their hands were making the universal motion for eating, finger tips together heading for their mouth, as if every egg in Bulgaria had been eaten just moments before we arrived to make our purchase.

Later each would tell a friend:

"Did you hear? The American teacher had guests for the long weekend?"

"Ya, I saw all three of them at the bus station, at the grocery stores, in the center, at the bakery and in front of the school." (They saw us in just one place.)

"They bought a two month's supply of food for just three people!"

"I guess the American doesn't know how to raise a garden."

"Not only that, they asked about buying eggs."

"He doesn't have chickens?"

"Don't they know this is the day before Easter?"

"They asked for eggs at Boris' shop, at Nedelka's, and at Donka's place. Sad, isn't it?"

"Those poor Americans."

Dying Easter eggs is serious business. As well it should be. Once they are dyed, they might end up at church, or on the mantle for the year to come, so it should be done with sufficient reverence. Just like other Easter eggs, Orthodox Easter eggs get dyed all different colors, as long as those colors are mostly red. But, in Bulgaria, you don't just crack the dyed eggshell on the counter before peeling it, salting it, and eating it. Here everyone chooses an egg. A red egg. Then, you ever so skillfully smash them together and see which one breaks. Depending on the angle of impact, the speed, and the skill of the holder, your egg might sustain this collision. If you are so lucky, and your egg lives through all subsequent collisions with every other egg in the room, it is honored with a seat on the mantle. And there it sits for the year, until Orthodox Easter rolls around again, and a new, fresher, redder, bigger egg replaces it.

If you are devout Orthodox, then you march your dyed red eggs to church with you for the midnight Mass that only happens on Easter. You have been fasting for weeks in celebration of this important holiday. You have gone weeks without eating any animal products. Just vegetables. No wonder you are taking eggs to church. You are so close to eating them, but you have to wait. It's all about the timing. You have to wait for the bell.

During the service, the priest comes through the congregation and blesses you and your eggs. The clock strikes midnight, and you break a few of those eggs, and eat them, ceremoniously ending your fast. You might smash your egg against someone else's, and find that one, unbreakable, superhuman egg that gets placed on the mantle for the year. Or, you might not. You might just eat two or three or four because you are hungry for the animal protein you have been starving for. Either way, the ground outside the church is covered with red eggshells the next day. There are trails of eggshells that lead away from the church in every direction, marking the way to the homes of all the devout followers.

Easter morning found us making a big sweeping loop by foot to the north and east of Iskar on the hills overlooking the town and the river. We had packed some food for a picnic and were looking forward to some time without the constant background noise from the city. No car alarms, no cars. No honking busses belching diesel fumes, no busses at all. Just the sound of shepherds talking to their dogs, the shuffling sounds and bells of sheep making their way around the hills overlooking town, and silence. In this Bulgaria, you could actually hear the sound of even the slightest breeze, blowing into your ear, the sound of birds singing, of plants growing, of the morning dew burning off as the sun got hot in the sky.

We just stopped walking, found a tree to sit under, and had our lunch. It wasn't in a park or a walled yard. There were no fences keeping us out, or in. There were no barriers. We were finally out of the city. As we ate, we could watch water buffalo off in the distance, see herds of milk cows grazing near the river, and there was nothing in between them and us. While we were near a road, it felt like we could have walked forever without having ever returned to modernity. This was what being a Peace Corps Volunteer was supposed to feel like.

Monday morning marked our last day in this other Bulgaria, the last chance to soak in the quiet and the calm of the small town before returning to our Bulgaria. It was Matt's last chance for good conversation, his last chance to talk on and on in English. I had re-whetted my appetite for a more idyllic volunteer experience, though I wouldn't have wished away the one I had. I wanted both. But, I guess the grass is always greener in the other Bulgaria.

Back at home, Kate and I immediately began preparing our little space for another week. We turned on the boiler so we would have hot water to shower in a couple hours. But this time, we felt lucky that we had a boiler at all. We prepared our water distiller, reminding ourselves that it was nice to have electricity to even run the distiller. We brought in our clothes that had been air-drying on the balcony, our clothes that eventually would be worn out from wearing, hand washing, and wearing. But not wear from working—not the type of work that most of Bulgaria still engages in on a daily basis.

What made these two places inside this one small country feel so far apart? It wasn't our physical surroundings. We could still hear chickens crowing in Plovdiv, the second largest city in the country. We were affected by the same weather. We got the same news. We had the same seasons and ate the same food. It was the people—the way they lived, spoke, dressed— that made all the difference.

In Iskar, residents didn't need a fancy vocabulary to milk a cow, or hoe a field, or carry water. Their vocabulary was simpler. Their clothes were more functional than fashionable, showing the signs of the elements. People looked like they had earned the years they lived, like they had fought hard for the time they had spent on this earth. They were missing teeth, and fingertips, and wearing Soviet-era glasses that were long due for replacing. But that didn't change their outlook on life, or their appreciation for what they had. They were as happy as anyone. Men wore hats and women wore head-scarves, not as fashion accessories, but as functional necessities, to shield them from the elements. Their life is here and now, their world is small, and their daily functions are uncomplicated by wireless internet or cars or computers. And they aren't any less fulfilled as people. Whether or not they have water or electricity or life's other niceties as we have in our Bulgaria, life goes on just the same.

We wanted it—that other Bulgaria—where the hardships we faced would have been in hard work and cold water and going without. But maybe what we did, and saw, and lived, and learned, and struggled through was comparable. Life goes on just the same.

Bryan Fassett also contributed "The Pig" to Part One.

BENJAMIN BAGGETT

Mongolia's First City Park

*Despite the Soviet mantra of solidarity and communal
development that surpassed race and borders, these concepts
often saw little application on the Central Asian steppes.*

SOARING OVER A MILE ABOVE THE GOBI DESERT INTO THE FLAT,
broad plains of Mongolia's central region, Peace Corps recruits
from Group Eleven were within minutes of arriving in the
capitol city, Ulaanbaatar. Out the window, the golden light
gilded sparse clumps of trees lining the south slopes of the
nearby foothills; others fingered along the riverbanks outside
the city's dense circuit of streets. As the plane descended, the
scenes gently unfolded, while shades became color and shadows became shapes.

As we neared the runway, the open plains turned to a desolate horizon with few signs of life. Hopeful thoughts of teaching or promoting environmental awareness began to dissolve
into the bleak scenes below. What happened to the images of
snow-peaked mountains, beautiful green grasslands, and for-
ested regions of sacred mountains shown in online travel logs?
The images must have been captured from somewhere else,
somewhere far from this central region of Mongolia, somewhere out there beyond the horizon. After all, a country three

times the size of France or two-and-a-half times the size of the state of Texas must have more to offer.

Those early moments of arrival soon passed into faded memory. Within one week, we had entered training an hour east of the capitol, in the small town of Zuunmod, or "100 Trees." The views from town captured the surrounding hills where dense stands of evergreens grew at the nearby nature preserve and monastery. The sacred mountain of Bogd Khan Uul somehow anchored the town with a silent, abiding calm presence, like an old man who has stood watch for some inordinate amount of time. This mountain was where Chinggis (Genghis) Khan's courts produced a code of ethics for conservation, protecting the natural environment by setting guidelines for tree cutting, grazing, hunting and appropriate hygiene (no urinating in the streams). It was apparent after only a few weeks that the locals had as much an appreciation for the mountain as we new arrivals did. Within the short period of training, we traversed its summit and became knowledgeable of its features. It had often been the subject of in-depth scientific studies, religious practice and pilgrimage, and summertime junkets. Weekenders used it as a getaway from the stresses of the rapidly developing nearby capitol city.

In the center of the town was a small park. A half-mended metal fence skirted the edge of its borders, and the inside was worn with two single paths crisscrossing the interior: one to an exit, the other to an entrance. The park was used as a cut through. Concrete animals hatched from some universal mold posed frozen in time as the weather eroded their surfaces. The location of the park was a logical center of the town, but it was somehow cut off or simply in the way, either dead or certainly dying. The park did not connect with the people, and no one really seemed to care. Above all, it really looked out of place, as many of the Soviet era constructions did by this time.

The roads leading out of town, crossed with makeshift jeep tracks, hinted at no discernible order or purpose except to get from one point to another. Rutted jeep tracks followed power lines, streams, and ridges. In addition to the damage from the jeeps, land in nearby towns was visibly stripped of forageables by countless herds of cattle, leaving small deserts behind. Strip mining for coal and other minerals left the landscape pockmarked. Mounds of tailings left refuse burning in the sun. Abandoned Soviet-style buildings dotted each town. Evidence of industry gone belly up was apparent in most all the stops between the capitol and my new site, over three hundred kilometers east. I had to remind myself that it was only ten years earlier that Boris Yeltsin had left office and the Soviet Union fell, leading Mongolia's economy down a bumpy if not disastrous road. It didn't seem possible that this much decay could happen in such a short period of time, but then again the decline began well before Mr. Yeltsin's sober epiphany caused him to leave the Kremlin.

Khentii Province, my new work site, was also the birthplace and the alleged burial place of the great ruler himself, Chinggis Khan. His 500th birthday, as I was reminded many times, was the next year. Upon arriving in town, we found the layout oddly familiar. There was a square in the center of town, tall Soviet buildings on the fringe, and in the middle of everything was the front stage display of the government offices. But there, only a short distance from the square, was another park. Similar to the others, it appeared abandoned. Upon closer look, we saw that it was completely off limits for the local population: a steel fence united all four corners, prohibiting any entry into the large interior of the two acres. Inside the fence's perimeter, a few shrubs clung to the sandy soil, and a lone tree staked its claim in the corner.

Upon taking my new assignment, to teach ecological principles, my counterpart and colleagues at the Hydrological and

Meteorological Center set the record straight. Indeed, the parks were of no use to the Mongolian people, at least in their present state. They explained to me that those parks were built for the Soviets and their families. They were in many ways, if not directly stated, simply off limits to Mongolian people. After the "transition," they began to serve as a cut through or, worse, just an abandoned piece of land overlooked by everyone.

Within the new post-Soviet education curriculum, the Ministry of Environment and Ministry of Education had taken a bold new approach to the sciences. The newly issued Green Book assisted teachers in making the transition to teaching Ecology in the secondary schools. The former curriculum only taught the hard sciences of biology, chemistry, and—if there were time or resources—botany. But ecology, the same science with humans factored in, had been added to the classroom for the first time. Topics such as the life cycle, pollution and its causes, environmental stewardship, and global warming were on the way to becoming common knowledge in the communities.

My counterpart had taken the lead on this project well before I arrived. One day as we were discussing teaching tools for use in an outdoor project, modeled after an outdoor instruction manual common to the United States, a discussion about the park started. The town could use a new park, a living park for learning the lessons now being taught in the classroom: a new outdoor classroom that reflected the values of this new education curriculum

Within weeks, the interest of the mayor, governor, and departmental heads had grown. They were ready to engage in making a new park for the community. Within several weeks, the project picked up donors. A man who ran a nursery donated over one hundred and fifty evergreen trees; secondary students and teachers began planting. A small grant matched by the city government covered the architectural design work, blueprints, fresh paint, welding, concrete stepping stones, river gravel, cement, and iron for construction of four new gazebos. By the first snowfall of the winter the park was completed.

A long winter blanketed the nascent trees just planted that summer. The paints had barely dried before the persistent freezing temperatures of the Siberian cold had set in. By spring the warm days returned, and the government held their opening day for their new park. The governor, workers, heads of department, and my counterpart gathered to announce the good news to the community. The park was officially opened that day. It was some weeks later that the question was asked whether the park was Mongolia's first city park. Someone replied, "It isn't the first city park in Mongolia, but, yes, it is Mongolia's first city park."

Benjamin Baggett served in Undhurkhaan, Mongolia, from 2000-02. During his service, he supported community efforts to build what might be Mongolia's first city park. He also, with the linguistic aid of his counterpart, taught rangeland management and secondary ecology lessons in the countryside and the provincial capital. Mr. Baggett is a Program Development Analyst with a community action agency. He and his wife live in Corvallis, Oregon.

REBECCA BOWMAN

✳
✳   ✳

Running

Sports can be a little different in a totalitarian country.

THE STUDENTS LINE UP. THEY STAND BEHIND THE CRUMBLED cracks in the dusty, cement path, an impromptu starting area circling the abandoned carnival grounds just off the awakening Caspian Sea. It's seven in the morning, and they have a good hour and a half before school starts. The girls are wearing skinny jeans and dress shoes. It's strange apparel for runners, but stranger still for a culture where girls usually only wear dresses. The boys wear the same, and one or two even sport a running suit.

The oldest boy lights up a cigarette and blows the smoke into the cool, morning air. He's fifteen, and the best runner at School #2. The other students mill around him…waiting.

The aging, blond-ified Russian teacher, Olga, heads down the "start area," a rock-scratched chalk line. The government ended support of sports curriculum like hers in Turkmen schools years ago, but because of her friendship with the director, she manages to stay on at School #2.

As the anticipation builds, Olga commands attention. She calls for a few boys to get ready. Some are pushed forward by their friends amidst elbows and snickers. Then, Olga blows her whistle and yells out the start commands, "*Nastart, Vnumenua, Marsch!*"

No one runs.

No one wants to be the first to take-off. After another few tries and a little harassment from Olga, three boys take off together. Olga's watch fails to work, so she counts aloud, 1, 2, 3, 4, 5, 6…

There are no lanes, so even with only three students, they jostle and jumble against each other as they try to be the first down the coastal cement path. The fifteen-year-old smoker wins, as expected.

The girls go after the boys. After three or four of the same false starts, they're off and running as well.

After the first few sprints, another boy, fifteen and soon-to-be graduating from the ninth grade, pulls up late into the carnival grounds. He's driving his father's thirty-year-old Russian lemon of a car. Coolly, he fires the engine four or five times, and smoke spurts into the face of the runners. It reminds one of a scene from *Grease*, except there's no dancing with pink poodle skirts and hula hoops.

The students are preparing for the big citywide race in three weeks. Since the government eliminated sports and sport teachers from schools a few years ago, kids have lacked the chance to play organized sports. This is one of the few chances they get to show their athletic prowess.

Unfortunately, after the race is over, it's unlikely that the students will get the chance to run again. It would go against cultural standards and custom. Therefore, this yearly race is a wonderful opportunity.

What about me? Well, I'm there as a Peace Corps Volunteer. I don't fit in, but I'm glad to run with my students. I like being with them, and since my language skills still don't allow me to communicate at the level I'd like, running serves to fill the communication gap.

Watching my students run, I can't help but compare what I see here and my own life. In "The America," running was different. We wore uniforms. We had tennis shoes. We all started the race at the same time, and there was usually a track. We worked hard, and running was part of our daily lives.

It frustrates me that I can't do more to help their energetic spirits. I can't give my runners the feelings I have had when I've run and trained and pushed my body to its utmost. I can't get them fancy uniforms or even a reliable stopwatch. I can only support them in their yearly race, even if their race is only on a crumbled asphalt path along an abandoned carnival area. Even if it is only a jog in jeans.

So here we are in Turkmenistan, my students and me. Just as they run today, I'm running down my crumbled asphalt path around the broken-down carnival of life. We'll circle the track, and I hope, they'll keep running.

Rebecca Bowman served as an English teacher in Turkmenistan, T-12, from 2003-05. There, she taught students and teachers, developed a computer center with local teachers, led a touring version of The Wizard of Oz, *and helped coach a girls' basketball team. Today, Rebecca teaches international politics at Luther College in Decorah, Iowa.*

NATALIE BRYANT-RIZZIERI

*

An Unexpected Turn

For some, the Peace Corps extends well beyond the two-year service.

AS IS OFTEN THE CASE, WHAT BEGAN AS A TWO-YEAR COMMIT-
ment to serve in the Peace Corps (Armenia 2003-2005) has
extended beyond those two years. I was posted in the city of
Kapan, in the southernmost region of Armenia. For two years I
worked at an orphanage and "special school," spending nearly
every day with children and young adults with special needs.

What began as an assignment turned into love and commitment to a group of people who had been marginalized.
This commitment was furthered and unexpectedly turned
into the creation of the first long-term group home in the
Republic of Armenia. The home, which opened in January
of 2006 (after the end of my Peace Corps service), provides
long-term rehabilitative care to a group of orphaned individuals with disabilities or mental illness who had outgrown the
Kapan orphanage.

Near the end of my service, I was informed that the orphans
with whom I had worked were to be sent away to the government psychiatric institutions. In the former Soviet nation of

Armenia, having a disability was deeply shameful for individuals and their families. The tendency during these years was to send members of this vulnerable population to an institution (either an orphanage or psychiatric hospital) where they would be "out of sight." As a result, Armenia's population with special needs still struggles to recover a sense of value and dignity: they are too often placed in institutions that cannot properly care for them.

The institutions are hopeless places that are cold in winter, without sufficient food and without the resources to care for the patients. After working and living side-by-side with the orphans in Kapan, I decided that with the support of many brave people in Armenia, I must make an honest attempt to create an alternative for my group of students from Kapan. Another former Peace Corps Volunteer, Bridget Anderson, who had also served in Kapan, joined me in trying to create a viable alternative for these people who had found their way into my heart.

Warm Hearth was birthed through the initial vision to provide happiness and peace for the orphans in Kapan. Through profound mercies, this vision has been realized one small step at a time, *and* continues to expand. Word of the project has spread literally around the world, and the first $80,000 of seed money was donated within a few months in 2005. With this money, the first home was purchased on the outskirts of Yerevan. We recently expanded to include five new residents who now live beside our initial eight residents. In this home, the residents are offered the holistic care that they deserve, rehabilitation opportunities, love, support, and safety. The hope is that they will be able to re-enter mainstream community life, slowly but surely.

Warm Hearth is the first long-term group home in Armenia. A local partnership has been formed with the Jermik

Ankyun Foundation, a nonprofit that was founded in an effort to focus exclusively on the plight of this vulnerable population in Armenia. The Jermik Ankyun Foundation is responsible for implementing the project and both the long-term and day-to-day oversight of the home.

Upon returning to the United States, I started Friends of Warm Hearth, Inc., to act as a support organization for the group home. Friends of Warm Hearth provides funding for the home and programmatic support, as the group home model had never been attempted in Armenia. We still collaborate with local Peace Corps Volunteers and staff. Returned Peace Corps Volunteers from Armenia and elsewhere who have relevant experience visit and volunteer at Warm Hearth throughout the year.

The Armenian government has recognized Warm Hearth as a pilot program for the deinstitutionalization of individuals with special needs. The legal mechanisms are now in place for the government to outsource funding to community-based projects that are offering service and care to vulnerable populations. As the government moves away from institutionalized care for individuals with disabilities and allows for private community-based homes and facilities to provide more individualized care, Warm Hearth has the opportunity to model quality care and be a part of this small revolution as the idea takes root and more homes are opened.

Warm Hearth group home is a new idea, but one with promise in a nation like Armenia. It has been an honor and a deep joy to be a part of this grassroots movement and to allow what began as Peace Corps service to remain integrated in my day-to-day life.

Natalie Bryant-Rizzieri served as a Community Health Volunteer in Kapan, Armenia, from 2003-05. During her Peace Corps service, she focused primarily on orphaned individuals with disabilities, a work which she continues to this day as founder and director of Friends of Warm Hearth, the first long-term group home in Armenia. She is also a poet and received her MFA from Lesley University. Her work has appeared in Crab Orchard Review and Connotations. Natalie lives in Queens, New York, with her husband and son. She makes frequent trips to Armenia.

SAMUEL ROBINSON

Smokestack Songs

*Every Volunteer feels disconnected from their community
and looks for a reason to stay at one point or another.
Sometimes the reasons come unexpectedly.*

THE VILLAGE STOOD LIKE A BIRCH TREE MARKED ON A TRAIL
leading to someplace promising. A rusty smear on an iron
horizon, it signaled the end of a long day's work for smelters
releasing precious metals from ore at a plant a few hundred
yards away. When the trail of gray smoke released from the
smokestacks reached the village, the workers knew they were
free to return home.

The ashy cloud lingering above the village acted as its only
beacon, a gray shadow hovering like a blanket neatly tuck-
ing in the fifteen hundred inhabitants living beneath it. The
cloud would grow until it immersed the village in a billow of
smoke, which would hover for a moment and then disappear
like an illusion under waves of dark wind, its solid complexion
dissipating into a million particles of combusted heavy metals
drifting aimlessly toward the village floor.

Once the embarking point for nomads headed to their
summer resting grounds in the Altai Mountains, the foothills
around the village later became a Cossack fort defending the

fringes of the Russian Empire. After the revolution, when maybe two or three small cabins constituted the entire village, the inhabitants were mostly peasants serving homemade potato vodka to transient loggers and woodsmen making a last stop on their return from the mountains. In time, straight lines of traditional one-story triangular houses were built with blue shuttered windows carved with crescent moons, hung like picture frames against wooden walls. Within this checkerboard of wood and earth, two stories of poured cement hardened into the cast of a schoolhouse, the production of the prototypical Soviet village complete.

Wedged beneath the red and white barber pole smokestacks of the titanium-magnesium smelting plant since its much heralded construction in 1965, the classrooms of the Vinnoye secondary school today are filled with the nostalgic orb of a leaden past, floating through slogan-slapped walls illustrated with posters of eager red-scarfed children. Since the fall of the Soviet political system, teachers have been asked to teach a new generation how to survive in a world where the state has become a parent with no dependents.

When I stumbled into Vinnoye, I was handed the dubious distinction of being an American in a region closed to outsiders for decades, a place suffering from enough nuclear fallout and heavy metal pollution that *National Geographic* awarded it notorious inclusion into the list of the thirty dirtiest places in the world. Fur-lined faces traced my movements with a typically local skepticism, the border of my unfamiliar American frame tinged with a fifty-year history of the Cold War, countless missing persons, and a winding staircase of secrets leading from winter food storage basements to the moon and beyond.

Suspicion of my purpose and longevity here was mutual. Even Svetlana, my teaching counterpart, was skeptical as she begged me to stay through the first week, preliminary spittle of doubt still tucked neatly behind my terse Western lips. Could I really teach English to children from square one, while trying to learn Russian alongside an English teacher who didn't even speak English? We both pondered this question for the first few months in front of classes dotted with curious patterns of children Svetlana referred to as "black minded."

Svetlana was a different type of teacher, one who juggled the lead ball of nostalgia with a brighter ball of curious hope. She stood against the board, somewhat moon-faced with eyes darting back and forth like meteors between her frost-blushed pale cheeks and forehead, her fingers hammering a piece of chalk into the board.

A trained music teacher, she had just completed a secondary degree in teaching English as a Second Language. Wearing neatly pleated sixties-era dresses with billowy blouses, she sat perpendicular to the class, warming our students up each morning. Nimble fingers running along an old and worn Belarus piano, she clanged out sweet, yet broken, renditions of English children's songs into the waiting ears of unkempt Russian and Kazakh children dressed in frumpy suits and dresses.

She was filled with ingenuity, passion, flexibility, a survivor of broken politburo promises and unfulfilled personal expectations. She was a believer in her and her family's role in the communist system of the Soviet Union of the twentieth century and in the capitalist democracy of the twenty-first, yet without the obvious contradictions of many of her colleagues. Her head undulating along with the rhythm, she maneuvered alongside the challenge of simultaneously teaching and learning a language in order to give her daughter Tanya the power of an education, feet submerged under the piano as she pedaled against the surface of the concrete schoolhouse floor.

The lack of interest of the students during that first winter was marked by frozen cheeks drooping against mittens and longing gazes reflecting against the plastic sheen of American pop star-studded notebooks. Mustering excitement out of students after Svetlana's jolted but inspired warm up songs was difficult without a continuation of the performance. Having never sung outside of the secure three-foot by three-foot stage of a shower, I didn't see my pop star shining in a place that lacked running water. So I curtly rebuked Svetlana's constant badgering of any form of articulate baritone participation in her songs, the basic fear of trying something for the first time too much for me. Our mutual suspicion of each other deepened with the onset of my first sub-Siberian winter.

With the first sprigs of highlighted green grass that first spring, a sharply contrasting confidence crystallized through the plane of frost that had leveled itself upon the village. The rite of new life barreled its way through me, leaving me unguarded for the first time from a stark landscape undergoing the trauma of rebirth. Svetlana, always stirring her subtle cocktail of patience mixed with forceful nudging, knew she had an opening. Coaxing this little piece of trust with the experienced hands of a motherly sculptor, she presented a new addition to her warm-up song repertoire that had an all too familiar melody. My placated defiance slid from between my front teeth pulling after it with flossy strings the melancholy heart of an inexperienced Peace Corps Volunteer. At first a whisper, "*yess....*" then a faint murmur bumping against the sides of every other note. "*All my troubles...so far away,*" then an undeniably American accent emerging from fissures in the ice, "*Oh, I believe in yesterday.*"

It took the song that has been covered more than any other song ever written for me to break through the icy chords of my own lungs. According to McCartney, "it's easy to rhyme those a's: say, nay, today, away, play, stay," which might explain its popularity in both the United States and the former Soviet

Union. My version, however, an overly cautious uncertain groan, lacked the same majestic influence. Despite this, the students responded in a refreshingly seamless chord of American accents. "*Suddenly, I'm not half the man I used to be*" flung itself toward the ceiling and walls soaking into the fresh whitewash. "*There's a shadow hanging over me*" slid its way through the open doors, down the early morning sunny corridor, "*Oh yesterday, came suddenly*" burst out the front doors of Vinnoye Secondary School finally jettisoning amongst the tufts of the cow-grazed schoolyard.

With each repetition of the song came new bravado. I was singing, Svetlana was playing the piano, and the students were starting to pronounce the English language in a halfway decipherable accent. We started experimenting with songs to teach not only vocabulary, but grammar as well, and soon the American pop icons on my student's notebooks weren't nearly as interesting as their two crooning English teachers performing private forty-five-minute shows, five days a week.

Sitting down for our now routine weekly lunch, I noticed a hesitation in Svetlana's hands as she wiped bright red beet stains from between her fingers into her apron. Unscrewing the lid of a jar of homemade sour cream, I heaved a generous dollop into my bowl of borscht and asked what was wrong. Svetlana tightened the corners of her crescent mouth and ducked into her bedroom returning with a long manila envelope, bound at the top with a red string wrapped around a plastic circle. She opened the folder and presented me with an X-ray of her head, a floppy over-sized piece of film highlighting the haunting shadow of a small brain tumor wedged within her skull.

It was the first time I had seen the listless glare of defeat in Svetlana's eyes. It was a look that on a dreamer's face resembles the contemplation of losing something greater than themselves. She sat beside me, her crimson beet juice-stained fingers working their way over a set of prayer beads one at a time, each brown sphere representing another unanswerable question. How would we continue our musical English curriculum? How would the students keep up their progress? How would her daughter continue her studies without the guidance of her mother? How could she continue moving forward when a gray ball of meaningless matter threatened her life?

My only consolation was the promise to keep on singing to our students.

And so I sang for Svetlana while she recovered, trying to fill her shoes in a classroom of weary students who missed the encouraging sound of her piano playing more and more with each passing day.

By the time she recovered and returned to the classroom, I found myself bowing to the pressures of teaching without her, my voice being drowned out by the growing ambivalence of our students. Svetlana re-entered the classroom with blurry vision, but a deeper focus to extract something precious from the ore that had constantly weighed down her hope for the future. At the end of our second year together, her efforts were rewarded when her daughter received an award as one of the top English-language speakers in the region. Tanya would start university in Russia the following fall and I would be free to return home, Svetlana and the smokestacks still bellowing upon a trail leading to someplace promising.

Samuel Robinson served as an English teacher in Kazakhstan, Kaz-18, from 2006-08. Samuel taught and learned Russian in a small northeastern village school. He earned a B.A in English at the State University of New York, College at New Paltz, and has studied literature at Oxford University. He was born, raised and still lives in Brooklyn, New York, where he founded and is a partner at Greenwood Robinson, a garden design and installation firm. This story is the winner of the Jason and Lucy Greer Prize.

JAMES MCHENRY, PH.D.

The Motherland

"Patience is bitter, but its fruit is sweet." —*Turkish Proverb*

AHMET KOKSAL WAS ONE OF THE HIGHEST REGARDED STUDENTS in the English Department at Ataturk University in Erzurum, Turkey. He came from a small village in central Anatolia located near Goreme, a site famed for its spectacular scenery and tourist sites. In contrast to some of his classmates, Ahmet was conscientious, hardworking, and dedicated to using every opportunity to improve his English language skills. He not only did exceedingly well in class, he joined a voluntary group that met after school to discuss (in English) topics relating to international relations and Turkish politics. One might have thought all this good behavior would irritate his fellow students, but Ahmet's friendly, open personality made him popular with everyone.

When a holiday period rolled around in the spring of 1967, Ahmet invited my wife and me to visit his family and experience life in his village. We were concerned about being an imposition, particularly because we had learned that Ahmet came from a family of modest means. Given the legendary, and by no means exaggerated, reputation that Turkish hospitality enjoys, our hesitation was appropriate. However, Ahmet waved off our concerns and insisted that it would be a great honor for his family to host us.

While the visit to the tourist sites was engaging, it was our luncheon with Ahmet's mother that imprinted itself most deeply in my memory. Following a meal that touched all the bases of Turkish cuisine, we were sitting around visiting and sipping tea, served piping hot in small bell-shaped glasses. On the floor was an elegant Turkish carpet, which I admired. I learned that the carpet, along with several others in the room, had been woven by Ahmet's mother. As we marveled at her handiwork, Ahmet looked across the room at his mother and paid her tribute in these words: "My mother worked for years, day in and day out, weaving rugs to sell so that I could attend the university and pay for my room and board. I would not be where I am today were it not for her love and her sacrifice on my behalf."

The look of pride and deep affection that passed over his mother's face was absolutely unforgettable. She then turned to us and thanked us for the part we were playing in contributing to her son's education. At that point, I'm convinced there was not one dry eye in the room. We assured her that it was our privilege to be Ahmet's teachers, particularly because we now had a much deeper understanding of our mutual debt of gratitude to her.

During the Ottoman Empire, the Sultans would appropriate unto themselves a variety of lofty titles, one of which was "the Shadow of God on Earth." I do not know if such a thing exists, but of this much I am certain: thanks to the U.S. Peace Corps, we were privileged to witness something magnificent that day as we stood within the shadow of a diminutive Turkish woman whose selfless devotion to her son had bound us together. And from that day forward, I've never looked upon a beautiful Turkish carpet without remembering her and wondering what story of unconditional love this carpet could tell.

James A. McHenry, Jr. served as an English instructor at Ataturk University in Erzurum, Turkey, from 1966-68. He was recruited to be the player/coach of the university's basketball team where he attracted the nickname "Arslan Jimi." (trans. "Jim, the Lion"). He has yet to recover from that compliment. Upon his return, Jim successfully pursued a doctorate in history, then worked for many years in nonprofit management and philanthropy in senior executive positions. He served as the Kansas Commissioner of Alcohol and Drug Abuse Services, as the director of the Kansas Child Abuse Prevention Council, and for the past fourteen years he's worked as the development director for the Topeka and Shawnee County Public Library.

✷
✷　✷

The Distance to Doubt: From Uzbekistan to Kazakhstan

Most Peace Corps Volunteers only get to serve in one
country in their lifetimes—Yen served in two.

I TOOK MY FIRST TRIP ABROAD IN THE YEAR 2000 WHEN I WAS eighteen. Armed with earnings from a part-time job, a friend and I saw Paris on a student's budget. We island- and bar-hopped through Greece and impulsively boarded a ferry to Israel to chase romantic prospects. En route back to Paris through Nice, I had my passport, return plane ticket, credit cards, and cash stolen. We somehow arrived at de Gaulle Airport, only to be dismissed by an unhelpful Air France ticket agent. Panicked and in tears for the frantic few hours before our scheduled flight home, I begged a calling card from a sympathetic stranger, convinced my family in California to shell out a for new plane ticket, and then called the U.S. embassy for clearance to fly and enter the U.S. with no identification. We landed in San Francisco giddy and unfazed with plans for our next trip.

Less than a year later, I found myself backpacking Southeast Asia with a college classmate. With scant planning and a meager budget for three months, we managed to experience the beaches, forests, cities and temples of Thailand, Laos,

Cambodia, and Vietnam. I saw the role that Western development agencies played in preserving the region's history; I also wondered how those same development initiatives altered the region's cultures and created industries that catered to tourists like myself. In spite of numerous mishaps along the way, I thought that relying on the mercy of chance, fellow travelers, and locals was a sustainable way to travel because things always seemed to turn out fine in the end. The adventure of being a young expatriate abroad tapped into my desire to explore new identities and new roles for myself. I saw the Peace Corps as an ideal way to continue traveling and develop a cosmopolitan worldview, while also exploring international development as a career path. Although I was attracted to the lofty mission of the Peace Corps, I joined mainly out of a willful commitment to a process of self-growth and self-discovery.

In January 2005, I arrived in Uzbekistan along with 63 other Peace Corps trainees in the UZ-18 cohort. We trained for three months in the capital, Tashkent, and I made rapid progress learning Uzbek. At the end of training in April 2005, I was placed at my permanent site in Urgench, a frontier town in the remote desert region of Uzbekistan's "wild west." Compared to the capital, the town's heat and aridity seemed to render life a few beats slower. I liked the way the turquoise domes on mosques shimmered in the heat, creating a mirage effect that was compounded by wandering camels. My host mother, Sanumjon-opa, owned a fabric stall at the bazaar, and her eldest daughter had just left to do similar work in Russia, leaving behind her three young sons. Sanumjon-opa's second daughter, Shakhnoza, remained unmarried at 27, forgoing the chance to start her own family to help raise her nephews. The family's hardiness and entrepreneurial spirit reminded me of my own sprawling family of sisters back in California held together by my stalwart mother. For those first few months, I was comfortable and quietly thrilled to live in Urgench: each new friend, each new experience familiarized me to an initially foreign and daunting place. My teaching counterparts, one an Uzbek divorcée, the other a married Tatar with two boys, and I were already known around school as a trio of sisters for our youthfulness and natural rapport. In a matter of months, we were versed in each other's romantic tribulations: Barno was looking for a fellow divorcé to marry, Dinara was struggling to raise two boys with a busy husband, and I was missing my boyfriend back in the States. Though I was careful not to romanticize their lives, I admired their purposefulness and resourcefulness. In those early months, they were my guides to the community and its resources, and they were key partners in strategizing new projects to improve the school.

That clear sense of purpose, optimism, and commitment I had in Uzbekistan abruptly ended on June 1, 2005, when I found myself in a Toyota Landcruiser bound for neighboring Kazakhstan with the outgoing Peace Corps-Uzbekistan country director, his wife, their ginger cat and three other similarly shell-shocked Volunteers. Our sudden departure from Uzbekistan was the result of a protracted visa struggle between Peace Corps-Uzbekistan and the Uzbekistani government. Before we had even set foot in the country, Peace Corps-Uzbekistan had been at odds with the local government over their refusal to issue two-year visas to our incoming group. We had arrived with three-month visas, only enough for our pre-service training; subsequent visa extensions allowed us to stay at our permanent sites for six weeks. Then the possibility of a two-year visa, however slim, became impossible after the Andijan incident on May 13, 2005, when thousands of Uzbeks gathered in a public square to protest the arrest of 23 local businessmen in the eastern city of Andijan. The Uzbekistani government crackdown was swift and violent, the government going as far as to close the city to foreigners and all media. The international community, along with the U.S., criticized President Karimov's actions and called for an independent investigation into what some human rights groups were already calling a massacre. In response, the Uzbekistani government allowed our visas to lapse with no hope for renewal, effectively signaling that our Peace Corps cohort was no longer welcome. This action was followed by the evacuation of all Western development and aid workers a few weeks later, including U.S. Embassy staff, the two earlier Peace Corps cohorts UZ-17 and UZ-16, and finally, by the closure of the U.S. Karshi-Khanabad air base.

In Urgench, I had two days to pack and say good-bye to my host family, counterparts, and students with no other explana-tion than the Uzbekistani government refused to extend our visas. The vast Kyzylkum and Karakum deserts that had kept me well insulated from the urgency of the news coming out of the capital and Andijan, also gave my Urgench community a disinterest and aloofness toward the events in the east. They promised that Andijan had nothing to do with us in Urgench and that Americans were still welcome in Uzbekistan. They believed that our regrouping in Tashkent was temporary and that I would return once the situation stabilized. Even as we talked, we all knew that my individual safety was not the issue but, rather, those political maneuvers beyond our control.

I flew back to Tashkent along with the rest of my cohort for our end-of-service conference, a ritual that seemed drained of meaning since we had barely started our service. In those few days in Tashkent, as we waited to be accepted into other Peace Corps programs or for return plane tickets home, I felt betrayed by the Peace Corps and by a romanticized idea of international development. Cooped up in a hotel with 60-odd devastated Volunteers, rumors and unconfirmed stories abounded as to why Peace Corps chose to send our large cohort to Uzbekistan in the first place. It was all too easy to assign responsibility and blame to the program itself. As I weighed my next step, I also weighed complicated questions with no clear answers. If Peace Corps had any inkling that relations with the Uzbekistani government were on unstable ground, was it prudent to send so many new recruits into such a tenuous environment? What were the aims of international development if the host country government did not welcome the agency invited to "help" them? In the inherently delicate relationship between local populations and international aid workers, especially those at the grassroots level, who was responsible for the lost opportunities and dashed expectations on both sides? Was human capital an effective aid, or would direct monetary support have been more effective? How could I maintain my optimism and idealism knowing that it was local communities and grassroots workers who suffer the brunt of political grandstanding?

Most of the UZ-18 Volunteers returned to the U.S.: some waited a few months to join other programs, but most were finished with the Peace Corps, perhaps exhausted by the tenuous environment of development. Hoping to redeem the journey in which I had already invested six months, I decided to cross the border into Kazakhstan to join a new cohort as a trainee once again. If the first three-month training in Uzbekistan was grueling, but necessary, the second three-month training in Kazakhstan was pure drudgery. I found Russian impossible to learn; the slurry syllables tangled up my tongue at every attempt, unlike the neat percussive sounds of Uzbek. At my new site at Taraz in southern Kazakhstan, I taught English language arts, business and computer skills, literature and teaching methodology to 17-to-19-year-old women at a pedagogical humanities college. Initially I was mainly interested in the ways that Kazakhstan was not Uzbekistan, and I suffered whenever I considered the extent of my emotional and psychic investment in Uzbekistan. Was there no recourse for the lingering disappointment I felt about my experience in Uzbekistan? Would my host family in Urgench think that I chose not to go back? After all, the state-run media did report that the Andijan uprising was contained almost immediately.

In my first year in Kazakhstan, I was forced to delve past my initial naïve impulse to merely experience and explore new worlds. I had to grapple with the question of what happens when one is no longer an 18-year-old tourist bar-hopping in Greece, but a part of the contentious world of international development and a trained worker with projects and expectations to fulfill. My students confided in me about teachers who demanded bribes for grades and diplomas. I then had to rely on those same teachers to co-organize conferences, training programs, and extracurricular clubs, even though I had begun to doubt their motivations. Were the teachers—whose already meager salaries were not only frequently months late, but also subjected to a variety of "voluntary" department collections— to blame? As a fellow teacher, I thought I could help improve my department by addressing corruption and encouraging grading transparency so my students were not subject to tyrannical teachers. Although my youthfulness and Asian features helped me blend in with local students and teachers, on days when I could not motivate attendance to my critical thinking or teaching methodology workshops, the value gaps between us loomed impossibly large.

In my second year of teaching at the college, I became good friends with a young English teacher who had been kidnapped to become the bride of a man she hardly knew. When I met her, she was already a year into the marriage with an infant son. Over tea breaks, I listened to her plot ways to leave her husband and save money for train tickets back to her hometown, but I could not suppress my frustration over societal injustices that trapped her in a violent bride-napping. I supported her plan and offered to loan her money; yet I wondered if she really wanted to leave or just needed a sympathetic ear. The two Peace Corps trainings did not prepare me for when a woman in my weekly Women's Club asked me to help her set up an online dating profile and navigate international marriage websites. If she thought a marriage abroad was her best option at a better life, who was I to condemn her choices? How could I inject my Western notions of gender equality into a conversation about bride-napping or online marriage services in Kazakhstan? I tried to disengage, to avoid the mess of moral ambiguity, but I was always pulled into the lives of these women by empathizing that it is human nature to seek a better life by any means.

I never became comfortable with the constant questions about my role in the larger picture of Western development practices, but I channeled that doubt into expanding the scope of my job by partnering with a local NGO to develop youth and community resource projects. My English language debate club attracted bright and motivated university students who used a foreign vocabulary to discuss domestic social issues that might have been too sensitive to do in Russian or Kazakh. One of my most memorable adventures was riding a twenty-hour train to Karaganda with my debaters to a national debate competition. Up against students who came from richer schools and cities with better resources, two of my students defied their own expectations and won the 2006 National English Debate competition. The victory took them on their first international trip to Istanbul, Turkey, to represent Kazakhstan in an international English debate. One of the debaters ended up studying in New York for a master's degree a few years later.

Although I was unable to recapture the clarity of purpose and unwavering commitment to the journey of being a Peace

Corps Volunteer that I had in Uzbekistan, in my struggle to meaningfully engage with my community in Kazakhstan, I learned to exist alongside unanswered questions about the goals of international development and my role in a world that, while still new and exciting, became increasingly complex and challenging. Before the Peace Corps, I might have considered myself a resilient person, but I didn't know how inflexible I was until I developed anemia due to an obstinate and irresponsible vegetarian diet. I found joy in seeing the initial shock and then understanding on my students' faces as they grasped the complexity of a Raymond Carver short story, whose deceptively simple syntax hid the layers of brutality underneath. I discovered that understanding different perspectives often led to ambiguity that could not be neatly resolved. In pursuing my initial goals of self-discovery and growth, I learned that personal strength was something as straightforward as consistency. It was challenging enough to do the good job that was expected of me as a guest in the country and for a community that came to rely on me. I focused on the quotidian relationships and on the day-to-day exchanges between my students and friends to define my success, instead of the larger goals of building local sustainability and mainstreaming development principles that were fraught with moral ambiguity. I learned to focus on developing an organic two-way flow of ideas to both influence and be inspired by those with whom I came in contact. And this was the most meaningful part of my Peace Corps experience.

Yen Le served in Uzbekistan, UZ-18, from January to June 2005 and in Kazakhstan, Kaz-17, from June 2005 to December 2006. She is currently pursuing a M.A. in East Asian Studies at Stanford University.

PETER L. GESS

Can We Pass Through Latvia, *Please?*

Even unpleasant experiences in the Peace Corps
are ripe with pleasant cultural lessons.

As you may already know, the Peace Corps and its Volunteers strive to accomplish three basic goals. The first and best known of these goals, especially among those unfamiliar with the Corps, is the technical exchange. This involves the teaching and learning between the Volunteer and her or his community hosts. Often, when someone mentions the Peace Corps, others conjure up images of digging wells for clean drinking water, of laying out irrigation projects for crops, of helping manage livestock, even of teaching mathematics and English. It is these arenas in which Volunteers are primarily engaged as they work to achieve this first and primary goal.

My Peace Corps group, Poland 8 (1994-96), was a combination of "small business development" and "environmental awareness advisor" Volunteers. This was the third group of environmental Volunteers to come to the country. According to the Warsaw central staff members, there was very little time to prepare sites for the first group, which arrived two years before my group. All of these Volunteers, 100 percent, were placed within various national parks around the country. For the next group, one year later, approximately half of the Volunteers were placed into the parks. And for my group, exactly two of twelve environmental awareness advisors ended up in the parks. I was one of these two, and found myself in northeast Poland—or Polish Siberia—living and working in Wigierski Park Naradowy (Wigry National Park).

At the time I arrived in Wigry, the park seemed to be the exception with its innovative approach. Under a progressive director, the staff and I launched a variety of public education and outreach activities designed to get students of all ages to the park to learn and experience its beauty. This initiative included activities such as authoring curriculum guides for classrooms, hosting field trips, operating summer field stations, holding Earth Day events, developing interpretive trails and a museum, and sending speakers to schools and community events. This educational effort was especially important for Wigry for two very important reasons. First, the forty-two lakes of the park were continually threatened by municipal waste streams, as well as agricultural and industrial run-off. Second, the park had only been created a few years before my arrival, leaving local residents bewildered as to why they were no longer allowed to hunt, fish, and gather mushrooms within its boundaries.

However, this all changed almost exactly one year into my service. The director, a trained biologist (unlike many of the other Polish national park directors, who were classic forest-ers), decided to let a bark-beetle problem run its natural course. Much of the Wigry forests were lost, and the spread of the beetle to nearby lands focused the attention of the national park headquarters in our direction. Rather than support the director, Warsaw saw fit to replace him with an old party loy-alist. Among rumors that the new director collected dog skins and sacked employees for being ten minutes late (we did suddenly have to sign in and out each work day), the staff withdrew from its innovative outreach and education efforts, and instead focused on traditional resource management. Under this atmosphere, I found it very difficult to share my technical knowledge with others in the park.

So I turned more to the second and third goals, to educate Polish nationals about Americans, and to teach Americans about Poles. Some of my favorite activities I did during this second year of service included hosting a local radio call-in show entitled "American University"; teaching environmental education at the local teacher-training college; playing basketball in a league of Polish physical education teachers; and using my bicycle as a way to travel around the country, with its seat as a conversation launching point to learn more about my new, albeit temporary home: Poland.

Wigierski Park Naradowy is located in the northeast corner of Poland, perhaps about twenty-five kilometers from both the Lithuanian border to the east and the Kaliningrad border to the north. I would often ride my bike along these borders, and especially in the latter case, wonder what lay across the other side.

As I became more adventurous and found that I could afford longer jaunts away from Wigry, I discovered the *Balti Express*, a train which ran from Warsaw, through Kaunus, Lithuania, then to Riga, the capital of Latvia, before landing in Tallinn, the capital of Estonia. Luckily for me, this train made an incredibly short stop in Suwalki, the Polish town of about one hundred thousand people just seven kilometers from Wigry. For something like three iterations, I boarded the train in Suwalki, rode it through the night, and arrived at Tallinn the next day. To this day, Tallinn remains one of my favorite cities. My fascination with medieval history dates back to my childhood, and within the old walls of the center of Tallinn, one can really envision how it must have been.

During the summer of 1995, I was excited to share my fascination with and love for Tallinn with my girlfriend, Jennifer, who was coming over for a long visit. (Remember that this period predates widespread use of the internet, especially outside of the U.S., and as a Volunteer I did not have regular access to a telephone.) But there was no reason to expect that this trip would be any different from the previous three that I had made.

The trip began easily enough. Jennifer and I got a sleeping car so that we would be more refreshed when we arrived at Tallinn. We knew we would be awakened by customs and immigration officials at each of the three border crossings, but perhaps we could get a little rest in between. The Poland-Lithuania border crossing went without a hitch. A much different experience was awaiting us at the Lithuania–Latvia border.

I knew that we would need a transit visa at this border, and I had always received them from the immigration officials on the train in the past. So at 3 A.M., when the knock on the car door awakened us, I had our passports ready. I began to get a bit apprehensive when I realized the Latvian border guard was taking a bit longer than usual with our passports. He did not speak English or Polish, but there was one phrase he knew quite well and kept repeating over and over again: "Is problem. Is problem."

The anxiety was screwed up another notch when this gentleman motioned for the two of us to follow him off of the train. In a bid to tether us to the soon-to-depart *Balti Express,* I purposely mimed to Jennifer that we should leave our luggage in the berth. But the guard would have no part of that, and escorted us back to our car and handed us our luggage.

We now followed him off onto the platform, where we joined a group of about eight Georgians just in time to see the train pull away and head off into the night. Jennifer and I turned and watched until the red taillights of the train winked out. We were not heading to Estonia that night.

Now about five guards escorted us around the front of the rather modest train station where a small van, more like a mini-van, was waiting for us. The Georgian family squeezed in, but there was no more room for the two of us. Again, with no shared language, the guards indicated we should remain there and wait for the van to return. And just for good measure, one of them—complete with machine gun—remained to keep us company.

We remained there for what seemed like days, but in reality must not have been for more than a few hours, as I have a clear memory of the rising sun. The beauty of that eastern, golden view contrasted starkly with the uncertainty of our immediate future. Our escort seemed genuinely uninterested in us (like this kind of thing happened all the time) and offered little insight into what lay ahead.

Finally, the same van returned for what was perhaps the strangest ride of my life. The drive, the morning, even the guards now seem nondescript, but the interior of that van will forever remain etched in my mind. Remember this was an official government vehicle, Russian-made, and upon climbing in I thought it must be the same as many others employed in Latvia and other Eastern European countries. We slid in the back and positioned ourselves on two long benches that ran the length of the vehicle. A guard joined us in the back, and one took his place up front next to the driver. But as we started on our way and my eyes acclimated to the dim interior, I realized a major cultural difference that you would not find in the U.S.

First of all, positioned on the dashboard was one of those plastic, grass-wearing, scantily clad hula dancers. Clearly not your standard government issue. I am not sure if memory serves, but I seem to recall some variant of Romanian gypsy music coming from the one center speaker with too much treble. And the hula dancer was keeping time, perhaps accenting with a pelvic thrust as we hit one of many potholes along the route.

But that is not this border security van's personal "accent" that caused me to go, "Wow!" Rather it was the cutouts of the naked women, mostly likely from a pin-up calendar, plastered throughout the back of the van. I looked at Jennifer, and we both tried extra hard not to laugh at the absurdity of it all. It is at times like this that a feminist in Central and Eastern Europe might take special offense, but one must really try to understand by seeing through a cross-cultural lens. This is really not unlike the naked-women condom packages I found staring at me from the thousands of kiosks all over 95 percent Catholic Poland.

After no more than a fifteen-minute drive, we arrived at a simple, wooden border guardhouse. The guards escorted us into a small room with a tall counter, and here we were reunited with the Georgian clan. A man who was obviously in charge—strategically seated behind the counter so we had to look up to make eye contact—motioned us over. Like his colleagues, he also did not speak English. After struggling for a few minutes to understand what he was trying to tell us, one of the Georgians came over and asked in broken English if he could be of assistance. Through a series of exchanges in a variety of languages, Jennifer and I began to piece together that Latvia no longer offered transit visas on trains entering the country. However, it was possible to get such visas when entering the country via bus.

Jennifer and I took advantage of a pause in the office bureaucratic processing of our documents to speak more with the Georgians. Although we never received the complete picture, it seemed that this family was only trying to get back to Tbilisi, their hometown. Unfortunately they lacked the proper documentation and authority to travel, and had been bumped from country to country. Their latest strategy was to get to Russia, then travel across that expansive country to get to their own. I was struck by how matter-of-factly they described their situation, as many Americans would have found the inability to freely travel incomprehensible and threatening, especially if it prevented a return to the U.S. In fact, more than one Pole told me during my Peace Corps service that the best thing about being an American must be the ability to travel when and whereever one wanted.

As frustrating as the situation was for the Georgians, at least for these few minutes they focused their attention and worry on the two of us. Jennifer and I were, and continue to be, genuinely touched by their concern. They certainly helped mitigate a rather stressful situation.

With the help of the Georgians, we learned that we would be escorted, via train, back across the border to a Lithuanian town. Once there, we would be able to purchase bus tickets for an "express" bus to Riga, where we would be reunited with the *Balti Express*, or at least the twenty-four hour later version of the original. So we bid goodbye to our new Georgian friends, and once again joined the company of machine gun-toting Latvian border guards. Sure enough, we were able to easily board a southbound train—at no cost—and in about thirty minutes found ourselves back in Lithuania.

I can recall very few details of that town, but it did have a rather frontier feel, complete with a layer of dust on everything. The town seemed to be just awakening, and the bus ticket office was still closed tight. The one very clear memory I have is of that god-awful public bathroom that we were desperate to use (it had been quite some time since we had been able to visit a water closet). Jennifer did not really want to talk about her experience in the women's side, but it is probably enough to mention that there was about a two- to three-inch layer of sludge on the floor in the men's room, some of which came from decrepit pipes and some of which flowed in from under the door during a recent mini mudslide.

Eventually the bus station opened, and we were able to purchase two tickets for Riga. The bus arrived shortly thereafter and was already crammed full of people heading to the Latvian capital. I have no idea from whence they came, but likely from small towns and villages in the region. During my time in Poland, I often felt a sense of pride when motorists or walkers stop to ask me for directions; I took this as a sign that I was adapting to the culture and society. But this was clearly one of those cases where we didn't fit in, and all eyes on that bus watched us move down the aisle. We were able to squeeze into spaces on the bench that stretched across the very back of the bus.

Several things caused that bus ride back into Latvia to be memorable. First, even though it wasn't raining, the bus was dripping something liquid in the back, right on our heads. Best not to think too much about that. Second, the man sitting next to Jennifer insisted in broken English that he read horoscopes for the two of us. And third, the sweater lady.

Apparently there is some limit on the number of homemade sweaters that one is allowed to bring into Latvia. As we progressed toward the border, a portly woman made her way down the aisle, asking if passengers would mind carrying a sweater or two across the border. By the time she got to the back, her giant red, white and blue-striped nylon bag was almost empty, so Jennifer and I took the last two sweaters. It was only later that I began to wonder if this was a smart decision on our part, considering our ongoing saga to get through Latvia.

When we arrived at the border, a new set of Latvian immigration officials boarded the bus. They made their way down the aisle, checking everyone's passports and visa documentation. This process went without a hitch until they came to us; when they saw that Jennifer and I had no visas for the country, we were once again escorted off the vehicle. Once again they asked us to take our backpacks with us, and again I worried that we would never make it to Tallinn. As we climbed off the bus, I could not help but notice the sweater lady's wide eyes at the thought of losing her sweaters. Her profits!

No pictures of naked ladies this time, and it was only a short walk to the control station. This time a younger man, who spoke some English, had us sit down at his desk. He was friendlier than anyone we had dealt with to this point, and he kept making jokes that neither of us understood (but we laughed along politely just the same). Without exaggerating, it took this man almost one hour to fill out one form in triplicate for each of us. He poured over our passports, studied our faces, made some more jokes, and excruciatingly slowly completed the forms.

Through this process it became obvious that we would be able to continue on our way—eventually—so that became one less worry. But now we had a new one. The entire bus of about forty people continued to sit at the crossing waiting for us, and now it was getting warm. Their trip to Riga was delayed by one hour. Anyone who has done much flying around the U.S. understands how irritable and impatient air travelers get at the slightest delays. Would the Lithuanians out on the bus be angry with us? And what about the woman who had trusted us with her sweaters?

Finally we were issued our transit visas. The total cost? An incredible zero Latvian lats. I was totally amazed that after all this, after all the personnel involved to make sure we were following Latvian law, after all the transportation, delays, and paperwork, there was absolutely no cost for the Latvian transit visa. One could wonder the sense behind such a policy. Indeed, as I have pursued a career as a scholar of public administration, I have often reflected upon inefficient and ineffective public policies. I can only think that Latvia was hurting itself as its two Baltic neighbors, Lithuanian and Estonia, were opening more and more doors to tourism and trade.

Anyway, we made our way back to the bus. The worries about the reception we would receive quickly evaporated as we climbed aboard amongst many worried looks. Not one passenger was angry with us for the delay; instead, every single rider was genuinely concerned about us. Although not much English was spoken, the universal "O.K." was used to express empathy: "O.K.?" "O.K.?" "O.K.?" These were joined by some reassuring pats on the arm by some of the more grandmotherly passengers. As touched as Jennifer and I were by the especially helpful Georgian family, we were overwhelmed with the kindness showed by this group. We asked ourselves, how many Americans would likewise go out of their way to help and express concern? It's not that I believe there is intrinsically anything different about Americans, it has just that we have become so busy and so impatient in such circumstances.

The ride to Riga was light and lively, and we tried to communicate with many of our fellow travelers. The sweater lady circulated the bus again, this time collecting her goods, and she was very thankful for our help. Jennifer and I tried to express, albeit inadequately, our gratitude at the humanity shown to us by these new friends.

And Riga turned out to be a pleasant surprise. Without this string of events, and the delay on our trek to Tallinn, we would not have had the opportunity to visit another great Baltic city. But most importantly, we were afforded an incredible cross-cultural experience, which has remained with both of us to this day. I have often used it as a teaching aide to support the third goal, to teach Americans about my host country nationals, the Poles (and the Latvians, and the Georgians, and the Lithuanians). And I would add that Jennifer and I were married about four years after my return from Poland. Who said long-distance Peace Corps relationships can't make it?

Peter L. Gess served as an environmental awareness advisor in Poland from 1994-96. Upon his return, he immediately went to work for the Atlanta Committee for the Olympic Games, before helping launch the International Center for Democratic Governance at the University of Georgia. He is now director of international programs and professor of politics at Hendrix College, Conway, Arkansas. He continues to have great adventures abroad, such as spending an extra week in Rwanda thanks to the volcano in Iceland.

GEORGE T. PARK

My Picture on a Plate

The frustrations of teaching were to be expected, but
the rewards could come as a total surprise.

"HOCAM, HOCAM. CAN I HAVE YOUR PICTURE?" ONE OF MY third-year middle school students asked me just as class was over for the day. *Hocam* translates as "my teacher" and that's how most students address their teachers in Turkey. It was late March, and as a Peace Corps Volunteer, I'd been teaching school in Kütahya since the end of September 1962. Kütahya is located in western Turkey and, at the time I lived there, was a medium-sized town with a population of about forty thousand.

"You want my picture?" I said, a little surprised. 3C was not one of my better classes and the student, whom I'll call Mehmet, certainly wasn't one of my better students.

"Yes, my teacher, please. I like."

A few days later Mehmet reminded me again, and after a bit of searching I found one to give him. It was a picture taken during my last year in university when a flat top and thick plastic-rimmed glasses were all the rage. The picture shows both, including the thick tape I'd wrapped around the arms of the frame where it was broken.

I taught five different grades or classes in Kütahya, one in each of the three middle school (*orta*) levels, 1, 2 and 3, and levels 4 and 5 in high school (*lise*). With the exception of my level 5 class, with only thirty students, each had sixty or more students, crammed three to a bench-like desk. A large number of students finished their education at the middle school level, with only those planning to attend university going on to high school. Quite a few more students dropped out at the end of the first year of high school, finding it too demanding. The course work was quite heavy, at least in terms of the number of different subjects to be taught. Second year students, for example, had sixteen different classes, including religion, history, commerce, Turkish, mathematics, geometry, physics, nature studies, social studies, agriculture, geography, sewing, art and physical education. Students had a choice of English, French or German, with most students opting for English and a much smaller number studying French or German.

There were three Volunteers teaching in Kütahya—Monty Peters, Leonard Flander, and myself. We all faced the same teaching difficulties. One set of problems resulted from the very large size of the classes. How can anyone teach a foreign language to sixty students, especially using the direct method, which meant speaking only English in class even though many students didn't study and didn't understand much of what was going on? I used to draw pictures on the blackboard, show pictures from magazines or other illustrations and do just about anything else short of standing on my head to try to teach new vocabulary. Sometimes it worked, but not always, and some concepts are simply impossible to get across without translating. I had the students repeating key words and sentences and doing substitution and other drills, but with sixty students, such an approach is difficult and often not particularly useful. It's quite impossible to tell who is repeating correctly and who is not.

With such large classes and with our limited Turkish, especially during the first few months, keeping order in class was always a big challenge. Other than "please repeat after me," the words we used the most in class were "don't talk," "please be quiet," and the less polite "shut up"—*konusma* and *sus* in Turkish. As frustrations increased, I became more adept at slapping students on the cheek from time to time to get their attention and keep them quiet. This kind of corporal punishment was widely used and even expected. I complained about three of my level 4 students to the school director one time. He immediately pulled them out of class and caned them on the palm of their hands in front of the other students. All three were crying and beet red in the face from embarrassment.

It was too much for me, and I never reported any more students for the rest of the year.

As one can imagine, with such crowded classrooms and three students to a desk, keeping students from copying or cheating on tests or quizzes was another difficult challenge. The only solution we could think of was to make up two tests, with every other student taking test A and the rest test B. This made it a bit harder to copy, but in the end probably didn't make all that much difference. A majority of our students would routinely fail any test we might give, so if they did copy from someone else, most tended to copy the wrong answers.

The second major problem we faced was lack of interest on the part of many of our students. In fact, quite a large number didn't want to learn English or saw no need to learn it. This was especially true in middle school. In addition, quite a few middle school students came from disadvantaged backgrounds. In such situations the help or support parents could supply, even if they wanted to, was often limited, including being able to provide a good desk or place to study. So the home environment was also something of a disincentive in many cases. As a result, we ended up effectively teaching only about a fifth to a quarter of the class, comprising a handful of boys and virtually all of the girls.

The girls were a godsend. In fact without them, we wouldn't have been able to teach at all, since hardly anyone else in the class would have been able to answer our questions or do exercises in class. We used to say that the girls studied more because they had to stay at home and weren't free to play sports or roam around the town as the boys were. This is partly true. However, in a conservative town like Kütahya, most parents thought primary education was sufficient for their daughters. Therefore only a small number of girls were sent to middle school and high school, and they came from homes where the parents were strongly motivated to give their daughters a more complete education.

By now you must have a rather poor view of the merits of Turkish education. I don't want to leave that impression. Class sizes were certainly a problem, and the curriculum needed much work and modernization, but overall those students who studied and worked hard could get a reasonable education. The problem was that only a relatively small number really worked hard, so the overall pass rate was shockingly low. The common complaint of all the teachers was about lazy students. "*Hiç çalışmiyorlar,*" they used to say—that is, "they never work or study."

All three of us worked hard to make our classes interesting by supplementing the rather boring standard textbook with more up-to-date materials, teaching folk songs, and acting out dialogues in class. I had the best time with my 5B class since they were my smallest class and understood the most English. I could read more interesting stories, discuss a wider range of topics, and get them to write more interesting short essays. We even sang folk songs in English on the school radio. It's possible that even today there may be one of my ex-students who still remembers "Oh Susannah," "A Hole in the Bucket," or "You Are My Sunshine."

To graduate from middle school and high school, each student had to pass a formal final exam. The exams were written, except for foreign languages, which were oral. With so many students doing poorly, we were very worried about how we would come out. None of us wanted to keep a student from graduating because of poor performance in the foreign language, certainly not at the middle school level. Since we had something like 180 students to examine, we kept the exam as simple and short as we could. In fact, all we did was ask each student an easy opening question such as: "How old are you?" or "How are you?" and then get them to read a passage in the textbook from which we would ask a few more questions to see if they really understood what they were reading. As each student left the classroom, he or she would tell the next student what the opening question was. Of course, we kept changing the opening question, which made for some amusing interchanges. A typical exam went something like this:

"Mustafa Özdoğan. Please come in." Mustafa walks in, sweating profusely and thinking if only he hadn't talked so much in class and studied more. He stands in front of a panel of three teachers, one Turk and two Americans.

"How are you?" Leonard asks.

"I'm fine, thank you," Mustafa answers after a bit of hesitation. We then give him a paragraph to read and see how he does. "Thank you, Mustafa. Please send in Ahmet Demiroğlu." As Mustafa leaves, he tells Ahmet in a whisper that the first question is "How are you?"

I take the lead this time.

"How old are you?" Ahmet smiles and quickly answers:

"I'm fine, thank you."

So I ask him again. If Ahmet still gets it wrong, we go on to the reading and see how he does. By the end of the exams, about 50 percent of our middle school students had passed what we thought was a very easy oral. Fortunately, at least as far as we were concerned, in almost all cases, students who failed English were also failing other subjects as well, especially mathematics. So in the end, none of our students failed to pass middle school solely because of English. At the end of the school year, I said goodbye to my students, as I would be teaching in a different town the next school year. Most I think were genuinely sad to see me leave. After all, I was the first foreigner most had ever had in the classroom. As a special treat on the last day of class, I let my students ask me questions in Turkish if they wanted to. Most were quite surprised to find out that their teacher now spoke reasonable Turkish. What did they want to know? The most common question was "Are there really cowboys and Indians in America?"

Oh, yes. About that picture Mehmet wanted. During the last week of school, my often less than well-behaved level 3 class presented me with a Kütahya ceramic plate with my picture in the middle. Kütahya is very well known for its ceramic industry, dating back many centuries, and Mehmet's father might have had some connection with one of the ceramic factories. On the back of the plate someone had written in Turkish: A keepsake from Kütahya Lise 3C.

The picture I'd given Mehmet was enlarged and reproduced faithfully in the center of the plate, including the tape around my broken glass frame. I still have it. In fact it hangs on our bedroom wall—a treasured memory from my year of teaching in Kütahya.

George T. Park served as an English teacher in Kütahya, Turkey, T-1, from 1962-64. George considers himself something of an international nomad having traveled extensively and lived abroad or worked on international issues since the mid-1950s, when he moved with his twin sister to Jordan where his father was working for the U.S. technical assistance program. Since then, he has continued to travel the world. High points along the way include graduation from high school in Libya; undergraduate study at the University of Maryland in Germany and at the University of Montana; his two years as a Peace Corps Volunteer; M.A. and Ph.D. in international and Middle Eastern studies from the Johns Hopkins School of Advanced International Studies; English teaching in Saudi Arabia; and two years doing program administration at the Ford Foundation office in Turkey. After a twenty-five year career with the World Bank developing and administering World Bank-lefinanced projects in Turkey, Cyprus, Costa Rica, Guatemala, and Pakistan, including a final four-year resident assignment in Warsaw, Poland, George retired from the Bank in 1999. George is married to Meredith, an equally nomadic Australian, and they have two children. They currently divide their time between Sydney, Australia, and Vienna, Austria.

SHERRY MORRIS

⋆

Soul Mates

Volunteers take part in all aspects of local life, including death.

DEATH IS ALIVE AND WELL IN UKRAINE. OR AT LEAST IT WAS when I was a Volunteer there from 1993 to 1995. Death appeared at the start of my service in the small town in central Ukraine where I was sent, and it returned at the end of my two-and-a-half years there. It also marked the whole in-between period where I got acquainted with lots of dead people, nearly as many as the live people I met. I got used to it after a while, but I couldn't keep straight who was who. We'd be talking about somebody—perhaps Volodia or maybe Natasha—and I'd have to ask, "The dead one or the alive one?"

I had only been in my town a month or so when I had my first experience with death, Ukrainian style. I was living with a math teacher named Galina Stanislovovna, but to me she was just Gala. She was (and is) a beautiful, joyous woman, with dancing blue eyes, long blonde hair and a figure that most men can't resist admiring. You'd never know she'd spent several years watching her eight-year-old son die of leukemia, his con-ditioned worsened by the Chernobyl explosion. She often said

136

to me in the small hours of the night, "In USSR Georgia they have special pomegranate juice. It could have helped Maxim. I could have tried more to get that juice."

Maxim's photo was the first thing you saw when you walked into Gala's lounge. You knew immediately the boy was dead. The oversized photo was a headshot, his school photo in black and white, with a large black bow tied round the photo. In contrast to his mother, Maxim had dark hair and dark eyes. He was probably very ill at the time; but he is smiling, and the smile even reaches his eyes. Perhaps he was thinking of his beautiful mother.

Maxim was the first dead person I was introduced to. He had been dead several years by the time I came to live with Gala, and I took his room when Gala offered to share her warm, cosy house with me. Her house had been part of the family home, which she and her sister, Lelia, had grown up in. They had split it into two separate houses when their parents died while Gala and Lelia were university students. Their parents were the second and third dead people I met.

I was immediately welcomed into their family, and luckily for me no more was ever made of my being a foreigner. Gala and I soon created a unique system of communication as her English was limited and my Ukrainian consisted of little more than "good day," "flowers," and "thank you." My Russian was even worse: I managed to combine *zdrasti* (hello) and *dasvidanya* (goodbye) into the incoherent *zdrasvidanya* so nobody knew whether I was coming or going. Gala, however, seemed to always understand what I was trying to say, and we hung index cards of the most useful words we needed in the kitchen.

In order not to overwhelm me, we decided everything important could be covered in roughly fifty Ukrainian words. But Gala and Lelia also learned vocabulary. A favourite word of Lelia's was "shaddup shaddup," which took on the meaning

of "You're in trouble and will not be allowed in the house."
She could often be heard shouting this to her husband, Misha,
when he came home drunk or the dog, Timosha, when he
rolled in something smelly. The phrase proved to be more
useful in this sense than in its standard meaning, so I never
bothered to correct it. It was in this slightly obscure way that
we gestured and guessed our way through half English, half
Russian and Ukrainian conversations. Gala was always the best
at communicating and understanding. Because I spent most of
my time with her, she and I grew very adept at figuring out
what the other person wanted to say, even if we didn't use the
right words.

Most of the time these charades were quite fun, and we'd
be in stitches watching each other act out complex ideas or
stories in ridiculous, exaggerated form. But there were times
when the things we needed to say were serious and the game
was not so funny. Gala explaining how her father died of a
broken heart three months to the day of his wife's death was
a sad re-enactment. Particularly when she explained that she
and Lelia had tried everything they could think of to keep
their father going. I never tired of watching and hearing their
stories. They told me the stories of the neighbours around us
as well. It seemed nearly every house had a death or tragedy
attached to it. I marvelled that so many people in such close
proximity had faced such adversity. If these people had been
living in America, they could have all gone on *Oprah*.

Across the road from Gala's there was a family with two
sons. I often saw the younger one, Arteum, climbing trees and
picking fruit with his older brother, Sasha, as I walked back and
forth along the puddle-riddled tracks from Gala's house to the
school where I taught English. He always called out "Hallo,"
and I would greet him in return. I saw the boys' mother,

Maria, frequently as well. She always seemed to be shouting at the boys, but Gala assured me they were a happy family.

I remember returning home with Gala from a visit to the capital, Kiev, in September. It was late, but there were many people standing around the lanes and entryways of their homes. It seemed everyone was up and everyone's light was on. Gala said to me, "Sherka, something happened." Sister Lelia met us at the gate. Her eyes red and puffy from crying, she choked out words I could not understand, but clearly something was wrong. I watched as Gala's hand went to her mouth, she dropped her head, closed her eyes and said, "No. Oh, God. Maria." Then she looked at me and pointing toward the house said, "Sherka, go inside." I knew she was thinking of how to explain what happened.

Through a series of gruesome pantomimes, they explained that Arteum, the nine-year-old boy across the street, was dead. *Oomer.* My word of the day. I did not doubt it, but could make no sense of it. I had just seen him the day before playing in the street. He seemed fine. I asked how, but couldn't grasp the words or gestures they made. His death seemed to involve a fall, but they shook their heads no when I asked, *"His head? His neck? His back?"*

Eventually they gave up trying to explain, and we sat in silence, heads bowed, listening to Lelia's sobs. I started watching people gather across the road at Arteum's house from Gala's kitchen window. Finally, Gala raised her head and her eyes were so empty. She said she was going to go to Maria, the boy's mother. I understood that only a woman who had lost a child could possibly comfort her. Gala asked if I wanted to go with her and Lelia. Even though I had only known Arteum a short time, I wanted to offer my condolences. I felt it was the least I could do, and I said I would join them.

Gala gave me a shawl to cover my head, and we crossed the road. The yard was full of people. There was a hush as I came through and I could hear people whispering "*Amerikanka. Amerikanka.*" As we entered the house, Gala found Maria. I barely recognised her, her features were so distorted from grief. They embraced, and I heard the words *Maxim, Arteum, God, heart, mother, good, son.* Then Maria saw me. She said, "Oh, look, Arteum, Sherry is here. The American is here to see you. She has come." I wasn't sure how to respond, and I hadn't thought to ask Gala what to say for bereavement. All I knew was *izvineeteye* a kind of "sorry," which was really "excuse me"—what you said when you wanted to pass by someone. Was that appropriate? If I said this to Maria would she think I wanted her to move out of the way?

I felt very awkward standing there. Suddenly we were going through to another room. It was small and dimly lit, and the first thing I noticed was the smell. There was an odor of cloves mixed with spices, but underneath was something else. A very old, heavy, clinging, mossy smell that was trying to take over the whole room. Gala was steering me toward the front of the room, past crying women, and I stopped short when I saw Arteum lying in a simple wooden coffin on the table. The room tilted a bit as I realized we'd come to do more than give our condolences. We were attending a wake right here in their home.

There would be no visit to a funeral parlor to view the body. As with nearly everything else in Ukraine, you did things yourself. This included preparing the body of your son for burial. Here, death was up close and personal, a hands-on experience. You washed the body, dressed the body and then laid it on the bed until the coffin arrived. The body was then laid out in the home. There were no discussions on how someone else would carry out "arrangements." No cards announced which funeral home to attend and when visitation hours were. There would be no undertakers arranging flowers, acting as hosts or ushering family members to a quiet room when overcome with emotion. You took care of your own, and it all happened right then and there, whether you were ready or not.

Gala took me straight up to the coffin, and I stared down at Arteum. He was wearing a black suit, and his blonde hair was neatly combed. He looked like he was sleeping, and I resisted the temptation to touch him. He wasn't wearing shoes or socks, and his feet looked so small. Was this real? All around me people were crying, and the smell was very strong and close. This was such an intimate, private moment for the family. What in the world was I doing here? The room was suddenly hot and I felt like everyone was looking at me look at him. I think I started to wobble. Gala saw I was distressed and told Lelia to take me home. Back at the house Lelia made me cups of tea, sang mournful songs and put me to bed. She stayed the night with me, and Gala stayed the night at Maria's.

The next morning when she came back, Gala looked tired and pale, but her eyes no longer looked empty. They were resigned. Accepting. By this time there were lots of people in Gala's kitchen. This was not unusual; her home was a meeting point for her wide circle of friends, and it was not uncommon to have fifteen people seated around a table that back home would have sat only four. What was unusual this morning was the tone and mood. Normally there was music and singing and talking and laughing in Gala's kitchen. I could not understand the conversations, but I could feel the merriment, the joy and the playfulness. This was not the feeling in the kitchen that morning. No one was talking, no one was smiling, there was no music.

Instead there were soft, quiet words of sympathy and sadness. My word for the day was *claudbistsche*: cemetery. We were going to the cemetery.

Eventually one of the Ukrainian English teachers came to Gala's. She was Arteum's class teacher and had brought the rest of the class for the funeral procession. She explained everything to me, though it still made no sense.

"Yes, Arteum is dead," she said. "He fell from a tree while picking nuts. He broke his liver and died."

"He fell from a tree and died?'

"Yes."

"How far did he fall?"

"Not far, maybe three meters."

"What does that mean, he broke his liver?"

"Well, he fell, but he seemed O.K. They took him to hospital and the doctors checked him. They said he was all right, that they would just keep him overnight to be sure. The parents went home to get him some things. He died before the parents got home. They hadn't realized he broke his liver."

I remembered how small and perfect he looked in the coffin the night before. There had been no sign of a broken liver. Just shattered hearts.

Gala told me it was time to get dressed for the funeral procession. I put on all the black I had, and we joined the large crowd of people who were forming in the street. It seemed we would walk to the cemetery, but I had no idea how far it was. A group of men showed up carrying tubas, a bass drum and an accordion. People stood in small circles talking quietly, and eventually six men came out of the house carrying Arteum in the coffin. They lifted him high over their heads, and as the coffin was still open we could all see him. It had started to drizzle. Did it matter that he was getting wet? Gala told me Arteum had a size 5 coffin, just like her son, Maxim.

And so we walked through the town to the cemetery. Arteum led the way, then Maria. She was escorted on either side by her husband and remaining son and sobbed her way along the route, followed by the rest of the family, then friends and classmates. Last of all came the musicians. They played the saddest tune possible from such jolly *oomp-pa-pa* instruments. As we walked, people came out of their homes and stood in their doorways and yards along the route. They threw white carnations as he passed. Some landed in the coffin, but most fell to the ground, creating a bed of flowers, which was trampled on by the rest of the procession.

I had no idea how far we were walking or where the cemetery was. It seemed we were heading for the school, but we carried on past it toward the forest. I was trying to figure out why we were heading toward the forest when I noticed various tombstones amongst the trees and that at some point the cemetery and forest melded. It was very different from the cemeteries I knew back home with their cleared ground of perfectly manicured lawns, every tombstone evenly lined up and laid out in organised rows. Those cemeteries were pristine, sterile places rarely visited, empty and lifeless. But here at the forest cemetery, there was lots of activity. There were birds singing, people going for walks with their dogs, a family was having a picnic. Here a cemetery was not an austere, vacant place. It was alive, in use by the living and the dead. I found it reassuring. Peaceful. I liked knowing there would be lots of trees for Arteum. It made me feel not so afraid of death.

We walked to the grave that had been dug by Arteum's uncles, father, and brother. In spite of the rain, he still looked perfect. The principal of the school came and gave a speech. She was an intimidating woman, built like a tank, with orange hair and steely blue eyes that dared you to contradict her. As she spoke there were many tears, many heads shaken in agreement, and the catch in her voice told me she was not the unfeeling woman she seemed to be. When she finished, a man from the local church led the crowd through prayers and songs. I noticed Gala was no longer singing but sobbing.

Suddenly everything stopped, and the men placed the lid on the coffin. They got out large hammers and long spikes from canvas sacks I hadn't noticed before. Maria started to scream then and the sound of the spikes being pounded in mixed with her shrieks. I realised Gala was leaning quite heavily on me. Eventually the hammering stopped, but the sound continued to echo around the trees and through my head. The men used thick ropes to lower the casket into the ground. Maria cried, "Arteum" and "my son" until she was hoarse, and they had to hold her back from the grave. I remember saying to Gala "enough," and I moved to the back of the crowd. I watched as everyone filed past with a handful of soil and threw it on top of the coffin. The men completed filling the hole and everyone placed flowers on the grave. This seemed to signal the end of the burial, and the crowd began to disperse. I felt a collective sigh of release from the intense grief that had bonded the mourners together. The sorrow seemed to have lifted somehow and the mood lightened.

Gala came back to me and said we would now go and visit Maxim, her son. As I followed Gala through the cemetery she pointed out various people she knew: a classmate who'd had an illness, the daughter of her close friends, a former teacher of the school. There were many, many tombs and nearly all had a chain link fence or gate around a small plot. With some tombs the gate was open; on some it was firmly shut. Some were very elaborate monuments, while others were more modest. The tombstones were all shapes and sizes and in addition to the name, date of birth and death, had a likeness of the individual carved in the stone. Some tombs had a text I could read: *We will always remember you*, said one. *A loving husband*, read another. *Our Angel* was on a baby's tomb. Maxim's read, *It's not true my son is dead, he's just not with me anymore.*

There was a bench just outside Maxim's plot and Gala instructed me to sit. From a locked cupboard beneath the worn, wooden bench she pulled out a pair of gloves, a bucket, a rag, a short broom made of twigs, a shot glass, and a bottle of vodka. Wordlessly she took the bucket to the nearest pump and filled it with water. She then began washing Maxim's tombstone with the rag. As the flecked, black marble became wet, his name, the dates and his image disappeared. The stone was momentarily blank. As the stone dried, the images reappeared, and I could once again see the boy who greeted me each time I entered the lounge. Gala then swept the tiled area around his tomb, tending the various plants and bushes she had planted within his plot. She plucked rogue twigs from the site and swept around the gravel and magnolias that bordered the posts of the chain-linked fence of Maxim's plot. She put one of the bunches of flowers in the metal vase that was permanently fixed to the base of Maxim's tomb. The final two bunches would be for her parents' graves that we'd visit next. When she was finished, she poured a shot of vodka, said, "*To your health*" and downed the shot. She then poured one for me and I drank, giving the same toast to Maxim's health. It was very serene sitting on the bench in the shelter of a tall chestnut tree.

In spite of the harrowing events of the past two days, I felt uplifted. The boys were in a peaceful place. There were birds that would sing to them, flowers that would blossom for them, family nearby that would visit them regularly and tidy their plot. All around me there was life. I could hear the school bell ringing in the distance and the sounds of children at play. It was like Maxim's tomb said: the boys weren't so much gone as living in the forest now. Gala tidied everything away, and as she left Maxim's plot, she made a point of closing the gate behind her carefully.

"Sherka, how are you?" She asked as she sat down next to me on the bench.

"I'm O.K." I answered. "It's nice here Gala. Maxim has a good place."

"Yes, he has a good place."

"Why did you close his door?" I asked.

She showed me as she explained.

"I don't want him to go out. If I leave the gate open, his *doosha* can go out. If the gate is closed, his *doosha* rests here."

"What is *doosha*?"

Further gesturing ensued and after a while I got it.

"His soul!" I cried in English.

"Yes, Sherka. *Doosha*."

I thought I understood. I understood how the dead remain alive, how a mother can cope with the most devastating loss and how death doesn't need to be feared and kept at a distance. We smiled at each other and hugged.

Gala now lives in the States where things are very different. There are no cemetery forests and Maxim's photo lives in her bedroom rather than her living room. But not everything has changed. She has an American son, and he knows he has a brother in the cemetery forest in Ukraine. Her American son is not afraid to talk about Maxim, and one day he will go and meet his brother there in the forest. He will sit on the bench, make a toast to his brother's health and both will agree that they are lucky to have such a beautiful mother.

Sherry Morris served as a TEFL teacher in Fastiv Ukraine, Group 2, where she taught English, drama, and a love of Halloween to secondary students from 1993-95. Sherry has been living in the London for the past ten years, where she divides her time between encouraging her broad beans and beetroot to flourish and lunching on the steps of St Paul's Cathedral. These and other entertaining activities get somewhat interrupted by her job as a Unit Administrator at Imperial College. Nevertheless, she continues to visit Ukraine for hearty meals and refreshing winter dips in the river Unava. She currently shares her flat with a mad Ukrainian, an even madder Russian, and the aptly named rat, Rattie.

PART THREE

GETTING THROUGH THE DAYS

SANDRA LEE ANDERSON

✶
✶ ✶

Visit to Karkamish

*The first Volunteer in town explores the
veiled lives of Turkish women.*

GAZIANTEP LIES ON THE SILK ROAD IN TURKEY, NOT FAR FROM
the Syrian border. In the fall of 1966, I was the only new
Volunteer in this city of 100,000. Southeastern Turkey, much
of it settled by Kurds, was considered to be a little like the
American Wild West. Even so, Peace Corps was sending
women there, and the city treated us well.

One weekend, four of us set out on a spontaneous adven-
ture to Karkamish—Carchemish in the Old Testament—one
of the most important centers in the Hittite Empire. June
Beale and Penny Feinberg worked in the local orphanage, Ann
Ringland taught at Boys' Middle School, and I taught at Girls'
Middle School.

Karkamish, just thirty-seven miles away from Gaziantep, is
an ancient site at the modern crossroads of the Euphrates River,
the Berlin-Baghdad Railroad, and the Turkish-Syrian border.
In ancient times, goods were traded across the river between
Anatolia to the northwest and Mesopotamia to the south. It
had been a major city for the Egyptians under Tuthmosis I

151

and Akhenaten, as well as the Hittites and Babylonians. The Babylonian King, Nebuchadnezzar II, defeated the Egyptians here.

Because we were going into a village, we dutifully donned our headscarves and black tights and then got on a bus, little bigger than a Volkswagen, crammed with twenty-seven people inside and six on top. June had to lean against a door, so a helpful woman from across the bus grabbed her arm and held onto it for the whole trip. June was a little uncomfortable and suggested that the woman might become tired. She said "no," with a big smile, so June in full gratitude grinned and bore it. And, of course, thanked the woman profusely later.

Ann, who spoke the best Turkish, got into a discussion with a man who started up a conversation. He asked why our eyes were *açık göz*, so open, so clear—he might have meant clever and smart—and here we were running around Turkey. He explained that it was not being from America because even Turkish men from America wouldn't *gez* (walk around, check a place out) as we do. Ann told him that we had all graduated from college, and he said that was it. He went on to comment that it was good that we are here because Turkey had much to learn from us and our liberty to come and go.

We arrived late in the evening, and there were no hotels open. The woman sitting next to me, covered in a black *çarşaf* from head to black stockings and shoes, offered to let us say at her house. Her son and daughter were with her. We had no idea what these people were like; we could only see her two eyes. Then the bus driver, a scroungy looking fellow, started pressuring us to stay with him. The woman pinched me and stuck her tongue out to show how the bus driver was ogling. And other women on the bus kept pinching Ann, telling her in emphatic Turkish not to go with the driver. We took their advice and got off with the family.

Our group traveled down passages between the walled adobe homes to their home. They had three rooms that opened on to a courtyard, so you had to travel outside to go between them. Invited into the main room, we settled down on the cushions. This was a well-to-do family, with nice rugs on the floors and walls, a bed and good china. Our hostess sloughed off the *čarşaf* and said, "Don't just sit there. Talk. Talk."

Every member of the family had to come shake hands with each of us and welcome us. Then a two-year-old boy brought the lemon cologne water to clean our hands, holding the bottle upside down, of course. Another boy, four years old, kissed the back of our hands, and pressed them to his forehead. He managed to wipe his nose on Ann's hand, but it's the thought that counts. In addition to the little boys, they had a very sick and thin baby girl.

In the course of the evening, we discovered that the woman was a real character! She had two sons and their wives in the town, and she had a daughter of our age she would not let marry. That way her daughter could always take care of her. She was the matriarch. She even took her grandson away from his father and brought the boy to live here because the father wouldn't send the boy to school.

She was the one who had chosen the wives for her sons. One girl, she just caught sight of in Nizip, a nearby town. The girl was good-looking and "clean" (meaning a good Muslim), so she offered $1,100, American money, for her. The girl's parents consented.

In Turkey, the way to be a good guest is to eat as much as possible and say a lot of "thank you's." But because there are usually ten servings of food in a meal, we ate somewhat gingerly. When the main dish came out, it was a hot pepper dish, and we half laughed: we knew we were going to have to eat it. Laughing was a mistake because our hostess interpreted that we were laughing at the food. They had felt that we couldn't possibly like Turkish food, so they had ordered from the local restaurant. We did like the food, told her that we loved Turkish food, and thanked her for the consideration.

That evening, the men were out, and the woman played Parcheesi with her daughter and daughter-in-law. Of course she cheated some, but what could the daughters do? They were all enjoying themselves.

When the woman was ready to say her prayers, she just pulled out a rug and began saying them in the middle of the floor, bowing to Mecca, while conversations continued on. After prayers, our hostess showed us that both she and her daughter had fingertips stained in red henna, so she asked if we would like to do our fingernails. They explained that a Muslim woman can't pray if her fingernails are white. The other three girls wanted to and did. I didn't because it was illegal for teachers in the girls' school to have hennaed hands. The woman gave me a hard time, and I was the only one without a red pinky.

At 8:30 it was time for bed. When we said we would sleep in our clothes, our hostess scoffed, bringing out nightgowns for each of us. I looked mine over to figure out which was the front side; she reassured me that the gown was clean. I explained why I was looking at it: I guessed that the yoke went in front. She laughed, "No," and demonstrated that the elastic goes in front. My ignorance.

We all crossed the courtyard to the bedroom with a huge mattress and blankets on the floor, and the woman and daughter sat down to watch us undress. We did it as modestly as possible.

We got into bed. The mother and daughter had another bed, but it was too small for both of them. So we all moved over for the daughter. The woman told us not to, and to enforce it, she pounced upon us, tickling until we moved back to our original places. Eventually the girl did join us. But we were giggling. So the old lady lifted the blanket and tickled our feet. It took a while to fall asleep.

The next day we visited some ruins of the old city-fortress of Karkamish. And as travelers had done for centuries, we waded across the Euphrates to the Syrian side of the border crossing, where we bought some goods, including instant coffee from the little open-front shops. Then we "smuggled" our coffee back, to the amusement of the soldiers guarding the border.

After a day of wandering, watching a wedding party with a weeping bride and eating lunch, we returned home. Our hosts told us we were not just friends—we were part of the family. And part of a family's responsibility is to protect its members. That morning some soldiers had come to the house wanting to take us to lunch. This was *ayıp*, a shameless act on their part. The two brothers yelled at them and reported the infraction to their commander.

When we parted from the family, we kissed the back of the woman's hand and pressed it to our foreheads, the first time we had done it. There were tears in her eyes at this sign of respect. We all caught the morning bus, and they took the baby into Nizip. A brother traveled with us the rest of the way to Gaziantep since women weren't supposed to travel without a male escort. He stopped by the apartment, so we were able repay some of their hospitality and arranged to send some food to help fatten the baby.

I have never regretted my two years in Turkey, and I have always felt that I was accepted and loved by the Turks.

Sandy Lee Anderson taught English in Turkey, T-13, from 1966-68. She spent her career working in central administration of the D.C. Public Schools, and now lives in Southern Maryland as a writer. She's maintained her friendships with Turks and worked over the decades to sustain Arkadaşlar, the group of returned PCVs from Turkey.

Mushroom Hunters

A Volunteer gets his hands dirty.

THE SUN HAD ONLY BEEN UP AN HOUR, SO THE SHADOWS WERE still long and cold as the tiny car bounced along the snaking, dirt road. Speaking Romanian is hard in the early morning, so I tried to stick to specific questions, ones that Doru could answer at length while I sat quietly and listened. As we reached Cheile Jietului, however, my child-ike wonder withered my will to sustain conversation. Cheile Jietului is a gateway (one of many) into the fairy tale kingdom that is Romania's wild places. So I shut up and stared out the window at the tortuously slow symphony of fall color on all sides of me: each note represented a different moment of passing, and every note was a symbol of the suddenly suspended transience of time.

Doru and I were going mushroom hunting, which seemed an apt way to spend a Sunday afternoon in the land of fairy tales. We crossed into the next county, Vâlcea, over a long mountain pass and came to a crossroad where scores of other mushroom hunters had set up temporary camps made of wood, plastic, and nylon. Doru told me that these mushroom hunters were after a different type of mushroom than we were, a kind that is exported to other countries throughout Europe. North of the crossroad, the road heads toward Sibiu, one of the more well-known cities in Romania. Ahead it goes to Râmnicu Vâlcea, and behind us back to Petrosani and the Jiu Valley I call home. The last time I was here was over a year ago, and since then a large portion of this road has been widened, graded, and paved. Doru told me this is part of an attempt to establish the area as a center for eco-tourism and to make it more accessible. It reminded me of all the other ways that Romania has been progressing around me since I arrived sixteen months ago.

We parked alongside a river with a crossing—a long, fallen pine tree. Doru poured two small glasses of strong, dark wine and we toasted. "For courage," Doru laughed before we cleared our glasses in a few, long gulps. Doru pulled on a pair of rubber galoshes and told me that he was going to wade the river. I had on hiking boots, so my route would be to "slowly" cross by using the tree. I climbed onto it and carefully began to step my way across. Now, as a person who is chronically clumsy, I figured the odds were at least 50 percent that I'd slip and fall into the water. True to my nature, two-thirds of the way across the river, I stepped onto a patch of rotting bark which disintegrated under my foot and threw my balance downward. I suddenly found myself suspended in the air, heading for a bad fall and a cold bath.

However, being chronically clumsy has its benefits: which is to say, I've adapted to my handicap. I'm really good at falling down. Instinctively, I kicked my right leg over my body and rolled my trajectory so that I was facing downwards. I planted my right foot ankle deep into the water, but I was able to catch myself on the log with both hands and raise my left leg over the river.

"Joe-ehl!" Doru yelled, as he quickly sloshed his way upriver. "Are you all right?! Did you hit yourself?!" Doru gave me his shoulder and helped me across to the far bank. I assured Doru that I had indeed caught myself, and that I was fine.

"You scared me," Doru said. "I have to be responsible for you," and I knew he was right. My seven Romanian mothers would scold Doru to death if I broke an arm or leg while I was in the woods with him. Doru seemed relieved, and passed me two large, woven, plastic sacks from the supermarket.

"Last fall I filled two bags," Doru said. "We'll see how we do."

He scampered over to a cinnamon-colored mushroom craning itself out of the supple earth. "These are what we're after," Doru told me, as he plucked off the mushroom's "tail" and passed the "head" to me to examine. I took mental notes: brownish and sort of spotty. Check.

Doru took the low ground, and I went higher. The hill was on a steep, north-facing grade, and the trees were dense. It had also rained lightly the evening before, so all roots were slick and the dirt was spongy. Each step I either sunk four inches into wet moss and pine needles or slid down a half meter over wet branches. Doru and I would leave our bags in a spot and sort of zigzag around, grabbing mushrooms, popping off their stems, and putting the caps carefully into our sacks.

Under a pine tree, in a place that felt noticeably more magical than the rest, I found two large mushrooms that weren't like what Doru had shown me. These two were a deep brown, and their heads came to distinct peaks. These were the sort of mushrooms you'd expect to find in a magic forest, safeguarded by overprotective gnomes. I carefully plucked the caps from the stems and bagged them. I heard Doru call my name, so I scampered across the hill so that he could keep me in his sight and wouldn't need to worry about me.

I instantly became aware that I had a problem. I felt like I was grabbing about four different types of mushroom. Some seemed more reddish than what Doru had shown me. Others had distinct, almost black "nipples" at their crests. Others seemed right, but were grey and rose-colored underneath. I took my half-full bag to Doru and asked him to inspect what I had collected.

Doru dumped the bag onto the earth and began picking through them. "No. No. These aren't good,' he murmured and I watched as he tossed away two-thirds of what I had found.

"Look," Doru said, handing me another "good" mushroom to study. The mushrooms I really wanted weren't brown and spotty. They were latte colored with the occasional light fleck of cream on top. And, underneath, they were a luminescent white that seemed so pure and soft that it almost sang lullabies.

I also showed Doru the two gnome mushrooms. "Oh, these! These are good," Doru said as he carefully took the two caps from me. "These are what the other mushroom hunters come after. You should have left the tails on them, but you didn't know. We'll try and sell them later for beer," Doru said and smiled at me before putting them in a separate plastic bag.

Doru and I moved on, and I now felt more comfortable recognizing the kind of head we were after. They start deep inside the ground, and grow upwards strong and solid. Hence, they're usually hidden under swathes of moss and dirt, or on the dim sides of uprooted trees. The young ones have domes, perfectly designed for pushing past the soil into the open air. Older ones flatten out and become wide, concave cups that catch rain. Because of the precipitation, the older ones are susceptible to mold and rot, growing fuzzy white beards and losing that glowing white sheen, trading it for a faded color like grave water. They are easy to uproot, tail and head together, and the two are separated with a quick, strong pinch at the neck.

When Doru and I wandered out of the forest about three hours later, he had two heavy bags, both two-thirds full. I was excited with my own contribution: one two-thirds full sack, and a second that was a little over a quarter full. Doru waded across the river with all four bags, while I slowly inched across the bridge again. This time, as odds would predict, I made it across without falling down.

Doru laid out a spread of canned meat, bread, sliced vegetables, salty sheep's milk cheese, and a beer for me. We ate hungrily, occasionally breaking apart our bites by talking about wildlife conservation, or how warm the recent winters have been in Romania. Doru and I ate heartily, and after the whole beer and another short glass of wine I had a small buzz. So Doru and I packed the mushrooms into the car and began the trip home.

Back at the crossroads, we stopped briefly so that Doru could sell the two gnome mushrooms I found along with two others that he had come upon. There was a group of hard-looking men hanging out around an electronic scale and a pickup truck piled with wooden crates. These were the mushroom gangsters. The crates were for gnome mushrooms that the men would buy from other mushroom hunters working at the crossroads camp. The mushroom Don was a squat man, and he held a wad of bills totaling a few thousand RON. A young crony in the pickup truck weighed our four mushrooms. They were 600 grams altogether. Although they usually sell for 25 RON per kilogram, the don gave us a 10 RON note. Doru didn't argue, so we got in the car and left.

In the car, Doru told me that the man was "making fun of us," but that he didn't want to argue. I told him it was fine. We had enough money for two beers, and that was alright with me. On the ride home, we blasted out of the fairy tale gate, and time suddenly latched onto us, hyperactive and anxious to make up for the three hours we lost away from it. There was sun, and countless packs of people grilling along this part of the Jiu River. I suddenly realized how sleepy I had become, and so I told Doru we'd have to save our beer money for another time.

"That's fine Joe-ehl," he smiled at me, and dropped me off at home. "I'll clean the mushrooms and give you some," and I told him that would be beautiful, but that I didn't want many. I said that I would rather go to his house so that we could eat them together, and spend our beer money. Doru replied, "This goes without saying."

Joël McClurg is a Colorado native who served in Romania. Aside from the usual Peace Corps accomplishments, he is excited that his Peace Corps experience has given him the opportunity to learn: how to dance the waltz (poorly), Kyokushin karate, and the subtleties of pickling and eating any vegetable (and almost any fruit) imaginable.

ROBERT SHORE

The Other Side

Chicken slaughter can also be a cross-cultural exchange.

"YOUR PEOPLE LIKE CHICKEN, RIGHT?" I DID NOT KNOW THE hunched, wrinkled figure before me. This was the first line of our first conversation. I liked it. I told him that we—Americans—did. He seemed relieved, as if I had settled some long unresolved bet. He had a worthless resource—three live male chickens—and now someone stupid enough to pay top dollar for them.

Ordinarily I might have taken issue with the phrase "your people"; but lately, I don't mind being pigeonholed from time to time. The more Mongolians tell me that I am one of the American people, the clearer it is that I am not. Every now and then, you need to be reminded that you are part of something, even if that something is chicken.

My roots are problematic. At age six I watched a Civil War documentary with my grandmother. After several attentive hours of *Sesame Street*-framed comprehension, I exclaimed in terror, "Gram, we lost." My grandmother, a Jewish woman from New Jersey, assured me with some conviction that *we* had most certainly won that war.

Raised in the south in a religiously indistinct family from the north always seemed to make me a default "other." In high school, I was a Jewish kid from a liberal family surrounded by good ole' boys. In college, I was a provincial country bumpkin surrounded by affluent Jews. I came to accept, and even nurture, this otherness.

Today, not much about me says "Georgia Cracker." I keep my Southern heritage in safekeeping for opportunistic donning of cowboy boots and uses of the word "y'all." But life in Mongolia has provided me some down-home legitimacy: I ride pretty well; I'm rather handy with both fishing pole and axe; and, off-roadin'/muddin' is a veritable transportational staple. Still, pioneer stock I am not. Unwittingly caught up in the muddle, three chickens sat precariously between pet cluck and potluck.

I asked my Mongolian brother Sanaa if he had ever killed a chicken—in Mongolian, "Have you seen killing a chicken?" He responded that he had never even *seen* a chicken. (Sheep, goats, cows, yaks, camels, and the occasional marmot; chickens were not suited to the nomadic lifestyle and, thus, never worked their way onto the Mongolian meat menu.)

"No problem," I said. "I've done this many times before. I just need you to help me."

It was the spoken equivalent of vomiting. Immediately, I wanted it back. Sanaa's look of premature excitement and admiration assured me that I would not have it. Panicked, I asked if he thought that the rest of the family would be interested in the execution of the exotic. I knew that his mother and father would not return from the countryside for two days. He nodded. I had bought myself time, and an audience.

Luke has a similarly rootless persona. He is from the rural plains, but in meeting him, you'd never guess he picked corn in the summers for extra cash. Still, I figured at the very least he could refer me to a poultry-savvy aunt. Stereotypes be damned, there was no Aunt Ethel. But by some odd act of chance, Luke had recently read up on all things chicken.

Apparently, chickens, in strange parallel with crocodiles, are brought to a partially comatose state when turned upside down. I presumed that this would be useful information, making things easier for all parties, feathered and not. From there, I clung to the hope that Luke had read some revolutionary methodological text, wherein the "like a chicken with its head cut off" hypothesis need not be tested. Apparently, even after so many centuries of potpie and salad sandwiches, there has been little innovation in the field. There is still no way around a firm chop.

Having received the information more quickly than expected, I had two full days to contemplate the task before me. Every time I ventured out of my *ger* I had to walk past the objects of my most fowl predicament. It took more effort than expected to avoid giving the little guys names and assign them human personality traits.

William Carlos Williams' poetic assertion that "so much depends upon a red wheelbarrow...beside the white chickens" started to make a bit more sense, taking on new and ominous tones. I held firmly to a distractive mantra: "delicious soup"— an unholy reversal of transubstantiation.

Two days passed. Everyone returned from the countryside. My Mongolian family and a small crowd of curious neighbors came out for the "show." Speculation about appropriate methods and the likelihood of my success began. I half-expected the assembly to start waving bank notes in the air, transporting the event to a South American cockfighting pit.

I had briefed Sanaa on how it would all go down. Though he only had to pull the string that had been fastened around each neck, he was part of the act, and wasted no time giving the crowd a privileged account of what was likely to happen. I wielded a meat-cleaver and a disingenuous look of confidence. I placed the first chicken on the chopping block. Sanaa pulled the string tight, and my stomach followed suit. Delicious soup. Delicious soup. Chop.

A single swipe initiated a surprising set of role reversals. A headless chicken chased my dogs around the yard, evincing shrieks of horror from the women and rapturous laughter from the men. In the faces of the children, I saw the sideways glances and grimaces that I knew I must have worn the first few times I saw a sheep butchered. For me, sheep were cost-effective Ambien. For them, chicken had no experiential referent. This was some bizarre ritual, executed by someone with esoteric knowledge of exotic creatures. As far as my audience was concerned, I was Colonel Robert Sanders of the Kentucky Fried Tribe.

The mythic cult of the chicken killers was an organic construction of group identity. No matter that I got the information from Luke, who got the information from a book. No matter that not one of my friends from home has ever killed a chicken. In the local consciousness, I am one of a people—and *my* people like chicken! And, for now, that is enough.

Epilogue: Delicious soup.

Robert Shore served as an English teacher and conducted tourism development in Mongolia, M-17, from 2006-08. Since returning, Rob has worked as a writer, producer, photographer, and part-time sophist. His writing and photography have been featured in the Fifth Wednesday Journal, Juked, Anderbo, *and on* The Best American Poetry Blog. *His essay "Time Travel" is forthcoming in the book* Resident Aliens. *He wrote and directed the documentary film* And Many More. *Rob currently lives in Washington, D.C., where he does new media for the FrameWorks Institute, a progressive think tank.*

J O R D A N   M .   S C E P A N S K I

The Eastern Regional

The Peace Corps sent Volunteers. The locals wanted ringers.

MAHMUT, THE PHYS ED TEACHER, COULDN'T BELIEVE HIS LUCK. Coaching a fledgling basketball program at a high school in the Turkish city of Elazig, he learned that the two new American teachers both played the sport. He and some of the older students had tested us on the court and found we knew the game. He concluded we were far better players than any he had on his team and immediately added us to the roster. John played what we probably now would call point guard. I, a bit taller, was a forward.

John and I started playing together during Peace Corps training at Portland State University. As a matter of fact, it was basketball that led to our being assigned to eastern Turkey together. In the summer of '64, some of the male trainees would show up early for the mandatory physical training class to play a few pick-up games. That's where the redneck from Winston-Salem met the Yankee from Yonkers. While trading passes and shots on basketball courts in Portland, Oregon, and Elazig, Turkey, and teaching English to as many as ninety students per class for more than forty hours a week, we forged a life-long friendship that led us to the same profession and homes ninety miles apart in the heart of Tobacco Road country.

The coach was rather excited about our chances in a regional basketball tournament to be held in the Turkish city of Sivas in March. As best we understood, clubs from all over the eastern part of the country would be competing, with the championship team going on to a nationwide event in Ankara. Mahmut saw the American players leading his team of burly Turkish schoolboys to the big time. There was, in fact, a third Volunteer who practiced with us on weekends and whose play was anticipated. Chris was assigned to the neighboring province of Tunceli, and he would regularly come to visit us. A good front-court player and ball handler, he added to Mahmut's confidence that he had all the elements of a winning team.

As tourney time drew near, Mahmut obtained permission from our school's principal for us to be absent from class for the few days of competition. Unfortunately, he had no influence with the Tunceli principal, who refused to give Chris any time off, thereby depriving us of a very important player.

We traveled to Sivas with Mahmut and our raucous seventeen- and eighteen-year old teammates, anticipating a stay through the championship game. Sivas had a Volunteer resident in the city, and in typical Peace Corps fashion, John and I invited ourselves to stay at his house during our time there. Where the rest of the team bunked is a mystery, but we were glad to have separate accommodations.

Opening night of the tournament saw us decked out in brand new warm-up outfits, specially purchased for us by the city of Elazig. As a huge crowd gathered in the arena and we did some pre-game shooting, we doffed the warm-ups, only to discover that our bodies were covered in sweaty lint from the unwashed jackets and pants. Attempting to pick as many of the green cotton specks from our arms and legs as we could, we took part in the traditional team salute to the audience and then gathered around Mahmut for some last minute guidance.

Our opponents were from the ancient city of Trabzon on the Black Sea. Famous in history as the Greek outpost of civilization that Xenophon and the 10,000 made its retreat to, it now housed an American Air Force facility high on a hill, nicely situated for listening to Soviet radio transmissions across the water. It seems Mahmut was not the only Turkish coach who saw opportunity in the availability of players hailing from the country that invented basketball. The Trabzon team included two large airmen, at whom we surreptitiously stole pre-game glances. John and I also engaged in occasional off-color banter, sometimes including comments about the referees. We assumed, of course, that no one nearby understood what we were saying. Just before tip-off one of the refs approached and in perfect English asked, "You guys ready to play?" As it turned out, we weren't.

I jumped center against one of the Trabzon ringers. He was at least five inches taller than I, and we later learned that before joining the Air Force he played some college ball at the University of Colorado. He easily won the tip. His American teammate brought the ball up court, passed it to him, and he proceeded to go over me and slam the ball through the hoop. John handled the ball for our team, and crossing the half court line found me for a long jump shot that hit nothing but net. Good start. Same play for Trabzon as before: American ball handler to American big man for another score. And same for the Elazig team and its Peace Corps Volunteers. "O.K.," I'm thinking, "we can hang with these guys."

That was the last time the score was tied, or even close. John kept feeding me the ball, but I could do nothing more, while on the other side the American airmen led what was shaping up to be a rout. John decided to do some shooting of his own, with mixed results, and the rest of our team concluded their Americans had choked. They started ignoring us and went to throwing up wild shots, sometimes from near half court, which only made matters worse. The game effectively was over at halftime.

We did come back somewhat in the second half, as John and I returned to a reasonable semblance of ability, but it was the proverbial too little, too late. Mahmut's dream of trophies and a trip to Ankara was over.

Later we went drinking with the two airmen (and the English-speaking Turkish ref) and became friendly enough to be invited to their quarters in Trabzon the following summer when we worked in a camp nearby. While on the base we ate real American food, drank real American beer, and slept in real American beds. We didn't, however, play any real American basketball. But then, we didn't in Sivas, either.

Jordan Scepanski, Dean Emeritus, California State University, Long Beach, taught English as a foreign language in Turkey from 1964-66. After entering the academic library world, Scepanski served as staff liaison to the American Library Association's (ALA) International Relations Committee and International Relations Round Table. He received a Fulbright Senior Lectureship to teach in the graduate program of the Department of Librarianship at Hacettepe University in Ankara and was later recruited to become dean of library and learning resources at Zayed University, an all-female national university with campuses in Dubai and Abu Dhabi, UAE. He and his wife Lea Wells work together as Jordan Wells Associates (Chapel Hill, NC), consulting on library and information issues and facilitating organizational and staff development.

MICHAEL BERG

Swearing In

"A guest belongs to God." —*Armenian Proverb*

MOST PEACE CORPS VOLUNTEERS WILL TELL YOU THAT ONE OF their best and most memorable days was their swearing-in day. It is the culmination of eleven weeks of hard work, and the day is full of excitement about moving to site within twenty-four hours. I, too, will not soon forget my swearing-in. I was extremely tired because I did not sleep the night before: not because of the anticipation or being busy with saying my good-byes, but because I was suffering from food poisoning. It turns out that the cow heart I ate a few nights prior was not treating me so well, and I spent all night traveling back and forth to the outhouse in the cold. When I got up in the morning, my host mom was skeptical about my leaving the house, and I had to assure her that I was alright. I survived the ceremony, had a Sprite in celebration afterward—as everyone else toasted their beers—and went home and went to bed.

The next day I awoke early to finish the packing that I was unable to earlier, and then headed with the rest of the Volunteers to go to site. My stomach was a little better, and I felt confident that I could make the three-hour drive without incident. As it turned out, I did need one bathroom stop, but it was no problem. When I arrived to my new host family, it was hard explaining that I was sick in the stomach. "Why?" was the question they kept asking. Had I forgot to wear socks in the house, or maybe I had been out in the sun for too long? The thought that it could be from bad meat or a parasite in the water was as crazy as the fact that I hadn't eaten in two days, which they immediately wanted to change.

I was treated with *dole-ma* for lunch, an Armenian specialty, and was told that dinner would be *khoravats,* which is a unique barbeque experience and the best and most expensive meal in Armenia. I decided to tighten my gut, loosen my belt, and dig in. I survived with only minor complications and was pleased with the food. The next day I was starting to feel a little better, when a group of men barged in with several bags of food, dead set on meeting the new local American, and naturally celebrating with another *khoravats*. I obliged, and figured that any good German ancestor of mine would tell me that the beer that the men brought would certainly help an upset stomach.

The following day, a little weary of all the food I had been eating and a few trips to the new outhouse later, I decided to cut it back to bread and tea to keep the stomach in check. This turned out to be as probable as finding peanut butter in the local store, and I was ushered away at 10 A.M. to a few villages over, and up in the hills. Here, to no surprise, we had another *khoravats*. I began to wonder how much chicken I could eat, alongside grilled vegetables and shots of vodka, when I was treated with honey fresh off the comb; literally, we were chewing the comb with the bees twenty meters away.

By this point I had forgotten just how sick I had been. The 2 A.M. runs to the outhouse, only a few days prior, seemed a distant memory. If offered cow heart at this last *khoravats,*

I would have said yes. I let myself get sucked into my new village, and as this happened the woes of my past months in Armenia disappeared. It was still several more days of meeting new people and feasting before I had a chance to settle down and relax. Maybe it was a bold move to pretend that I was fine and to dig right in, toasting away. Maybe it could have made me much sicker. But maybe I would get sicker anyway. And this way I had a local delicacy, met new friends, and had something to help my mind escape.

Michael Berg served as a middle school English teacher in Armenia, A-15, from 2007-08. There he lived in a remote refugee village where he worked on a number of secondary projects including teacher trainings and English clubs. Originally from Maine, Michael now lives in Washington, D.C., working as a contractor for the Department of Defense, while also completing a master's degree in Strategic Security Studies and pursuing a career at the State Department.

DONNA BRADEN

Babushka and Chickens

Which came first? The chicken or the chicken nugget?

IT WAS SATURDAY, A COUPLE OF WEEKS AGO. I WANTED TO CHECK
out the store up the street that sells household equipment. I had
been by there another day, but it was 1:15 P.M. and the store
was observing that Ukrainian tradition: closed 1:00-2:00 for
lunch. The concept of attracting customers with convenient
hours of service apparently has not quite penetrated the new
Ukrainian market economy. So on Saturday morning, I made
my way up the street, thinking with a self-indulgent smile that
after I finished at that shop I would, after all, be only about a
kilometer from the city's one and only fast food establishment,
McDonald's, and I could pop over for a Big Mac.

As I approached the busy traffic circle, I passed a clump of
evergreen trees in the parking area. Seated on a folding stool
near the trees was an elderly woman, a *babushka*. Beyond her,
among the greenery, I saw several large hens scratching in
the dirt. It seemed like an odd place for chickens. Then I put
two and two together and realized that she was there tending
the chickens. This was hardly a rural area. I was walking less

173

than 100 meters from a large traffic interchange and less than 300 meters from the main bus station! She surely lives in the neighborhood, and that area is nothing but huge apartment buildings. I pondered why she would be *there* with chickens.

After a few steps more I came to the conclusion, later verified by friends who lived here longer than I, that, yes, she keeps chickens. The eggs are her main source of protein. Perhaps she can even sell a few. And those funds will buy cereal, or a bit of milk. My well-informed friends also explained that in the area I was in, many apartment dwellers have small storage huts, built in rows between the apartment buildings. They are hidden from the street by the nine-story buildings so I wouldn't have noticed them, although I have seen them in other areas. Those huts probably serve, besides storage, as housing for the chickens. And the woman takes the birds carefully across the street occasionally for fresh air and a chance to root about a bit as range birds are meant to do.

As I walked by her, I was dealing, both intellectually and emotionally, with the reality of her life. I started to reach into my purse and offer her a few hryvnia. But, I thought, and probably correctly, she might be quite hurt, if not insulted. She is doing what people here do; she is making it on her own. Such tenacity. Such resourcefulness. She didn't have her hand out like some of the others. I walked on by, feeling a little like the New Testament Pharisee who "passed by on the other side," but not at all sure I should take other action. I may never know.

I found the household equipment store open for business. I looked at the merchandise carefully. I didn't buy anything that day; it didn't seem necessary, after all. And I realized that a Big Mac didn't seem all that necessary to my well-being that day either. I went on to the central market for the really necessary shopping I had to do, the open-air market where most general shopping is done. The *shashleek* (shish kabob) at my favorite eatery was tasty, as I knew it would be, and my having my lunch there kept more money in the local economy. I'm sure McDonald's didn't suffer. That Big Mac may taste better another day.

That's reality, at least as I see it. Now. November, 2000. Here. In Ukraine.

Donna Braden served in Kryvyi Rih, Ukraine from 1999-2001, after a career in several fields in both business and not-for-profit areas. She is the mother of two daughters and now has three granddaughters and a grandson.

ROLAND MENDOZA

✦

The Wheels on the Bus Go Round and Round

Missing life's little inconveniences in Mongolia.

THE DRAGON CENTER LONG-DISTANCE BUS STATION IN Mongolia holds a special place in my heart. As exciting as the planes are in Mongolia—what with wires hanging off the wings and pilots carrying bottles of vodka on board and hearing rumors that U.N. people were banned from flying on them due to crashes and safety concerns and whatnot—it still just couldn't touch the minibus for adventure. Whereas the plane ride ended just as the insanity started to sink in, the bus provided a nice thirty-plus hours to absorb the madness, and lunacy knew no bounds once that door slid shut behind you.

I miss bus seat bingo where I had the chance of being stuck in the back of the bus and doing my best to stave off frostbite or being put in front of the heater vent and being slowly roasted alive over the course of the trip. I miss the big hot sweaty Mongolians who keep trying to lean up against me like I was some sort of pillow while they sleep and elbowing them wherever I could for their trouble. I miss the pleasing *thonk* a human head makes as the bus hits a bump and causes the person's head to quickly pull away from the window it was using as a pillow and then knock back into it. I miss the second and just as pleasing ★*thonk*★ as the person continues to try to use that window as a pillow despite what just happened.

I miss being one of the fifteen-plus people—and those fifteen-plus people were rarely skinny—sardined into a bus that fits nine comfortably. No, there was always at least one wrestler and a fat drunk and an old lady with a giant box/bag/child on their lap squished into that bus somehow.

I miss arriving somewhere at 3:30 A.M. and not knowing where the hell I was going to be spending the night because the person I'm supposed to be staying with wouldn't open the door and being left with no other option but to spent the night in the stairwell of the apartment building.

I miss *tsuivan*, the best damn stir-fry I've ever eaten from these tiny, four-family compound-oases in the middle of nowhere who could put it out at a moment's notice at all hours of the day and night.

I miss learning all kinds of crazy tidbits about Mongolian culture and history on the bus, like how after Mongolia backed Russia in the Sino-Soviet split, the Chinese and Mongolian border patrols used to take shots at each other from their posts back in the '70s. I miss people I don't know always probing into my personal life for no reason whatsoever. I miss how the bus would break down and add anywhere between one and six hours onto the trip while the driver did something crazy-magical, like fix the alternator with a fork and a rag, or better yet drive a dying bus six hours back the way we came because that was the closest place to get the parts he needs.

I miss the adrenaline rush from being in a bus with the driver falling asleep at the wheel. I miss pondering the safety of traveling through steppe and forest on muddy rocky non-roads in a vehicle that could be rendered totally inoperable simply by turning on the radio. I miss watching mud swallowing up buses like dinosaurs in a tar pit and wondering how long it would be before ours suffered the same fate. I miss carsick children spewing up like fountains because it was just so nice to see the Mongols finally perturbed about something during the trip. They took the most absurd things in stride on the bus, oh, but get a little vomit on the shoe and it was all over for them.

I miss watching the mesmerizing dance of snow and fire sprites while warming up by a tree the passengers had set on fire in the middle of blizzard while we waited for the van to get up and running again.

I remember that last one well. After the initial hypnotic effect wore off, all I could think about was how perfect it would be if the entire forest were to go up in flames and we all died. I had my epitaph all thought out:

Here lies Roland Mendoza
Loving Son and Brother
He was burned to a crisp in the middle of a blizzard

Once you got in that bus, all bets were off and anything could happen. Even though it could be extremely frustrating when things weren't going your way on the bus, things could always turn at the drop of a hat and most times did. Life felt spontaneous and chaotic and vibrant and just plain old more real back then. Here in America, all I do is go to work, after that pick up the misses from work, after that go home, eat and sleep. Rinse, wash and repeat. Nowadays the only thing that ever changes is where to eat out when I get paid and that's already lost its novelty. The bus never did, and I miss my adventures.

Roland Mendoza served in Chandman-Undur, Mongolia, M-12, from 2001-03. In English, Chandman-Undur roughly translates as "tiny village in the middle of nowhere," that's only called a "village" because no one uses the word "hamlet" anymore. He taught the people how to speak English, at least that's what he tells people when they ask, not that anyone ever does. In exchange, the people taught him about what's truly important in this life. Talk about a lopsided trade. He made a triumphant return to Texas with his utterly amazing and devastatingly beautiful Mongolian wife Tugsu in 2007. They are currently kicking around somewhere in the rainy Northwest. By day they fight the good fight against homelessness (mainly by preventing their own...lousy economy). They spend nights drinking wine, holding hands, occasionally fighting over something stupid Roland said or did, and advancing their plans for world domination, not necessarily in that order.

MARANEE SANDERS

Trip to Akjakent

*Where but in the Turkey of the 1960s could your nurse be
a Chinese-speaking first cousin of Ernest Hemingway?*

SPRING IN TURKEY WAS GLORIOUS TO SEE. PEOPLE IN GAZIANTEP
burst out of their front doors to stroll up and down the wide
sidewalks. Located in southeastern Turkey, Gaziantep is on a
high arid plateau only forty-five minutes from the Syrian border. Families had been cooped up during the cold winter and
emerged arm in arm with mothers, children, grandmas, sisters,
brothers, and husbands who weren't at work. Most Gaziantep
women wore headscarves and long coats outside, whether it
was freezing or sweltering. At the teahouses, men sat at sidewalk tables staring at passing families and the blossoming trees.

There is a wonderful word in Turkish for this experience—*gezmek*—which means to walk about leisurely and look
at things. Since my arrival in Gaziantep in November, I would
gezdim whenever I could. My job involved teaching at the
Girl's Institute and in nearby villages. The best part of my job
was traveling to villages weekly. My Peace Corps supervisor
arranged with the governor of the province for the loan of his
jeep and a chauffer to transport me to one of the nearby villages.

The chauffeur's name was Kasim, which means November. Although tall and graying handsomely, his front tooth was missing. He arrived wearing a khaki military coat with matching jodhpurs. He must have been the age of my father, but later when I knew him well enough to ask, he said he didn't know his age. He said perhaps he was born in November, but his mother didn't know how to read or write. In the village where he was born, people didn't keep track of age.

This was to be a special week. My principal, Muderhanim, wrote to the village teacher in Akjakent well ahead of time to make arrangements for our visit. I looked forward to returning to Akjakent because it was picturesque and because I would enjoy teaching with my Peace Corps colleague Judy Johnson from Wisconsin.

Kasim picked us up, along with a week's worth of teaching materials and personal belongings. The governor's jeep overflowed with fabrics, doll stuffing, food, pots, and teaching aids as we headed out of town. We sped along the blacktop until it became a dirt road, and then veered to the right through bumpy brown fields. Sometimes the villagers plowed right over the road, so Kasim knew the way even if it was through a hayfield. We were to stay with the village teacher, Goksel, and her family.

We could see Akjakent atop a steep hill overlooking budding orchards. An impressive arched aqueduct built by the Romans was still in use. A small river flowed at the base of the steep hill. Women with baggy pants rolled up to their knees stood in the water beating a Turkish carpet. Our jeep roared up the steep hill and came to a lurching halt. We stepped out onto dusty cobblestones and unloaded our gear inside the walled gate. A narrow street led in between the mud–and–rock walls of the houses.

As we were shown to her house, someone ran to get Goksel. Her two grandmothers, sisters, and her brother from

Nizip rose from their tapestry floor cushions as we arrived. They brought us the traditional Turkish tea served boiling hot. We stirred our sugar cubes, making clinking sounds against the glasses resting on gold-rimmed glass saucers. Goksel arrived and after some visiting, asked us why we were there. It dawned on me that perhaps the principal's letter hadn't arrived. They obviously didn't know we were coming. We explained in Turkish that Muderhanim had written last month to arrange a week-long workshop for students. Their faces fell when they heard we were staying for a whole week. Nevertheless, they made us feel welcome and brought in our belongings and teaching supplies. Kasim had already driven off in the governor's jeep.

Goksel's brother left that night for Nezip, and the rest of us slept in the same room on mattresses that emerged from wall cupboards. We were honored with thick satin coverlets topped with snow-white sheets embellished with crocheted zigzag trim. Even though it was spring, we were covered as if the snows were coming. One grandma was very short. We called her Little Grandma. She prayed on her goatskin rug frequently. She kept a close eye on us. During the night if we pushed our blankets off, Little Grandma covered us again. We woke sweating in the warm spring air.

Little Grandma told us about her hardworking and industrious son Ahmet. When no one else was around, she came to tell me that Ahmet was very clean, very clean…"*cok temiz, cok temiz.*" Since she stressed how clean he was, we referred to him as "Mr. Clean." She thought I would make a perfect match for Ahmet. During our stay he visited each day, though he lived an hour away in Nizip.

The next day we started teaching with "Innovative Clothes Washing Methods." I brought a wooden plunger I hoped would make washing easier. Judy was very clever and made a washboard out of an old chair and some twigs. We borrowed a washtub and demonstrated how to wash with the plunger and washboard, saving a trip downhill to the river. We taught sewing skills as we made cloth dolls and wrist pin cushions. Our students were girls between eight and fourteen years old, wearing bright floral dresses of red, yellow, or green, worn over baggy pants. Each wore an embroidered scarf over her long dark hair. The girls seemed as fascinated by how strange we were as by what we taught them. No Westerners had passed this way since the Crusades.

In between classes, we lunched from large copper trays, while seated on the floor of Goksel's one-room home. While the food was prepared, I gazed out the window, which looked straight down forty feet onto the steep road that lead up the hill. Below me a man pulled a camel carrying a huge bag of flour across its back. Boys soaked their feet in the stream. I had the sense that life continued much as it had been since the Romans built the aqueduct centuries before. The Grandmas came in carrying hot tomato vegetable soup, bowls of unripe plum buds, homemade flat bread, yogurt, and strings of figs encased in sweet hardened syrup. The food was delicious. The Grandmas let out approving belches.

The next day I demonstrated how to feed a baby. I prepared mashed egg yolk, mashed liver, and cream of wheat as alternatives to hot spicy adult food. Turkey had a high infant mortality at weaning age. I asked Goksel to bring in a baby to demonstrate how delicious the food was. Young babies aren't accustomed to solid food, crying and spitting up on their clothes. I learned early on to ask for an older baby, as they were better eaters.

This time they brought a baby dressed in a bright orange and purple floral dress, a yellow hand-embroidered cap, little gold earrings, and with permanent tattooed X's on her temples to keep away illness and the evil eye. Luckily for me the baby ate well, and the demonstration was a success.

However, all afternoon our stomachs churned. Judy and I made frequent trips to the outhouse. The toilet had two raised footprints with a hole in the middle. Interesting worm specimens dotted the floor. We continued our classes, enjoying the wonderful meals, and having the runs.

On the fourth day, Judy awoke quickly to run to the outhouse. I heard a crunching sound as she stepped on my glasses. Without my glasses I couldn't see more than a foot in front of me, so we decided to catch a ride back into town with the brother from Nizip. I let Judy sit between us. Maybe he would be interested in her instead of me. Our plan was to pick up my contact lenses and stop at the old American Missionary Hospital for diarrhea medicine. At the hospital we explained our four days of diarrhea, nausea, feeling faint, and the worms in the outhouse. The doctor put us in the hospital immediately. We couldn't believe our good fortune to lie in regular beds with light blankets.

Our nurse, Isabel, was a first cousin of Ernest Hemingway. She supplied us with enough reading material on him to last a month. Her father was a missionary in China, so she grew up speaking Chinese.

We were so dehydrated, we couldn't give any urine samples. Three times a day we received back rubs, greatly improving our morale. We wondered if we had any of those interesting worms, but the doctor said, "No." By the time I finished *For Whom the Bell Tolls*, they decided we were well enough to return home. Judy took a bus back to Iskenderun. I slowly climbed the stairs to our fourth floor apartment. Sitting by my window, I watched folks below stroll the sidewalks. I thought about how much I loved Turkey and the generous village people. I missed Little Grandma who was so kind to me; I wondered what they were doing in Akjakent.

Maranee "Mimi" (Jones) Sanders taught Home Economics in Turkey, T-3, 1963-65. The Peace Corps experience was an immense influence on Maranee, who returned to Turkey to visit her daughter, a Turkish language major attending Boazaci University in Istanbul. After the Peace Corps, Maranee changed majors, receiving a master's. in Modern Dance and became department head at Portland State University. Currently she teaches dance in an old church where she and her husband reside. Two years ago she returned to Turkey to perform in an International Dance Festival with Mythobolus Mask Theatre and saw old friends from her Peace Corps days.

ASHLI GOLD

* * *

Champp

What could be better than dinner with a friend?

I HAD COME HOME FROM A HARD DAY OF WORK TO FIND ALL OF my host family gone, which was odd, because there was always someone at home. What was odder still was that there was a horse in my backyard. But after two years in Kazakhstan, I was hardly surprised by anything anymore, so really, why *not* a horse? I walked out to the horse and start talking to her.

I had recently moved to the Chemolgan to begin my six-month stint as a trainer to the incoming group of Peace Corps Volunteers. This was an amazing job and a fabulous experience, but at the end of the day, it still meant that all of the dear friends that I had made over the past two years in Turarkent now lived thirteen hours away. By bus. Suffice it to say, I was a bit lonely. Hence why I'm now speaking to a horse. But, the horse and I hit it off. We quickly made friends and I even gave my horse a name: Champ! After a bit of PCV–horse bonding, my host-dad came home.

"There's a horse in the backyard!" I exclaimed, "How come?"

He responds, "It's for my sister's wedding."

Which made perfect sense to me—the people of Kazakhstan were, once upon a time, nomadic herders who depended on horses for transportation and on particular holidays, to act as a platform for wrestling contests. Horses were also signs of wealth and status in the time before the Soviet Union. Of course you would give a horse to your youngest sister. What a perfect way not only to show your economic status, but also to wish prosperity on the nuptials of your sister.

"We're going to cut it," he added.

I'm pretty sure I heard that wrong.

"Cut it?" I repeated.

"Oh, yeah. I have some horse cutters coming by tomorrow morning to cut the horse. As the eldest in the family, it is my job to provide the wedding feast."

In addition to all of the other facts about horses that I had linked to the Kazakh culture, I had forgotten a pretty big one. Horsemeat is considered a delicacy here. Now, this wasn't the first time that I had been exposed to the concept of eating a horse. Honestly, I had acquired quite a taste for equine flesh during my time as a Peace Corps Volunteer. It's delicious—tastes just like roast beef. What I found really disturbing here was that my host father was going to be cutting *this* horse and that I had just spent twenty minutes making friends with dinner for 200 people.

In the spirit of hospitality and cultural discovery my host-dad invited me to come the next day to witness the horse-cutting—after all, it's quite a display of Kazakh culture. And, he said, I wouldn't even have to take the whole day off. The horse-cutters weren't coming until ten. I declined this invitation. I just couldn't watch Champ go out that way. We were buds.

The next morning, I stood grim-faced in front of the Peace Corps trainees who lived in my village. I was facilitating a session on how to make reading assignments more interactive for students, but my heart wasn't in it. I kept looking at the clock. As much as I willed them not to, the seconds ticked unyieldingly by. At ten o'clock I stopped talking and cocked my ear toward the window. I don't know why, but I thought I would hear something—a call from the president of Kazakhstan issuing a reprieve perhaps? Instead I was met with the puzzled whispers from the seven trainees sitting in front of me. I steeled myself and went back to the lesson.

That evening, after a full day of methodology instruction and observing the lessons of the future Volunteers, I come home from school to find pieces of Champ all over the backyard. Literally. It seems that cutting a horse requires a lot of room.

My host aunt walked up to me as I set my bag down in my room and let me know that I was just in time for dinner.

"Yum," I thought. But I knew that I had to. To decline an invitation to eat with the family would be extremely insulting, especially when that meal consists of fresh horsemeat and vodka toasts to the life, fertility, and fortune of the bride-to-be and her beau.

I sat down on the ground next to my host aunt at the *stol*, the tablecloth that had been laid out. There was quite a spread. Flat bread *lapioshkas*, various and sundry *salati* (salads) made with carrots, beets, and mayonnaise, elegant shot glasses and a full bottle of vodka for toasting, tea kettle and tiny cups, and a big empty space in the middle for the main dish. I was told that on this night, we would be dining on *kurdok*. Ah, *kurdok*, in my opinion it is the most underappreciated of all of the Kazakh dishes. Most American palates just cannot appreciate the combination of cottonseed oil, onions, and organ meat that comprise this dish. But I am not most Americans. I love *kurdok*. It is my single favorite Kazakh food and a taste that I have not been able to replicate since. It's chewy and grainy and oily and amazing. And fresh *kurdok* is even more delicious. I tried to resist, but I couldn't. I ate a big, heaping plateful. Then I had seconds. It was too good not to. Champ was delicious.

As the party wore on, the elegant shot glasses began to be filled with the best Kazakhstani vodka. First my host father toasted, since he was the host of the party. He gave a beautifully worded speech about his wishes for his sister and her soon-to-be husband. Then it was my host aunt's turn. She gave a similar toast the fortune and future children of her niece. Then the next person went. And then the next. After a while, it was my turn to toast the wedding. As everyone had already had a few and it was considered to be good luck to have a guest give a toast (especially a guest who had come all the way from *Amerika*), I decided to make a request before I raised my glass. I said that I would say the beginning of the toast in Russian, but that I had something to say at the end that I could only properly express in English. The family quickly consented. I raised my glass high and in my very best Russian wished the bride and groom happiness and good fortune.

Then I added in English, with equal conviction,

"I drink now to Champ. She was a good horse, but made for an even better dinner!"

Ashli Gold served as a primary and secondary school English teacher in Turarkent, Kazakhstan, Kaz-17, from 2005-07. There, she worked with students from grades 2-11, organized a summer youth leadership camp, and ate kilos and kilos of horsemeat. Following her time in Turarkent, Ashli moved to Chemalgan, Kazakhstan, where she worked as a Volunteer Training Assistant and assisted in the facilitation of the Pre-Service Training for incoming Volunteers. Upon her return, Ashli continued to be involved with education, and is now a Special Education Teacher in Washington, D.C.

LAWRENCE LAWSON

* * *

A Convergence of Angles

Time spent in developing countries looking forward, often means a lot of time spent listening and looking back.

HER FACE TANNED THE TEXTURE OF A WORN CATCHER'S MITT beneath her pastel kerchief, a *babusya* sat folded within her faded floral skirt. "*Nasinya*," she called out. "*Nasinya*." Resting between her knees was a nylon sack filled to bursting with thousands of black, unshelled sunflower seeds. In the old woman's lap were scraps of newspaper pages, each rolled into a cone. For 50 kopeks—10 U.S. cents—you could get a dose of Ukraine's national street food. Everyone standing around me was stocking up.

That *babusya*, and a beer tent, were doing business prompted by Ukraine's first FIFA World Cup appearance in Leipzig, Germany. Led by expat captain and national football hero Andriy Shevchenko, the Ukrainian national football team was to play its first-ever World Cup match as Team Ukraine that day. A fourth of the population of L'viv, in western Ukraine, turned up in Park Kultury—the Park of Culture—to watch the historic match against Spain. A gargantuan, 40x60-foot LCD screen was hoisted up and lashed to a metal scaffold to facilitate the process.

To get to that television screen, my wife Karen and I walked through a maze of cobblestone streets—reminiscent more of L'viv's distant Central/Eastern European past than its recent Soviet one—behind a thick column of Ukrainians draped in the colors of their national flag, blue and yellow, and in their national flag itself. Veering in and out of traffic, with its acrid gasoline and smoke smell hanging like a lingering spirit, we followed the chants and laughter and excitement past the tram tracks, under the shadow of the Dynamo sports center, and toward the Romanesque columns and arches that frame the park's street-side entrance.

Stopping just past a row of patio tables and orange umbrellas emblazoned with the "Hike" beer logo, Karen and I stood beneath the giant screen. We watched a man with a dark moustache wearing sky-blue overalls fumble with a wrench and a nest of wires. Fifteen minutes before the match, the man was still fiddling, his head turned upward toward his work.

Hundreds of young Ukrainians continued to arrive, blowing into plastic tubes to produce foghorn-like sounds; they chanted, "U-kra-yi-na! U-kra-yi-na! U-kra-yi-na!" Every face was turned toward the still black LCD screen. Waiting, but maybe not believing.

My wife and I, however, were believing. Always. When a woman sells fruit at the bazaar, we take her words as truth. We believe it's fresh. The city said it would show the football match in the park. We believed. We arrived and saw the television strung high, technological fruit hung from a metal tree. We believed. As the man in the sky-blue overalls fiddled, producing neither a single noise nor a colored image, we believed.

At five minutes to four, a short man with sunglasses picked up a microphone and thanked the crowd for being so strong, for being so good. "There are technical problems with the television," he said. "If you want to see the match, you should go home now."

We couldn't believe it.

Without protest, the crowd broke like ants over a summer lunch. Karen and I stood shaking our heads. "Maybe they'll get it fixed," I said. And there we went again. Believing.

As the crowd filed away, I wondered when Ukrainians would get a break. When they'd have a reason to smile for longer than only a few moments. A good, long smile. One that hurts the face. One that carries hope, ushering in the next day, month, year saying, "I'm feeling good, and I expect that to continue." Maybe a football team can bring that. If only the television could carry the promise.

But broken promises and disappointment seemed to be a Ukrainian curse.

Consider our landlord, a sweet, older man with winter birch hair and soft, blue eyes. If we have a problem with the apartment, he'll be over to act the *maister* with his tools and spirit. At the end of the month, just before we took off for a trip across the country to work in some summer camps, Yuri came over to collect a few tools and rent. As always, we got to talking. He asked us how we enjoyed L'viv, and we told him how beautiful his city was.

"*Brudno*," he said. It's dirty.

"Well, it's the best city I've been to," I said.

"In Ukraine?"

"Yes. My favorite city in Ukraine." Though I haven't seen all of the country, I think I've seen enough to make the call.

"Eighty kilometers to the west is Pshemyshl. It used to be Ukrainian. Land a hundred kilometers into Poland used to be Ukraine," he explained, leaning on his white cane, which he is far too young for.

"Pshemyshl," he continued, "is a different world. It's cleaner than here." He continued to talk about the convergent and then divergent paths Poland and Ukraine walked. He drove home the reason the differences between the two countries exist. "Radyanskiy Soyuz." The Soviet Union.

"The East can't understand us when we talk. And we can't understand their psychology," he explained. The west of Ukraine, under Soviet rule for only the years between World War II and the fall of communism in 1991, has a detectably different mindset than the easterners I've met and the people of the central region where I once lived. The east and pieces of the center were Soviet for far longer. The east and the west make up separate, but equal, personalities in the body of Ukraine. They even speak two different languages, the west, Ukrainian, and the east, Russian—and the center, Surzhik, which is a mixture of the two—and pretend they cannot understand each other's tongue.

"Lenin," he continued. "Do you know Lenin?" Everyone knows Lenin. Towering statues of him adorn many city centers of Ukraine, his bronze eyes watching. Watching.

"Lenin said, 'Without Ukraine, Russia cannot live.' We are rich here, but it's been taken away. We had gas here, but it was sent to Moscow. Now it's being sold back to us." He broke off here, set his jaw. "They sent the gas away. They sent people away." He looked at us, and we said we knew. We'd read the stories. Free trips to Siberia. One way. We never know what to say when he brings this up. Yuri was born in Russia. Near Japan. In a camp. We can never understand.

What we are coming to understand is that Yuri is here. His smile is here, his glittering, blue eyes. His family has the good qualities you wish for in people. Talent. Energy. Happiness and warmth. His button-down, red-and-white striped shirt lifted with a breath. The conversation changed directions. "If you need any help while you are gone, give us a call. We can help you." He offered his hand.

"*Shchaslivo,*" he said. Good luck.

Then there is our former host mother—our Peace Corps history has given us four real, plus one adopted, host mothers in seven months—who fondly remembers her cheap sausage. How bread used to cost less. How there were jobs and there weren't so many drunks in the park. She owns her apartment. She has a job—earning $100 a month as a college teacher—that supplements her $67-a-month pension. She favors Western-leaning Ukrainian politicians, but lambastes the American government for discrediting a recent Belarusian election.

"How would you like it if someone came into your house and told you that everything you did was wrong?" she once asked me over a plate of homemade potato-stuffed pasta. She told me that they had jobs in Belarus. They weren't drunks. Sausage was cheap.

Yet she still favors progress over what Ukraine had before. This paradox—wanting to move forward, but being reluctant to release the past—is etched on face after face in a country the size of Texas. Though it is difficult to obtain visas, some Ukrainians do see other parts of the world first hand; others see it through television. They see the way of life in other countries, and some Ukrainians want that. To them, it seems that their country is moving too slowly to fulfill their desire. For others, the country is moving too far, too fast. Candidacy to the European Union is ludicrous, consideration of joining NATO sacrilegious.

To me, it's symptomatic of the paradox that envelops Ukraine. At the same time happy and sad, hopeful and hopeless, smiling and scowling, warm and chilly, spacious and cramped, gas and brake, all and nothing, health and disease, brilliance and ignorance, beauty and beast, east and west. Only after Ukraine has found its path—averaged the angles of all the corners it still has to turn with the corners it already has turned—can the convergence of these lines be understood.

Now the World Cup. Game one ended 0-4, Spain over Ukraine. The team didn't look like it was even trying. Walking when it should have been running, sulking when it should have been scoring. The city of L'viv sulked right along with them. Right up until FIFA World Cup, game two: Saudi Arabia versus Ukraine.

Karen tried getting the match on our small, black-and-white television that came with the apartment and receives, on good days, about two and a half stations, one in Russian. We decided to stay in for the night. It was too far to walk down to the park, and the giant television probably wouldn't work anyway. I had some cinnamon apples drying in the stove, and a home-cooked meal sounded better than another night in a piz-zeria. So I took over the television, twisting the plentitude of knobs that decorate the set. Turning the television 15 degrees away from the wall and giving it a few smacks seemed to be all the magic we needed: at 6:50 P.M. we heard a snippet of the Ukrainian national anthem. We settled onto our once-a-bed-now-a-couch-better-than-nothing, popped open a bottle of L'vivske beer, and waited to see if the signal would drop. To see if the team could carry the hope of a country. And to see if they could score.

Four minutes into the game, I was screaming. Rucol popped a shot past the Saudi keeper and the stadium, faces blurred behind a light dose of static, erupted. Ukrainian flags, dark grey and light grey to our eyes (better in color) shook like they were finding the steps to a new national dance. U-kra-yi-na U-kra-yi-na! U-kra-yi-na! pulsed like aluminum cans were crushing through the speakers.

1-0.

At 36 minutes, Rebrov made it 2-0.

Suddenly, I wished I'd tried the park. Wished I was sitting among the Ukrainians, awash in that sea of yellow and blue.

At 46 minutes, Shevchenko slammed the door with a header past the keeper, and I tried not to cry.

3-0.

As the game's outcome closed in, the Ukrainian national team never let up. They attacked and attacked again. They didn't give up, didn't go slack. And at 86 minutes, they were rewarded with a kick by Kalinichenko that sailed like it had a mast.

4-0.

U-kra-yi-na! U-kra-yi-na! U-kra-yi-na!

And then, *kinets*. The end.

Fireworks blew up directly over the park where, just one week before, a television had remained black. We stood out on our balcony, overlooking a twisting, cobblestone road, and watched our neighbors as they leaned out their windows, looking for the fireworks, smiling. For the rest of the night, Ukrainians danced through the streets of L'viv, igniting car horns, hand-held foghorns, and their own voices, letting everyone know, well into the dark hours of the morning, that there was something to scream and yell about. That a team of men wrapped in yellow-and-blue soccer uniforms might indeed be a light in the gathering dawn.

Pochatok. A beginning.

Lawrence Lawson served as a secondary school English teacher as part of a Peace Corps Masters International program (through the Monterey Institute of International Studies) in the Ukraine, Group 29, from 2005-07. There, alongside his wife, he ran or participated in camps that raised awareness about human trafficking, HIV/AIDS, and the role of youth in leadership. He also taught English courses at the L'viv National University in Ukraine. He is currently working as an assistant professor of ESL at a California community college and is completing, with his wife, a memoir of their Peace Corps experiences.

JOAN HAMMER GRANT

✻
✻ ✻

Thanksgiving in Turkey

When you're far away from the usual amenities that accompany your holidays at home, you do the best you can.

NOVEMBER 1962, BANDIRMA, TURKEY. IT'S THANKSGIVING AND I'm feeling blue. No family, no football, and especially no Thanksgiving feast. I'm far from home, teaching English in a Muslim country. My students have never heard of Pilgrims and Indians and probably don't care about their gathering together to celebrate the harvest and friendship. They surely have never seen a football game, although they are rabid fans of their *futbol*, our soccer.

But it's Thanksgiving and I should be thankful, especially since I landed a plum of a Peace Corps assignment. Bandirma is a beautiful small seaport town on the Marmara Sea several hours south of Istanbul, but far more conservative than that metropolitan center. My Peace Corps site-mate, Carolyn, and I got a small top-floor apartment on a hill overlooking the harbor. The view from our window would be wonderful, but for the fact that the terrace outside also holds the wash lines for the entire building, so the scenery is perpetually blocked by waving laundry.

In addition to its beauty, Bandirma is a "plum" because of the receptivity, hospitality, and kindness of the people. Carolyn and I are not only the first Peace Corps Volunteers here, we are also the first Americans—if not the first non-Turks—to live here. Our arrival in late August caused a major stir and generated an overwhelming welcome. Even now, we are followed daily by small troops of children, some who want to learn a few English words, others who are just curious.

Our teaching assignments are great, too. A full load of middle- and high-school classes and a school principal who has afforded us much freedom. Thus, we were able to start an English club after school, a student-run English newspaper, a student theater group, and English classes for adults in the evenings. With so much work to do, we still have endless social obligations—responding to many dinner invitations and especially attending *guns* (pronounced "goons"), which are teas that various women put on each week. Since Carolyn and I don't want to offend anyone, we go to all the *guns*—as many as ten to fifteen per week.

Frankly, I'm exhausted. I'm also sick. I have a perpetual cold that's turned to bronchitis, and my coughing is so bad that the Turks are worried that perhaps I won't survive. Teachers and neighbors are plying me with home cures, ranging from herbal teas and soups to rubdowns with olive oil and hot pepper.

Maybe it's my physical deterioration that has me down in the dumps this Thanksgiving, but I'm determined to rally. I have no afternoon classes, so I decide to surprise Carolyn by making a real Thanksgiving dinner.

I grab my string shopping bag, some money, and a fistful of handkerchiefs and head out to the market. First stop is the meat market, to buy a turkey. Simple enough? Not here.

The meat market is in the center of the town market. A dozen small butcher shops encircle a plaza where the "meat" is kept alive, on-the-hoof. The butchers only slaughter one animal at a time. The carcass hangs in the shop and the buyer points to a section. Leg? filet? liver? Then the butcher slices off the chosen segment and wraps it in paper.

Meanwhile, huddled in the plaza are the next victims: long-tailed, curly-wool sheep marked with dots of colored dye that indicate the owner. Butcher Ali might use blue dots, while Mustafa's sheep sport red ones. It is not unusual to see the face of a kitten or two peeking out from between the dye-dots on a sheep. The meat market is a favorite place for stray cats, which live off entrails tossed out to them by the butchers. Since Turks believe it is bad karma to kill a cat, and few Turks would consider keeping "the filthy animals" as pets, stray cats abound and vie with each other for food and shelter. The mother cats no doubt long ago spotted the woolly sheep as great places to park their offspring while they are out hunting up food. The sheep, for some reason, seem to tolerate this; hence the cute kitten faces nestled on tomorrow's supper supply.

But my mission today is not lamb chops, its turkey—called *hindi* in Turkish. I head for my favorite butcher and ask for a *hindi*. Looking dismayed, he says he doesn't have any. (Come to think of it, I had never seen turkey served in any Turkish homes, but I was sure they must be available.) In my weakened state, I become teary-eyed, saying, "But I must have a turkey. Today is our American *bayram* when we eat turkey."

The word *bayram* strikes a chord with the butcher. In Turkish, *bayrams* are not just holidays, they are religious holidays, and therefore quite sacred and serious. The butcher panics and runs out of the shop to gather with the other butchers. After much discussion about the American teacher who MUST have a *hindi* to celebrate her *bayram,* a plan is laid. The butcher comes back and tells me "not to worry"—there are no turkeys in Bandirma, but the butchers will find a very large chicken for me. Will that do? I smile through my tears and thank him.

The butcher pulls up a stool for me and dispatches a small boy to fetch a glass of tea. In a flash the boy returns, holding a Turkish-style tea tray with one finger, which balances two tulip-shaped glasses of dark tea and a small dish with a pile of sugar cubes. (Turks drink endless glasses of tea all day long, and they consume it with enough sugar to cause early diabetes.)

After about ten minutes, I see another small boy running toward the butcher shop, carrying a big fat red chicken in one hand and a white one in the other. The chickens are clucking furiously, maybe because they know where they are headed, but certainly because it can't be much fun to be hanging upside down with hands gripping your legs.

The pleased butcher then asks me to choose a hen. It doesn't matter to me, but the white one looks fatter and cleaner, so I go with *beyaz* (white). To my surprise, the butcher takes the hen, ties string around its legs, and hands me the bird—alive and well and complaining loudly.

I hadn't expected this! Even though I'm a meat-eater, the thought of killing something myself is not in my nature. I don't want to look like an American wimp, but I just couldn't do it. So I hand the chicken back to the butcher and, since I don't know the word for "kill," I make my request by indicating a chop to the neck with my hand.

The butcher gets the message. In a flash he whisks the chicken to his chopping block and with one swing severs its head, spraying a bit more blood on his already bloodstained white apron. Then, with sign language, he asks if I want him to pluck out the feathers. Indeed I do.

When the hen was nearly nude, except for dozens of small pinfeathers, the butcher wraps the bird in paper and puts it in my string bag. He refuses to accept payment, insisting that the chicken is a gift for my *bayram*.

After picking up carrots, potatoes, onions, and some flavorful tangerines for dessert, I head home to prepare the Thanksgiving feast, which I know will be a challenge. Our kitchen appliances consist solely of a two-burner hot plate hooked up to a cylinder of natural gas. In lieu of a real oven, we have a movable, top-of-the-stove tin oven that looks like a miniature Quonset hut when placed on one of the burners. It has a door on front, but the interior is only large enough for about three baked potatoes. My fat chicken is never going to fit.

I turn to the only other kitchen gadget available, a pressure cooker recommended by the Peace Corps office in Ankara. I have never used one before and worry about blowing up the apartment or something. But it will hold the chicken, so it will have to do. Since I can't understand a word of the Turkish instructions that came with the cooker, I turn to the cookbook I had brought from home and look up "pressure cooking." On page 12, it says, "Just follow the simple instructions that come with the cooker." Thanks a lot, Fanny Farmer.

I decide to turn my attention to the chicken, which is still quite warm, since it hadn't died that long ago. The feet are still attached, but I screw up my courage and hack away at them until they finally fall to the floor. Next I turn on one of the burners (which have to be lit with a match) and singe off the remaining pinfeathers. I am feeling pretty proud of myself . . . so far.

Setting the chicken aside, I prepare stuffing, using bread, onions, olive oil, and thyme. When I am ready to stuff the bird, though, I realize it was missing the usual convenient opening where the stuffing goes. Uh, oh, the innards are still in there. Well, I had dissected a cat in Biology 101, so I take a scientific approach to what otherwise would seem a gory experience. I cut a slit by the anus, reach inside and start to pull stuff out. The entrails are even warmer and bloodier than the outside of the chicken. In my determination to be "scientific," I start to name the parts as they slide through my hands. Ugh.

Back to the pressure cooker. I cram the stuffed bird into the pot, throw in the carrots and potatoes, put in some water, and crank the top down tight. Carolyn would be home from school soon, and I figured that in an hour, the entire delicious feast would be ready.

I set the table and pull out a container of wine from the cupboard. Of course we have no such luxury as a refrigerator, so the white wine will have to be served at room temperature.

Carolyn is delightfully surprised by my efforts, and we sip some wine while waiting for dinner to be ready. When I open the cooker after an hour, I find that, even though the vegetables look done, I can't even dent the chicken's skin with a fork. Oh, well, maybe a really fresh chicken might take a bit longer to get tender.

A half hour later, the chicken still is as hard as a brick. Another glass of wine is in order. By 7:30 P.M., we are getting very hungry, if not a little tipsy. I open the pot once more and the damned bird still won't yield. By 9 P.M., we have had it. Carolyn is now griping and I am frustrated and coughing my head off. The Thanksgiving dinner is going to be served NOW, do or die. Out comes the chicken, still tough, as only a really old bird can be. It is surrounded by the most overcooked vegetables ever.

We are starving, so we cut off whatever meat we can manage to remove and proceed to chew and chew and chew. We wash it all down with the last of the wine and completely forget to say "Thanks" for our blessings.

All in all, it was the most memorable Thanksgiving in my life.

Joan Hammer Grant served in Turkey, T-1, from 1962-63. Joan was born and raised in New Jersey and graduated with a B.A. in history from Bucknell University. She went directly from college to Peace Corps training with the first group to Turkey. Grant taught English in middle and high school in Bandirma, Turkey, and Denizli, Turkey, and during the summertime she lived and worked with a Turkish midwife in Akcapinar village. Post-Peace Corps, Grant worked with the AFS International student exchange program in New York City. Joan moved to Maine in 1971 and since then has worked as a newspaper reporter and later editor of a weekly newspaper.

BRUCE MCDONALD

✳

The Fourth of July

Language training is sometimes about soft summer nights and fireflies.

THE FOURTH OF JULY! BULGARIA'S INDEPENDENCE DAY IS THE third of March, so in Bulgaria, July 4th was just the day after July 3rd. We were a few weeks into our training in Panagyurishte, a city with its own revolutionary history, on what would have been our American holiday, learning about the language and ways of the Bulgarians. But there would be no break from our training schedule. There was a nod to our national day in the language curriculum, in that we learned an all-purpose greeting for wishing each other happy holiday: "*Chestit praznik!*" The word for independence, to give the day its proper due, has six syllables and sounds like a little song: *nezavizimostta*.

We had two hours of language classes and then, for the English teaching program, a two-hour practice workshop with exercises for getting students to communicate verbally. Then after lunch came the "community orientation walk," part of the "culture and customs curriculum." On her walk, my wife Mary—in a different group from mine—visited a museum that had once been the grand home of a prominent family still living in the city. There she heard the story about how in the days of the 1876 April Revolution against Ottoman rule, the family took in a large group of women and children and old people and hid them in a concealed room in the basement from the Turks who violently suppressed the uprising. A member of the family hiding the group was tortured and died without revealing it. Years later when the Soviets arrived, the family was evicted and the building appropriated for use by the Party members who were in charge of the district. That family is still prominent in town, still displaced from their ancestral homestead, and everyone knows their story. A shrug says, "Yes, but what can they do now?"

My group took its field trip for the afternoon to a kindergarten where we saw what they called a four-step program, four distinct levels of learning for children three through six. Most notable among these, in my mind at least, were the real electric stove in miniature size, and the real knives, spatulas, sharp cooking forks and kitchen implements for instructive play. Dangerous? Another shrug.

"These things are in their homes, aren't they? It's better they should learn."

Although the Fourth was not a Bulgarian holiday, after the day's school activities there was to be a celebration for us anyway. After all, anyone who knows Americans knows what this holiday means to us. At least the people in Panagyurishte do. After our classes, we went home and met with our host mother, Krassimira, to take her with us to the Fourth of July party being given on the grounds of the museum, the very place with grim and sad history that Mary had just visited. Krassi's sister Magdalena and nephew Rumen were to meet us there.

Along the twenty-minute walk to the other side of town— a sort of informal culture and customs lesson—Krassi greeted people she knew. By this time, we knew to remain silent unless spoken to. Bulgarians do not acknowledge or make eye contact with people they do not know. To do so, as we would expect to be customary in a small town, is considered vulgar. Naturally we had made that mistake regularly for the first few days in Bulgaria. On our first night in the country, several of us had greeted an older man, and he had been so taken aback at the audacity of it that he went a few paces ahead on the sidewalk then turned back and shouted after us, asking what nationality we were.

We thought, "Uh-oh, what do we do now?" But he was friendly, even excited. He told us—in a torrent of words that could only give us the general idea of what he was saying—that *komoonizam* was bad and *demokratzia* is good, and he liked Amerikantzi and hoped we liked his country. It was a very effective communication, done with scowls and smiles and hand gestures and tone of voice more than with words. And that in itself was a lesson, a valuable template for effective communication.

That had been our first night in Bulgaria, though, and now after several weeks of learning about the people's ways and customs, we knew that such an exchange was a rarity. And so we tried to practice being normal, not offending people by trying to make them talk to strangers. On the way to the party, Krassimira stopped and talked to a woman with a child. They said something about the celebration, I think about the fireworks that were to be set off and how the noise would scare the dogs. The child did not speak since she was not spoken to, and Mary and I followed the same pattern. We gave a polite goodbye at the appropriate moment, after being invited with a glance and a nod from Krassimira.

Our path took us past the center of town, by the hotel and past the place where the bazaar is set up on Saturdays. The museum grounds had become festive, decorated with red, white, and blue paper chains and paper stars hung from the trees. The crowd grew to several hundred people: the sixty-seven of us in training, our teachers and Peace Corps staff, most of our host families, and some of their extended families.

The evening's festivities began with a speech by the mayor. Radost, one of my favorite language teachers, translated. Although His Honor was making an effort to keep it simple for us, we wouldn't have understood much between "Welcome to Panagyurishte" and "Thank you and good evening." I think most of the enthusiastic applause, which the mayor took as a tribute to his fine speech-making, was for Radost.

After the Mayor spoke, a small group of us, Mary and I included, took the stage and sang the "Star Spangled Banner." We had practiced it the day before, a cappella. There was a remarkable lump-in-the-throat feeling in singing our national anthem there, under those friendly circumstances in a welcoming place so far from home.

The menu was an approximation of what was understood to be American holiday barbecue food: little brown spicy sausages and chicken sandwiches, with beer and soda, sold in bottles with paper cups provided along with them, upturned over the opened bottle. We were expected to fill the cup and leave the bottle with the vendor. Somewhere along the way we had learned it is considered crass to drink out of the bottle, though as the party went on some of our younger members regressed to their college habits. The stray bottles were conspicuously collected for return, by a child sent out for that purpose to make sure none were lost. The drinks were served in the European way, cooled only by being kept in the shade, with no ice involved in their handling. Over time, we came to enjoy our drinks at whatever temperature they could be had, and in some places where ice was available, that became an added treat in itself.

After dinner, a musical group, the town's own brass band, was introduced and started playing on a little open-air stage under the big oak trees in the courtyard. First a few marches, then a set of unfamiliar tunes that were some kind of folk music. Neither the marches nor the folk tunes caught on with the audience, and about nine o'clock the band had knocked off, the sky was still light, and we had about run out of things to say. There's just so much you can do with a vocabulary of a few hundred words and, of course, improvised sign language and smiles.

But darkness did come, and with it the big fireworks display got everybody's attention, with a lot of *oohs* and *aahs* and applause at the end: just like back home.

The music picked up again, with cassette tapes of Bulgarian and American popular music played on a boom box placed on a chair on the stage. We joined in the dancing with a folk tune, the kind of Zorba dancing I have always associated with Greece. I learned the step after a little fumbling and it was fun. Then on the more contemporary music we danced and danced, more than Mary and I had done in a long time. Mary and Krassi took turns dancing with me and with each other; we all danced with groups and with nobody in particular sometimes. It was fascinating listening to the Bulgarian pop music that was so unfamiliar to us; yet our teachers and our new family members all sang along. How many things there are like this; things that are integral to the way people understand the world and that are so unknown and unheard of to those outside their circle.

Krassi tried to explain one song about "Summer Nights" to me, picking out words enough to get me to understand that it was a song about a night like this.

One might not have thought that a cobblestone courtyard would make a good dance floor, but everything about this

Fourth of July was a little different. The night was warm and everybody was soaked with sweat, and it was one of those times when the least little movement of air feels like a gift from heaven bringing cool refreshment that makes you smile just thinking about it.

Walking home along the dark, quiet street—late for a school night—Krassimira startled when something flew into her hair, and she instinctively knocked it away. She realized it was a firefly, a word we didn't know when she said what it was. She explained by making a buzzing noise and finger motion for a flying bug. She pointed to a lighted window, then pointed again with her hand open and closed like a blinking light. A *svetulka*. We looked for them the rest of the way home and didn't see any more. So then we knew there are fireflies— *svetulki*—here but not so many as to take them for granted. Kind of like the fireworks, and like special celebrations on soft summer nights.

Bruce McDonald (along with his wife) seved as an English teacher in Pazardjik, Bulgaria, B-12, from 2002-04. In addition to classroom teaching they both volunteered at an orphanage and with an NGO providing guidance, recreational and educational programs for youth in the Roma minority neighborhood. Now Bruce works part-time writing and editing articles about real estate, and the couple participates in volunteer work with a wide variety of organizations. He says they are both enjoying learning new things from their grandchildren.

ROBERT NAGLE

The Art of Losing Things

"The art of losing things isn't hard to master." —*Elizabeth Bishop*

ABOUT TWO WEEKS BEFORE THE EVACUATION, THE CURRENCIES were going wild, and I had to change my lek back to American currency before it lost any more value. I had rent money, grant money, and money for future travel. In one week, the value of the dollar dropped 25 percent. It was to be a repeat of the hyperinflation found in Bulgaria. I walked with a sense of urgency past Skenderbej Square in search of the man with the best rates. I took pride in my ability to figure out exchange rates and the best value for them. I brought about $300 or $400 and a calculator. I found a man with the best rates, sat at a café with him and counted my money.

But in my haste I'd made a mistake. Instead of looking for the best rates, I ended up exchanging my lek with the man who had the worst rates for the dollar. I didn't realize it until the next day. I discovered my error at the same time I discovered that fifty more dollars were missing or unaccounted for. I frantically searched my bags in the hopes that it had fallen somewhere. Perhaps I traded it the day before. Perhaps the man who did the money exchange accidentally took it. Maybe I should go back the next day and ask if he was $50 over. That day and the next were spoiled. How could I have been so stupid! And I for so long had prided myself on my quickness with numbers!

The $75 I had lost was nothing to sneeze at either. To someone living in America, it was an annoyance, but in Albania, it was about two weeks of living expenses. I couldn't believe it. Suddenly I became more conscious of what I was spending. Perhaps I didn't need that extra bag of Cheetos on the way to the Peace Corps office. Perhaps I could skip the Stephen Center (the only American restaurant in town) a few times. My misfortune was too embarrassing to mention to other Volunteers. I should have known better. But my loss was an mere inconvenience compared to what I witnessed when a series of collapsing pyramid schemes caused many Albanians to lose everything. Looking for a high return on their lek, they had made a mistake.

Sometime in November 1996, I visited my Tirana host family and mentioned the Peace Corps director's warning about the pyramid schemes. I'd heard about it on and off before; a banking Volunteer had told me as early as 1995 that Albania's biggest company, Vefa, was probably a pyramid scheme. The story started hitting the Albanian newspapers in that month or the month before, but the dangers warned of by the newspapers seemed more hypothetical than real. Nelson, the new country director, prepared us for contingency plans and talked about possible scenarios for the next year.

At first, Bashkim, my host father, didn't understand what I meant by "*schema pyramida*," and then when I mentioned "*fajde*," he replied that yes, he had invested money just recently. I stared at him with surprise.

"Did you invest a lot?" I asked.

"Yes, a few thousand dollars, why?" My heart sunk as I realized the implications. I explained to him what the embassy had been fearing. But how can you tell a man that the two-year's worth of salary he'd invested was probably gone? Of course, he was concerned and wanted to know exactly what I heard. But I knew only sketchy details. He had invested most of his money in Gjallica (the investment company based in Vlore) and some in Vefa. He planned to use the profits to buy a taxi and become a taxi driver. His business as a drink shop owner was worsening. It was hard work, the profits weren't great, and his shop was not large enough to compete. He was renting from somebody, and the owner wanted the land back. I tried to tell Bashkim that I really didn't know if he would get his money back. I was only an English teacher and shouldn't be trying to give people investment advice.

Upon returning to Vlore, I tried to spread the word about the schemes to my Albanian friends at the university. Or at least to find how many of them had invested their money. Some like Abdyli, an English professor, waved off the question together. "Where would I get the money to do such a thing?" I mentioned it to Ermelinda, the best business student at the university whose father worked for Vefa. What did she know? What had Vefa been telling her dad?

She smiled and shrugged. "Nobody knows these things. Maybe it is a good investment, but how can anybody find out?"

She said it with a bit of good cheer, as though merely wishing would make the schemes work.

By 1996, signs were growing ominous. One scheme revealed itself for what it was, but still people continued investing. One firm set up branches in major towns and villages to take people's money. As long as everyone believed the system would work and could encourage their friends it was a safe investment, the pyramid would continue indefinitely... that is, until it ran out of people. But for someone to refuse to invest was to hurt everyone else. It was almost unpatriotic. Although Albania was close to a free economy, its members easily fell victim to the same groupthink from communist times.

In a similar way, the old socialist economy depended on the people's confidence in the system to work. If only everyone did what they were supposed to, the planners thought, then socialism would work. Any shortcoming in the economy was a result of the "human element" (corruption, bribes and profiteering) infecting the overall system. But goals were not met, officials took bribes, a black market began to emerge. These things became the economic scapegoats instead of the system itself. The only way for socialism to work was for everyone to invest their full time and loyalty to it.

January was a peculiar month. The government had wrested concessions from the pyramid schemes to pay out or else. Or else what? Nobody really knew. People hoped that things were not as bleak as they seemed.

In mid-January, I took a nice trip to Bulgaria to sightsee and visit Elton, an Albanian student studying at the American University of Bulgaria. He and all the other students (who were mostly business and economics majors) were following the economic developments of Albania through the internet. Every day we checked the computer postings for the latest updates on the pyramid schemes. We read with astonishment about the protests in major cities, including Vlore where I lived. All of us were clearly nervous and full of dire forecasts. We joked at the hell that would break loose when people realized they wouldn't be getting their money. I half-jokingly mentioned to Elton that there could be a coup or revolution by the time Elton had summer break. But even that seemed like a wild hypothetical. On the ride home, my bus was detained at the border for an ungodly amount of time. By the time I arrived in Tirana, I heard there were more riots and burnings of public buildings. It seemed unreal.

In response to the riots, the government promised to give people the money they lost. That kept the people quiet, especially when the government gave February 5 as the day that people's money would be paid back. It was a dumb thing to say, but the protests forced it out of them. When the Foreign Minister visited Lushnje to speak to the protesting depositors, the rioters kept him hostage in a soccer stadium and (it was rumored) put a leek covered with cow shit in his mouth. There was no telling what could happen, and Berisha made the easy choice: tell the people what they want to hear.

But to promise to reimburse investors was absurd. The money was gone, and the government certainly couldn't pay the millions that had disappeared. A few days later, the government said it needed a few more days to analyze the accounting of these firms. Later, the government said that not everybody would be compensated immediately, only small investors. Then, the government said that the people would not receive their money, but simply a savings book stating the amount owed them. Then when the government distributed these savings books, the books stated that the money was to be paid not by the government, but the investment company. Protests were called for by opposition parties and newspapers, but the government said that they wouldn't grant them the necessary permit to have one.

By that time, investment schemes were the only things people talked about. At a large family gathering, all the four- and five-year-olds babbled the names of all the pyramid schemes to their parents' laughter and applause. Once on the sidewalk, I ran into the mother of a teacher I knew well. We made small talk for a while, and I asked her if they'd invested in the pyramid schemes. She looked at me wearily, and said, "Yes, but let's not talk about it anymore." Something about that memory stays with me, the old woman on the sidewalk nodding her head and telling me not to talk about it. I remembered then that I was just a foreigner, that the pyramid schemes were no longer proper subjects for small talk. They were something to discuss in private, arguments better to avoid. After all, nobody liked to publicize their own stupidity.

First semester finals were coming, and so was the February 5 deadline when Gjallica promised to distribute its money. I remember when I first heard it; I was talking to the English department head about a final exam when yells came from outside, and a mass of rowdy-looking men were marching toward the university square. A good hundred police were escorting them. They went inside the square, and what did they do? Yell chants and jeer at the police; it was not a political meeting but a pep rally devoid of messages. No banners, no speeches, no symbols of protests, just singing and swearing and shoving. About a hundred students and teachers were still inside the school building staring in amazement. After twenty or so minutes, the mass of people started to walk back into town. Most of the onlookers inside resumed their usual business, but at the sound of scuffling noises, I glanced out the window again.

Men were throwing rocks at the policemen, and soon after the police started firing: right in front of my window! People were scattering around, students were crowded around the windows watching the action outside although this clearly seemed to be the dumbest thing to be doing. I went into a room with all my first-year English students. They were scared and excited and nervous. One girl, a nineteen year old named Orgis looked over at me, smiling. "Do you ever have this kind of thing in America?"

That Sunday morning, I woke up earlier than usual to do my morning shopping. I walked down the main street, intending to stop by another Volunteer's house. As I walked along, I could see a small mass of people gathering together for another street demonstration. Before I knew it, the group had grown larger and was walking in the opposite direction toward a barricade of twenty riot police. The demonstrators (a rowdier group than the families that marched during the week) started throwing stones, and the riot police stayed crouched behind their shields, enduring the abuse. I scurried up to the fifth-floor apartment of my friend Stuart. The first words to come out of his mouth when he opened the door were, "Why the hell are you here? Are you crazy?"

We stayed in his apartment glancing out the window as the police were gradually outnumbered and started firing at protesters. But too many people were throwing rocks. Underneath our apartment balcony, middle-aged men were throwing down rocks to break them into smaller, more throwable pieces. The riot police—20 against 300—had no choice but to retreat into a restaurant. The crowd followed them, breaking windows, trashing plastic furniture on the balcony and ultimately taking the riot gear, guns and clothes from the policemen inside. Thirty minutes later the crowd had dispersed (I later heard that the policemen were escorted naked to another place), and the main street returned to its usual hectic pace. The memory of what had just taken place had seemed to evaporate. Even Stuart, rattled by the whole thing, asked me not to tell everything that had happened to Peace Corps. Because if I did, "they're going to send us out of Vlore for good."

But by afternoon, images of this event had been transmitted all over the world. Then half an hour after it was over, I felt safe enough to walk twenty minutes to my apartment. The streets and sidewalks were busy with people: friends, neighbors and co-workers. At an intersection I ran into some shopkeepers who were neighbors. I said hello, asked them how they were, told them what I had seen.

"*Sali Berisha eshte gomar! Hadjut!*" (Berisha is an ass! Thief!) The people demanded the money that the government stole from them. When I tried to say that it was the pyramid schemes, not the prime minister, that had stolen their money, the men—my friends—started arguing fierily that Berisha was a thief. More people were walking toward me to participate in the discussion. For once, I didn't feel safe. What was I doing trying to have a political discussion 500 meters from a riot area?

The next day I arrived at the university to give students their grades for their final exam. Later, after all the grades were given, Marcela who had been sobbing in her desk about her grade (B-), came up to me and asked in a tearful voice to explain why she received such a low grade. I knew Marcela well. She was a dark-eyed girl with strikingly beautiful black hair, the daughter of the city's district attorney. And although her English wasn't fantastic, she knew how to argue and did everything to ensure high marks. I quickly scanned the test and tried to read my scrawls on the test, but Marcela had already left the room in tears. Fifteen minutes later Peace Corps told me to evacuate Vlore for the capital city, Tirana. I returned to class and announced the news hesitantly to my students. I didn't know when I would return, and I certainly didn't expect that I wouldn't return again.

I still think about that hallway meeting with Marcela. How strange that in the midst of a vortex of political violence that would sweep her town over the coming weeks, this girl's preoccupation was her grades. And yet how normal! And then came a letter from Elton, the student with whom I had joked about the coup, that lamented not the fate of his country, but the loss of a girl who had rejected his romantic advances. Communist leaders made the mistake of thinking that individuals actually care about larger social and political issues. But the individual's first concern is himself and the world he inhabits. Franz Kafka, for instance, barely mentions in his diaries the war taking place in his country. We may criticize this blindness, but self-absorption is perhaps the first privilege taken away during times of crisis. It takes real courage to cling to it.

Robert Nagle is a Houston-based fiction writer who served as a TEFL Volunteer in Vlore, Albania, from 1995-97. His latest writings and stories can be found on the idiotprogrammer blog. His collection of essays, Noncrappy Things from my Blog *was published as an e-book in late 2010.*

CHARLENE PEÑA

One Steppe at a Time

*An invitation to dinner is more than just
about the food. It's the culture.*

GETTING THE WIND KNOCKED OUT OF ME HAS A NEW, MORE LIT-
eral meaning. After fighting against the powerful wind causing
me to trudge through the vast steppe that was my village, I
had what I referred to as an "only-in-Kaz" moment. It was
something I would not have had to deal with if I had stayed
in my hometown. With wisps of hair getting in the way and
blocking microsecond periods of vision, my surprising reaction
was a recollection of the joy and wonder of my Kazakhstan
life for two years. How I'd come to develop an affinity for my
Kaz-life struck me like the wind in my face.

Facing cultural differences—like bathing once a week in
the hot, steamy *banya* and being pushed and poked like a piece
of skewered and barbecued *shashlik* at the coat check after a
concert (because the idea of standing in line would make too
much sense)—brought many "only-in-Kaz" moments within
my first year of Peace Corps service. But with only one more
month to go in my term of service, these infamous "only-
in-Kaz" moments weren't as frequent. I liked to think it was

because I'd adapted, was better accepted in my community, and able to bargain at the bazaar. However, there was nothing quite like being invited as a guest to a *gosti* to produce an altogether new "only-in-Kaz" moment. A *gosti* never failed to be a mix of surprises and comfort of good company. The basic rundown of a formal *gosti* had three parts and uncannily embodied a lot in my life in Kaz. There were the unexpected, the expected, and the personally dreaded experiences.

Experiencing a *gosti* meant I did not always know what could be included in the cuisine being served. Once, at a Kazakh wedding, teachers from my school were excited about serving all the first-rate horse meat and sausage stuffed in intestines to me, the foreign guest. I figured if it was high quality, it had to be tasty…and tasty it was. Another time, though not exactly for a party, I went to the bazaar and saw a lady selling pizza. My taste buds were celebrating, but then we (my taste buds and I) found that Kaz pizza could only be made to perfection with mayonnaise. A little unexpected; but, ah, mayonnaise pizza sauce now has a special place in my heart.

However, the award-winning surprise had to be what a friend of mine termed "meat jell-o." I first came across this delicacy when my Russian host family had set the table for a *gosti*. They had spent morning and afternoon stewing over the stove. On the table I found *holadetz*. It consists of meat, usually pork, and congealed meat fat. Let me just say this: thank goodness for the staple bread and for tomato and cucumber salad. The cuisine was never terrible, just a little surprising at times.

After the main course and its surprises, I was able to anticipate a good cup of freshly brewed chai. This other part to a *gosti* really meant hosts and guests alike would soon have access to tea and plates and plates of cookies, cake, chocolate, candy, and fresh fruit when in season. The dining table was always transformed into a golden-ticket winner's dream. After a salad course, the first course, then the second main course, chai at least made me feel like the heat melted everything I had just eaten and made room for all the sweets. The chai course was the part wherein I could additionally expect more entertaining events and conversations. The old grandmothers, the *babushkas*, would sing their beloved Russian oldies or tell stories of life when they were part of the Soviet Union. I may not have always been able to comprehend every word, joke, or idiom spoken during teatime, but one thing was for sure, I learned something new with every cup of chai.

Throughout the main meal(s) and chai were all the required toasting and shots taken with one's choice of vodka, cognac, or wine. I more often than not dreaded this part of the *gosti* because I was never able to hold liquor well, so my friends have assured me. I've noticed two types of drinkers: the kind who get extremely quiet and the kind who get extremely talkative. I am different from both. Let me clarify.

With all the *gosti*s, I've found that I'm my own type of drinker, the kind who neither gets too quiet nor talkative but, rather, very red. No one was ever as sly as my host father in creating a reason to celebrate, regardless of whether guests were over for dinner that night or not. My first purchase for Siberian-worthy winter gear at the bazaar was made with my host family, and upon arriving home, my host father had said that it was tradition to drink to all purchases made at the bazaar. Another time, he asked me to have 100 grams of vodka with him because it was Astrology Day. He was no alcoholic, but he enjoyed finding a reason to celebrate. There was also a Teacher's Day party when other teachers gave me their spiel about the benefits of vodka. In case anyone ever asks, I'm fully aware that vodka is full of vitamins, will apparently keep me warm in the -40 degree winters, and is wonderful for getting out clothing stains.

Sitting around at each *gosti* for a few hours or so also gave me time to think about life, especially when I shamefully zoned out because I couldn't quite follow why people were debating over something about something that a neighbor had said and caused someone to say something that upset the neighbor. So here's what I've come away with from two years of *gosti* under my winter coat: It was never about what I was eating or drinking, it was who I was with. After the eating, drinking, talking, and sitting, there usually was dancing, complete with whooping, yelping, head bobbing, and hand clapping. People were never self-conscious about how they danced. People never worried about their troubles. People delighted in each other's company, and that was reason enough for celebration.

With or without harsh winds, daily bathing, standing in lines, meat fat, chai, or vodka shots, the people of my Kazakhstani village have significantly altered my views on the important things in life. Through the difficulties I'd faced and the community I'd found, I wouldn't trade my "only-in-Kaz" moments, not even for a miracle pill that promised to never allow me to turn red after multiple shots of vodka.

Charlene Peña served as a teacher of English as a Foreign Language in Kazakhstan, Kaz-17, from 2005-07. She primarily taught students from grades 2-11 at local village schools, collaborated with local teachers for creative lesson planning, and developed a small English resource center in the community library. Once back in the U.S., Charlene worked with a non-profit organization for refugees and asylum seekers, and went on to pursue a dual-degree master's program at Columbia University.

Homecoming

In a land where the guest is king, Volunteers
must also play host from time to time.

FINALLY SPRING WAS COMING TO ERZURUM. IT WAS APRIL AND the sun was shining, the snowmelt was dripping from roofs, and running in rivulets down streets and sidewalks. Looking out my window beyond the balcony, over the rooftops of the city, I could just barely discern spidery dark veins of soil and water emerging against the dazzling whiteness that had blanketed the long valley since November. Outside the building, and even up in our sixth-floor apartment, I could hear someone hacking away at the ice on sidewalks that had formed from thousands of footsteps tromping on layer after layer of winter snow.

We had a day off from classes at Atatürk University, where we taught English. My husband, Jim, was out playing basketball with some of his students at the city gymnasium. I had a couple hours of complete solitude, and I wanted nothing more than to be left alone. The challenge of operating in a foreign culture was exhilarating, but often exhausting. Language acquisition was a daily, moment-by-moment effort, and was frequently encumbered by trying to comprehend the attendant cultural cue, or in awkward moments, to discern the cue that had been misunderstood.

Glancing up from the book I was reading, I cast my eye over our apartment, noting with distaste that, as usual, there was a layer of coal dust on the bookcase, the desk, the window sill. I should get up and clean it off. I should put on my coat and do the grocery shopping. The coal stove glowed opposite my chair, warming my feet, and I turned back to my book, escaping happily from reality and obligations.

The knock on the door startled and annoyed me. Not caring to return to reality, I thought of ignoring the knock, pretending I wasn't home. But of course, if it were a neighbor, she'd know I was at home and would continue to knock. I heard the giggles and children's voices echoing in the stairway, and my curiosity was provoked—that, plus the fact that children were usually quick in their errands and easily dismissed. I went to the front door and opened it to four adolescent girls from the orphanage. The girls smiled shyly at me, waiting to be invited in. Of course I asked them to enter, wondering all the while at their presence, and hoping we weren't all going to get into trouble for doing something unofficial. I also wondered if I should offer them tea, the hallmark of Turkish hospitality. Hot tea served in tiny, bell-shaped glasses had warmed my hands and my heart in many Turkish homes during that long winter.

We had met the girls and other children when we began tutoring at one of the three orphanages in Erzurum, a provincial capital in far eastern Turkey, more than a mile high in a valley of the Palandöken mountains. Our official assignment in that city was to the English Department at Atatürk University, and we had been teaching there since the beginning of the fall semester of 1966. But we had wanted to participate in our community in other ways, and so we volunteered at the orphanage to tutor English, a foreign language required in the public schools.

From the beginning of our tutoring at the orphanage, their home, the building itself underscored the gray and unrelenting cold that often represented, at least in my imagination, our life in Erzurum. Winter in that city seemed interminable, starting in September with cold rains that fell onto the bare grays and browns of the mountains. By October the first snows had begun, crowning the mountains with powdered sugar and making the city streets slushy. By November the whole valley was a brilliant white, blinding on sunny days, and bitter, bitter cold at night. The streets were thick with snow-on-snow packed into layers of ice. From then on the snow continued, lingering well into spring, the last snowfall arriving in early June. The rarefied air of the city carried the constant perfume of smoke from the wood and coal stoves.

The buildings, and particularly the public buildings, stood tall, gray, solid, and cold. They looked as if they were constructed to withstand adversity in whatever guise—weather, change, political opinions, ethnic battles, time. They called to mind street scenes from *Doctor Zhivago*. Their long, looming windows staring down at all who passed by reminded me, more than anything else in the city, that Russians had fought for Erzurum, and had won it several times before 1918. Our Peace Corps years occurred in the midst of the Cold War, and those darkly glaring windows seemed to reflect the mystery, myth and misunderstanding that existed between the Soviet Union and the United States.

The orphanage matched the bleak physical ambience of the city. It was a ponderous building, entered through tall stone steps to the front door that stood sentinel over the narrow side street descending from Cumhurriyet Caddesi, the Avenue of the Republic. The building was constructed of huge, dark stone blocks, and had large, barred windows. Inside, the ceilings were high, with a single lightbulb hanging in each room—certainly no cozy, low-lit, localized seating arrangements or individual desks with lamps. This was something that had leaped out at us as we began our tutoring.

It was the children who provided the warmth of the institution. They adored our interest in them, were excited by each visit, and dropped whatever they were doing when we arrived in order to greet us noisily. They called us Jim *ağabey* (big brother Jim), and Sue *abla* (big sister Sue). They danced for us—the lack of musical instruments made not a particle of difference. They would gather into a circle to dance, or would dance in pairs, or even singly. Those not dancing would clap hands and intone the "*nai-ni-nai-nai, nai-ni-nai, nai-nai*" rhythmic tune that accompanied their different steps. Girls danced more than boys, especially the older boys, who played soldier, lining up, drilling and marching whenever they could.

The day of the girls' surprise visit to our apartment, the oldest of my young guests quickly indicated that they couldn't really stay for tea. This girl was Mualla, a tall and responsible young woman whose younger sister, Gül, was a part of the foursome that day. These two girls were not truly orphans, I remembered, but had moved into the orphanage with their newly widowed mother when she was desperately seeking a way to support her family. The mother now served as one of the cooks at that institution. Of their present visit to our home, Mualla explained that they had just stopped by on the way home from school and were expected back at the orphanage, but they had wanted to see where we lived. I hesitated, but not because I felt their interest was an intrusion. One of the cultural attributes to which I was adjusting, indeed which I now mostly enjoyed, was the candid curiosity of Erzurum citizens about our personal lives and activities. My hesitation occurred instead because I suddenly felt embarrassed at the state of our apartment. Whether I looked at it with American eyes or from a Turkish point of view, it seemed shabby to me. The ubiquitous coal dust, from which I never managed to liberate our home, did not appear in any Turkish home I had entered, from the most humble dwelling to the most luxurious domicile. Turkish women kept their homes spotless. Then there was the big empty room in which we were standing. It should have been our living room. Our limited budget had allowed limited furniture; that fact plus our concern about staying warm in the winter had helped us decide to put the coal stove, our one desk and the two chairs into the small room off the living room— the room we now called the study.

My hesitation lasted, in reality, only a nano-second. I found myself smiling in response to the girls' shy curiosity, and I began to show them the four small rooms that constituted our apartment. Their delight at my invitation, however, quickly overruled any shyness, and they began to explore in four different directions, each one happily calling to her friends at every new discovery. They were charmed by everything! The hot water heater in the bathroom, created with a small stove beneath it, in which we had to build a fire when we wanted a hot shower, was a source of exclamations, *oohs* and *ahhhs*. The wooden cupboard that held our dishes in the kitchen (which I had painted) and the one in the bedroom where we kept our clothes (that was still unpainted wood), were marvels to the girls. Indeed, I confessed to them, they had been built by the previous apartment dweller, who had been an engineer. Where I had perceived a poverty of furniture, they found great luxury. Our tiny study with the two chairs was a wonder of domesticity. "Jim *ağabey* sits here at night when he's reading or grading papers, and you sit here!" And then from the bathroom sink came another shrill of delight. This fixture was not really in the bathroom, a room much too small to hold it. The bathroom contained the Turkish toilet (two foot treads and a hole in the floor for the drain) and the hot water heater-cum-shower. The sink was attached to the wall outside the bathroom door, and opposite the kitchen, and at the moment all I could see was the gray dust coating the fixture, or showing the rivulets where water had begun to wash the grime into the sink. There stood one of the girls grinning from ear to ear, however, and another stood at the kitchen sink, exclaiming, "Two sinks! You can wash your face here and Jim *ağabey* can wash his face there (the other sink) at the same time!"

I stood in amazement as the girls sought out each corner of the apartment, delighted by every detail of quotidian life. The kitchen table was welcoming, they exclaimed, the curtains were beautiful, and the bed, covered with Peace Corps-issue sleeping bags and topped by the Turkish *yorgan*, looked like unparalleled comfort. Still giggling and shrilling their delight in happy voices, they kissed me goodbye and departed as suddenly as they had appeared.

I stood in what, ten minutes before, had been solitude in an empty apartment. I listened to the girls' voices descending the stairs. Below them the hacking away at the ice on the streets continued. The sound seemed to announce, "We're breaking through! We're emerging from the ice world!" I could hear the shouts and laughter of children running home from the school up the street.

Susan Fleming Holm served as a Volunteer in Turkey. She went on to become the Dorothy Donald Professor of Modern Foreign Languages at Monmouth College in Illinois and entered phased retirement in 2008 to spend more time on writing. Teaching in a liberal arts institution has allowed her to marry her professional discipline (Spanish language and literature) with her love of Turkey and all things Turkish—a love born during her Peace Corps years. While at first glance these two fields of interest may not seem to have much in common, there are truly many ways in which they connect, both historically and in literature, from Cervantes to Juan Goytisolo. She spent her last sabbatical in 2007 in Turkey, examining what Turkish women see as changes in their lives in the past forty years. She contributed a chapter, "Conversion in Erzurum," to the anthology Tales from the Expat Harem: Foreign Women in Modern Turkey. *Susan is proud to say that both of her children grew up understanding that most of the rest of the world doesn't speak English as a first language, and both have used a second language in their professional work. Her two very young grandchildren include expressions from Turkish such as "İnşallah" "Maşallah," and "çok yaşa!" in their active vocabulary!*

PART FOUR

CLOSE ENCOUNTERS

✦
✦ ✦

I Love Lucy Moment

A little learning is a dangerous thing. —*Alexander Pope*

I HAD AN *I LOVE LUCY* MOMENT TODAY.

You know those moments, don't you? It starts off innocently enough: There's some minor technical problem that's been bothering you, and you think you can solve it easily enough without anybody's help. So with your good old American independence and know-how, you're going to go out and do something about it...only to wreck it up more. Maybe Ricky's been really dismissive of your abilities and has been tight-fisted in buying what you want. Maybe getting a job packaging chocolate at the chocolate factory to earn some pocket money sounds good, because after all, how hard can it be? You like chocolate. You can put chocolate in a box. It's gotta be simple. Then, suddenly, before you know it, you've got your mouth crammed full of chocolate and you're shoving more into your shirt pocket as things start spinning out of control and you wonder how you got yourself into this mess.

After moving to Ust-Kamenogorsk, a city in the northeast region of Kazakhstan, for my placement teaching English at a

233

university, I was lucky enough to be referred to an apartment that contained an old washing machine. Having put in my time in the village getting the "authentic" Peace Corps experience of washing my clothes by hand for several months, I was looking forward to the prospects of not having to devote several hours to washing my clothes only to have them come out looking dirtier than before. However, modern conveniences like a washing machine often present their own complications, as I soon discovered.

Upon my return to Ust-Kamenogorsk, after teaching at a summer camp in Pavlodar, I came home to a small puddle of water collecting underneath the washing machine. Investigating this, I found that the rubber hose connecting the hot water valve to my washing machine had been slowly leaking. Because the handle to open and close the valve had broken off some time ago, I couldn't close it off to stop the leak.

Easy enough to fix, right? Buy a new handle to screw onto the old valve and some plumber's tape to seal off the leak on the hose. I even take a picture of the "before" setup on the valve so that I can proudly show my handiwork off on my blog. I tramp off to the bazaar.

Walking past each of the shipping containers that were now converted into stalls, I head toward the back of the bazaar where tools are sold. I stop at a stall where an enormous Russian woman with flaming red dyed hair is tending shop. She has a box of valves sitting out. Red eyes me as I sift through a mess of valves until I find a valve with a handle that resembles the broken valve at home. I try to haggle with Red to buy just the handle and not the whole valve, but she won't hear it. She picks out a few other ones to offer me if I was price-conscious. "*Eto russiski, chyeteristo tenge,*" This is Russian-made, four hundred tenge. She grabs another and tosses it at me. "*Esli ti hochesh kitaiski, dvesti tenge.*" If you want the Chinese-made, it's two hundred.

"Are the Chinese ones bad?" I ask in Russian.

"It's probably why the handle on your old one broke. Buy the Russian one."

I pay the woman for the new valve and some plumber's tape and set off back home with my treasures.

At home, I happily unscrew the handle off the new valve and install it on the old valve, beaming at my ingenuity. I don't have a monkey wrench, so I'm scraping by with a small pair of pliers I found in a tool drawer in the house. I turn the pliers, following the righty-tighty rule until it's tightened to my satisfaction. The handle looks great on the old valve. All right, time for a test run.

I turn the new handle. It doesn't move.

Huh, that's weird, I think to myself. Maybe after being on for so long, the mineralized water left a buildup on the inside of the valve. I try again, this time pushing a little harder. Should be easy enough once I get the valve moving.

The valve gives a little bit. I can feel it turning ever so slowly, so I apply some more force to turn the handle all the way to the "closed" setting. Then suddenly I hear a sickening *CRUNCH*.

Hot water begins to spray out of the hole where the valve once was (now firmly in my left hand, still attached to the handle) like a fire hose. Hot water. EVERYWHERE.

The water is blasting out, soaking my entire body and the shorts that I'm wearing (which at this moment happen to contain my wallet, sunglasses, passport, and digital camera.) My first instinct is to cover the hole with my hands and screw the valve back onto the hole. I'm screaming like a little girl, using every curse word in the book in every language I can think of as I'm pushing at the hole where the water is shooting out through.

As I'm grasping blindly at the valve, I quickly realize that my attempts to screw the valve back on are futile, because in my efforts to close the valve I've snapped the valve clean in half. Part of the valve is still stuck inside the pipe itself, preventing anything from being screwed back in. In my desperation to stem the water flow and buy myself some time to think of a plan, I jam my palm over the hole itself. This only serves to spray the water upwards toward the ceiling, shorting out the light bulb.

So now I'm standing in the dark, soaked shirt to shorts, with water flooding the floor of my bathroom. The floor begins to feel weirdly soapy as the water gets to the box of detergent on the floor as well. I grab a plastic basin and try to redirect the water flow toward the bathtub, where there's a drain. This, like my palm idea, only proceeds to make things worse by redirecting the water over to where my dry clothes are hanging from the last wash. Suddenly, it occurs to me that there's a water shut off valve in the toilet room, which is right next to this bathroom.

I slam the door shut to prevent the water spraying out into the hallway and run to the toilet room. I reach behind the toilet and fumble wildly for the water shut off, mashing my cheek up against the toilet tank to reach the valve. I reach the valve and turn it off. The good news from this action was that I was able to stop my toilet from leaking, but the valve seemed to have no effect on the sickening "*Pssssssssssssssssssssshhhhhhhhhhhhhhhhhhhhhhhh*" emanating from the next room as the hot water continued to spray out.

Time to call for reinforcements. I run out into the hall, soaked head to toe, and desperately pound on the door of my neighbor. Sergei, a gangly Russian teen living next door with his family, answers the door in his white briefs.

"Sergei! Is your dad home? The valve to my washing machine from the pipe broke and it's spraying water everywhere! I need to shut off the water!" Of course, this is in my broken Russian, and Peace Corps language training never covered home plumbing repair, so my desperate pleas for help came out more like "Sergei! Your dad home? Water washing machine! Broke! Water! Hot Water! How close water!?"

Sergei's dad is not home, of course, but Sergei runs to my bathroom and offers to use the plastic basin to try and redirect the water back into the tub while I get help.

"Go downstairs to the first floor," he yells at me from the bathroom, standing in his briefs and white socks, "Find the superintendent! It's the black door!"

I run downstairs, leaving a trail of water as I get to the first floor, and I pound frantically at the door. A woman answers, I look inside, it looks like an office space.

"*Da?*" says the woman, her eyes slightly open with surprise, as she looks at the strange foreigner, soaked head to toe, gibbers at her in broken Russian.

"Super, he here? Water! Hot Water! Water. Washing machine. Water broken! I need close water!"

"Not here!" she says, as she tries to close the door on me, no doubt thinking I'm an escaped mental patient.

I jam my arm in the door to stop her from closing it, and I gasp, "Where's the super? Who can help me? Please, help me!" She seems to respond to this, and tells me to go to the second floor and knock on the door, where the super lives.

I run to the second floor, and ring the doorbell.

Of course, no answer.

So I run back down and pound on the black door again, begging the woman to help me.

"I don't know how to turn off the water," she says. "The master water valve is in the basement, but it's locked, and you need Nikolai Ivanovich (the super) to open it because he has the key to open the basement." I beg her to make some calls for me, to which she agrees.

I run back upstairs to my apartment to check on Sergei. My wet shoes squish with each step. Sergei is stripped to his underwear, fighting the futile fight to stop the floor from flooding. He's bailing the water from the floor to the tub. I tell him that the super isn't in.

Sergei, without looking at me, screams back, "There should be an extra key to the basement with the director of Lumix, the clothing store on the first floor of the building!"

I run downstairs, and tell the first woman on the phone (who is now frantically calling all of the neighbors to try and find Nikolai). She says O.K., and runs out to Lumix to ask the director. The director comes out, and tries the one key she has.

Of course, this doesn't work.

"You need to find Oleg Anatolovich, the director of the sport equipment store!" I run over with the woman to the sport equipment store on the other end of the apartment building, and find Igor, who denies knowing anything about any key, ever.

Twenty minutes have passed already. I'm running back and forth asking if anyone knows where Nikolai is. Everytime I run upstairs to check on the apartment, it's starting to look more and more like a sauna. Steam is everywhere. Walking into the apartment is like walking into a bad Halloween haunted house with a fog machine gone wild. After some more frantic pacing, I let out a huge sigh of relief as I spot Nikolai Ivanovich pull up in his old Lada. He waddles out of his car, scratching his balding head as I run up to and start pulling him toward the basement door to shut off the main hot water valve.

"I can't do it," he tells me. "The café on the first floor is remodeling, and they blocked off access to the main water line, so I can't access it from here. What's wrong with your valve? It's a *kitaiski* valve, isn't it? Can't buy the Chinese ones, those are garbage, gotta go with the Italian ones."

I'm about to lose it. I'm flooding the third floor of the apartment complex and the super wants to talk about the relative qualities of pipe fittings based on origins.

"O.K., what do we do next?" I say to him through gritted teeth.

"Well, we have to find Igor Yevgeninovich, the owner of the café to unlock the back door." Nikolai picks up his phone, and starts making calls.

I run up to check on the apartment. The bathroom is flooded and the water is coming out into the hallway. I run back downstairs to find Igor arriving at the scene, who luckily lives in the apartment building down the street. Nikolai again insists on pointing out and debating with Igor the inferiority of Chinese valves.

Igor walks slowly toward the back door of the café as if he's on a Sunday stroll, unlocking it and walking in while listening to Nikolai's wild proclamation on the superiority of Italian valves. He goes down into another basement accessible only through the café with another worker, examining pipes here and there along the way, trying to figure out which pipe shuts off the pipe in my house. After about five minutes of poking and touching, he twists a valve and looks at me.

"Well," he says, waving his wrench upwards, "Go see if it's off."

I run back upstairs, and I can still hear the sickening "*pssssssssssssssssssshhhhhhh*" from outside the door. I look inside, Sergei's given up on bailing out the water into the drain, and has resigned to just pulling on the door to keep it shut. The water isn't off. I run back downstairs and report.

Igor and Nikolai both scratch their heads a bit, and mutter between the two of them, "maybe it's in the other basement? But we don't have the key for that…we'll have to call the super of that section…" My eyelid twitches a bit upon hearing this.

"Maybe turn off all pipes? Try all!" I gibber more, having more or less accepted that I effectively have a pool in my house now.

On a whim, Igor pulls out a gigantic wrench and turns off another valve and tells me to check again. I run back upstairs. My assumption that it was just a pool was wrong. My house is actually a sauna. It's difficult to see anything in the house because of the amount of steam, but as I walk in, splashing water everywhere, I'm relieved to see that the water has ceased. Sergei gives me the universal thumbs up and staggers back to his house.

I go back down to report, and Igor instructs me to call the KCK, which is a plumbing service. The plumbers arrive thirty minutes later to repair the damaged valve.

"What happened?" they ask.

"Valve, broke off, water everywhere," I reply.

"Ahh...yeah, those Chinese valves are worthless, can't trust those. Gotta go with It–"

"Italian or Russian, I know, I know," I interrupt. I listlessly hand them the new Russian valve that I had bought earlier and they fix everything for me.

While the plumbers are working on the job I should have called them for earlier, I mop and clean up the new Olympic-sized swimming pool in my bathroom and corridor. They finally fix the valve for good and turn on the hot water supply again for the building after about an hour's work. I pay them and they leave. I casually look over their handiwork and find that they had left the old broken valve on the washing machine, the original source of all my problems. I pick it up to see the manufacturer and can't help but laugh as I run my thumb over the rusted out "MADE IN ITALY" sign stamped into the broken valve.

Jay Chen served as a University English Teacher at East Kazakhstan State University in Ust-Kamenogorsk, Kazakhstan, Kaz-17, from 2005-08. There, he taught over 500 students over a course of three years, staying an extra year to complete a multimedia language center at the University. In May 2011, he received his Juris Doctor from University of California, Hastings, with a concentration in International Law. He is the editor of this book.

✳

Boss Visa

*The Soviet Union saw vast networks of railroads developed
through the nation. Following the collapse of the Soviet
Union, borders were drawn up, but the railroads still
crisscrossed across borders. Few experiences were as stressful
for a Volunteer as an encounter with the transit police.*

FOR NO APPARENT REASON, THE TRAIN STOPPED AND SOLDIERS
began checking compartments. It was 8 A.M., August 1994.
Gabriella, a Moldovan-born English professor, had joined
me for two weeks' vacation in Moscow and St. Petersburg
to celebrate my thirty-fourth birthday and my first train ride
out of Moldova in a year. We taught at the State University
Alec Russo in Balți, an industrial city of 250,000 known for its
cognac factories. Feeling exhausted but gratified, we'd boarded
the train in St. Petersburg, destination Chisinau, Moldova's
capital. This required three days of travel, with border crossings
through Byelorussia, the Ukraine, and into Moldova. We'd
weathered delays, track changes, long lines, and were running
nearly a day behind schedule. Not bad by Soviet meltdown
standards.

Perhaps the Ukrainian soldier sensed that Gabriella and I
were in love because a look of anguish reddened his features.
A willowy blonde with watery gray-blue eyes, he studied my
passport with such curiosity that I had to assume he'd never

faced an American. I'd bribed, danced the *hora*, and polluted myself with vodka and wine in consort with *apparatchiks*, ex-KGB operatives, train conductors, gypsies, cops, retired Ministry officials, students, teachers, and soldiers alike. Though armed and in uniform, this boy reeked of virginity. He told me I'd have to get off the train because my three-day Ukrainian transit visa had expired during the night.

Gabriella protested that no one had said a word at the borders of Russia and Byelorussia. She explained that we were colleagues, and I worked through a program called Peace Corps, new to the former USSR, funded by the U.S. government. As a Volunteer, I received no pay for teaching. By mid-August, we both had to return to work.

Earnest, solemn, perhaps a little drunk on power, the soldier insisted nothing could be done. In Byelorussia, I'd bribed a conductor fifteen bucks so Gabriella and I could have a bunk where we'd made love as the stars rolled past our window. I considered bribing this soldier when another one appeared, just as young. After a year of greasing palms, I'd learned it was impossible to do so once a second authority figure appeared. Gabriella began to cry, begging them to reconsider.

As she pleaded our case, both soldiers appeared to respect her fine Russian diction (she'd been raised on military bases in Siberia). This didn't stop them, however, from shoving me down the aisle and out the train's open door.

Cell phones, at that time, along with laptops and Internet connections existed in rare quantities, even among Moscow's elite. I'd asked Gabriella to contact the Peace Corps office in Chisinau if she didn't hear from me during the next two days. I had no idea how I'd get in touch with her, but I'd worry about that later.

Watching the train roll out of sight, I heard the echo of her tears in all their sincerity. I felt paralyzed and dizzy with anger.

Not about my fate, but hers. How could those boys have done that to a woman so lovely and one of their own? It was another example of the cruelty I'd seen Soviet citizens inflict on each other, and I assumed it came out of frustration.

I inventoried what I had: some Moldovan coupons, my passport, a plastic sack that held short pants and a t-shirt, and $60 dollars worth of crisp new greenbacks. Nobody accepted bills that were creased, torn, stained, or more than five years old.

Making my way to a small square building where a dog slept out front next to a bench, I gauged the horizon, saw no trees, and wished I'd brought a hat. I dawdled near hollyhocks that stood as tall as the building and scented the air. No breezes stirred. Behind the building, I found an adjoining room made of limestone blocks. Its two window openings without glass, its door squeaking, I entered and addressed two uniformed soldiers. One remained seated, indifferent, a cigarette glued to his lower lip as he played a hand-held computer game that sounded little blips. The older one, fair-skinned with a mustache and an orangeade tint to his short hair, faced me across a desk and asked for my passport. Not thinking, I handed it over.

He tried to speak English, blanching when I told him in Russian (Gabriella had been my teacher, and that's how we'd met) that I spoke his language.

He asked my nationality. I told him American.

"No." He scowled at me. This was his game, not mine. "Your nationality."

I held my ground and repeated myself.

Sounding angry, he insisted that American was a form of citizenship, a system, not a nationality. I disagreed, but kept my lips sealed as I watched him take a form out of his desk, instructing I read and sign it. It stated I had no translator and lacked a correct transit visa. I could have my passport if I signed. I did so. He didn't return my passport.

A new pair of soldiers arrived, and the old pair left. The new supervisor could have doubled for the old one, except he wore no mustache. A crystalline glint hardened his hazel eyes. His wing man didn't play computer games; he held a Kalashnikov in two hands and kept it pointed at me.

Grabbing a fly swatter off the desk, slapping it against his thigh, the supervisor circled me as I sat and pickled in my own juices. He asked if I wanted to hear a joke. Why not? He shared it in a vivid style, rife with details, and I was careful to laugh even when I didn't grasp the humor. I kept a wary eye on the Kalashnikov. Twice in my life I'd had a gun pointed at me. I relied on a trick I'd used in both cases. Biting my lower lip, I breathed through my nose and imagined a smooth lake at sunrise.

He filed my passport into his shirt pocket. Trains to Kiev would pass through, but he couldn't say when, probably late at night. Nobody knew anything anymore. Only God knew. He leered at me and suggested I relax in front of the building. Eventually, I could get to Kiev and buy a transit visa there. Trying not to sulk, I told him I lacked enough money to pay for a night in Kiev, a transit visa, and a train ticket to Chisinau.

He shrugged and ordered me out of his building.

I wandered down the railroad tracks for a while, found a bottle and smashed the anger out of my system. I looked around. The horizon made me feel puny. The tracks angled off into a haze of heat ripples. Much of the land had been tilled, stretching like sun-scorched rhino hide and motionless in every direction.

While I hiked back to the building, I decided to ask for permission to board a train to Odessa rather than Kiev. I'd be closer to Chisinau, about three hours away. The ticket would be cheaper, perhaps leaving me enough to afford a visa.

With the sun at its noon peak, the building an oven (nothing was air conditioned or refrigerated in this part of the world), the supervisor's face gleamed with sweat. He seemed impressed as he smoked a cigarette, pondering my suggestion. I asked if Odessa had an airport. Could I buy a transit visa there? He said maybe. I should wait out front. He'd make a call. His man with the Kalashnikov led me out.

I had the sun to measure time by. About an hour later, the Kalashnikov poking my ribs, I was ushered back and granted permission to ride to Odessa, but had to wait until 5 P.M. He asked if I'd exchange five American dollars for 150,000 Ukrainian coupons. I said I had no idea if that was a fair rate. Toying with me, he joked that as an American I surely missed toilet paper, and wouldn't all those coupons come in handy? This brought sniveling laughter from his sidekick. Then he chased me out.

At the front of the building, under a sign that read *KACCA*, my spirits rose when I saw through the ticket window a woman seated behind her desk. She wore the customary Soviet blue smock. I tried to get her attention, but she ignored me.

A railroad man appeared. Paunchy, with the bulbous nose of a drinker, he wore a bright orange vest. I asked if I could buy a ticket to Odessa. He shrugged and walked away, mumbling, "It's your problem, not mine."

The dog still lay asleep. My forehead baked. I sat on the bench and napped, hour by hour more thirsty. As five o'clock neared, the sun began to cool, and there arrived two skinny boys with primitive fishing gear, followed by an old man with a girl, perhaps his granddaughter. They stood in line at the window as if this were proper etiquette. The old man got the woman's attention. She shouted, "Go away."

More villagers had gathered, true peasants, looking as if they'd emerged hunched over from long hibernation in the earth, their faces wretched with road grime and sweat, their backs bent, many no doubt having walked a great distance to meet their train. Two stout women in wool skirts and beat-up slippers, their opaque nylons and long-sleeved sweaters over legs and arms like thick beams, each gripped in red hands one corner of a burlap sack of potatoes and onions, lugging it between them one slow step at a time. They wore bright yellow and orange kerchiefs on their heads, their faces seared a dusty crimson, their eyes a bit mean. Over their shoulders hung gym bags, and as they put them down I saw they were packed full of loaves of bread, jars of homemade sour cream, and tubes of kielbasa.

They dropped the big burlap sack on the platform and sat on it, their backs to each other, hands on their knees, scars and scabs in plain view as they sighed and lolled about on their heavy bottoms. They ripped hunks from one loaf of bread, using a knife to carve kielbasa and onion, looking annoyed by heat, flies, and mosquitoes as they chewed ever so pensively with their black teeth, and they sweated, drinking now and then from an unlabeled bottle that experience assured me was full of the moonshine the Ukrainians called *gorilka*, the Russians called *samagon*, and the Moldovans called *rachiu*. I'd been treated to them all, distilled from ingredients that ranged from rotten apricots to apple cores, lengths of wood and strips of leather. In the words of poet Andrei Codrescu: "Drinking is a Russian religion with a complex metaphysic."

At quarter to five, the ticket window opened, a line formed and I waited my turn. I explained everything to the woman. She refused to help me without my passport, so I ran back to the soldiers, interrupting their session with a bottle of vodka, a loaf of bread, and a raw onion. The supervisor looked annoyed. He said no ticket, no passport.

I ran back to the window. A sleek long-distance train had arrived from Russia, olive green with lots of cars and sleeper compartments and a red star fixed to the locomotive's nose. "No," said the woman. "Get your passport."

Hurrying back to the soldiers, desperate now, I begged for my passport. They scowled at me as if despising any show of weakness. Teeth clenched, I waited, watching them each down 100 grams of vodka from the same glass.

At last, bleary-eyed and looking bored the supervisor flung my passport out a window, laughing as I chased after it. I ran to the ticket woman, who took my money. All other passengers had already boarded. The train had slowed but hadn't really stopped. The woman shoved the money back at me, crying, "Go, go, go."

I was too late. Doors had closed, the train rolled and I ran alongside, yelling "Stop" until sweat stung my eyes and I gave up. My ribs heaved as I tried to catch my breath. Muttering, cursing like a lunatic, kicking loose gravel, I stumbled over railroad ties, blind with rage. As I moved further away from the building, I reminded myself that I had my passport back and could now do as I pleased.

Spotting a linden tree, I crossed what seemed an endless plowed field and crashed in its shade. I rested a while, the echo of Gabriella's weeping still fresh. I thought about her family, and how they and so many other Moldovans had given the best of what they had to help me. I'd been treated like a prince in village homes with dirt floors, in homemade saunas, in sparely furnished block apartments without heat or running water. I'd listened to peasants and intellectuals alike explain how they'd woken up one day to learn that thousands of rubles they'd squirreled away had been devalued and rendered worthless. The Marxist dream they'd studied and sworn allegiance to, no longer existed. No new money, only coupons. No rule of law to help those in cities like Bălţi where unemployment hovered at 90 percent and packs of wild dogs and drunken men assaulted the innocent by night.

How they waited in line all day to hoard whatever they could find, to learn again no bread or milk had arrived, and it seemed no worker would ever get paid, no pensions would come, nor would there ever again be gas or electricity. The old lived on memories and nostalgia. Hadn't it been a golden time? The young dreamed of what might be if only they could get out. Anywhere but here. One day a vigorous leader would rise up, and a new economic system would replace this decaying outmoded engine. Who was a peasant to trust? Old kopeks and ruble bank notes spoke of a nightmare of loss: Stalin's trains, gulags, nearly 20 million dead in World War II, pogroms, the overnight disappearance of family members, many of whom had fought Nazis in defense of a new bold nation that in theory would never resort to fascism.

My face to the sun, fists clenched, I screamed until my vocal chords hurt, and I felt better. I walked railroad tracks until my feet grew blisters inside sneakers that turned black from pumice and creosote. The sun like a lozenge stewed in its dim orange glow.

Vast angling fields of wheat began to shrink into a quilt of smaller garden plots. In the distance, people tilled crops by hand, their bodies tiny in silhouette against a spreading wash of crimson. A slender dirt road with dried wagon ruts emerged from between two plots and ran parallel to the tracks. I took it. Walking became easier and I felt safer, at ease, in a different phase of what I thought of as my boss visa adventure. Who would believe it?

Runnels of sweat snaked down my back as I moved on inspired by the sight of a factory smokestack on the horizon. Goats munched grasses along the road. I cursed myself for leaving my knife and matches with Gabriella. I smiled at the sight of a motorcycle with a sidecar, its headlight on, idling in a field. A man and a woman unearthed lengths of what appeared to be asparagus, stuffing them into the sidecar. Only a sliver of scarlet lit the horizon. The sidecar full, the woman rode behind her man, both hands around his waist as they bounced out of sight.

I kept a dogged, sputtering pace. Passing a woman with a young girl, my voice brittle and cracking, I asked if Moldova was far and whether a town was nearby. Startled by my accent, she pulled the girl close to her skirt. I asked about a bus or train, but she refused to answer.

Slapping at mosquitoes, walking on, soothed by the amber twilight that settled over the earth, dank evening air cooling my face, I turned right at an intersection and headed down a tree-lined dirt road fragrant with fat green leaves. Passing limestone block walls, the rusting metal and paint of the hammer-and-sickle insignia at the center of an arch that ran high over a gated entrance chained up for the night, I heard dogs barking, my pace brisk as I kept to the road. I reached a sign for Mardarovka, 10 Kilometers. Chickens clucked in matted chicory and fragrant onion grass. Houses appeared, with high steel fences painted green and blue, trimmed in white, their gates shut, each a self-contained compound with fruit-bearing trees, a corncrib and a pungent barnyard aroma.

A trio of teenaged boys, each in sandals, t-shirt and polyester sweatpants, sized me up. I hurried past them. One I would talk to, but not three. As I neared a limestone block building, a dog chased me out of the dark. I sprinted away until nearly running over a burly peasant woman. After dodging me, she picked up a rock and heaved it at the dog, nailing it on the snout. Then she shooed it off with a big stick. Winded, a bit stunned, I thanked her and asked if there was a train station nearby. She grinned with a whiff of malice tainted by alcohol, showing a full metal jacket of gold teeth, and raving in slangy Ukrainian that I didn't understand.

Around midnight, I found a train station, and a startling amount of activity. I used a dollar to buy six bottles of water and some large confections of baked dough and white cheese that the Moldovans call *placenta*. What did the Ukrainians call them?

Bread and water had never tasted better. I drank three bottles, Arcasul brand, which was Moldovan and meant I was getting closer. I couldn't find a public phone. I asked about busses and trains. There used to be a bus to Chisinau, but like everything else it couldn't be relied on. Yes, I was still far from the Moldovan border. My best bet was a train coming from Moscow through to Odessa.

My spirits lifted, I sat in the grass in front of the station and listened to The Scorpions sing "Winds Of Change," one of Gabriella's favorites and an anthem for the Perestroika generation. It played from a kiosk where villagers could buy cigarettes, Snickers bars, vodka and homemade cassettes. Ace of Base was singing "Happy Nation" when the Odessa train arrived. I bribed a female conductor with a five-dollar bill. She gasped in delight and led me to a berth I had to share with two older men who argued that it was their berth; they'd paid good money for it. The conductor ignored them. Neither man looked happy when they saw my filthy socks and bleeding feet. My sneakers off, I climbed up into a bunk and passed out.

I arrived at two A.M. to a bustling Odessa. Briny air, cleansed by an occasional breeze off the Black Sea, hugged my skin. I walked sidewalks heaved, sunken, pitted and dusty, a faint whiff of the sewer about them. In Lenin Square I found a park and under a row of plane trees slept on a bench until a flashlight beam awakened me and two uniformed cops asked for my passport, looked it over and explained I couldn't sleep there, but could join others in the train station where it was safer.

Leaving those cops, I felt grateful as I returned to the station and sat on its granite steps, joining many others, some waiting for rides, some loitering. I watched the streaming of traffic, most of it taxis circling a rotary that was home to an outdoor café called Arena, with sea-blue lights around a water fountain and a disco glitter ball that peppered nearby buildings, trees and dozens of white plastic café tables and chairs where young new Russians drank under Pepsi and Coke and Camel cigarette umbrellas. As the song "Lady in Red" filled the night sky, a woman approached and asked if I needed an apartment. Her eyes lit up as I explained my situation. She knew a place where for a hundred cash per night I could sleep on the floor.

A crew of sidewalk sweepers appeared, most of them humorless old women in kerchiefs and blue smocks, some barefoot, some in slippers, each stooped over short-handled brooms that looked like thorn bushes. They kicked up enough dirt to scare the mob, about thirty strong, off those steps and around the station to a side entrance.

Like many Soviet public buildings, the train station was massive, but old enough to evoke Odessa's international past with its mix of Italian and French architecture, four polished marble staircases, and a domed cupola roof. From the top of the centrally located staircase, a monolithic statue of Lenin gazed down upon those who entered. In this case, a wee-hour army of drunks, homeless beggars, cripples, and seasoned drifters carrying sheets of cardboard to sleep on. I watched them quickly turn the station into a dormitory as they occupied each sliver of floor space. I had to step around their bodies, some of them already snoring, until I found a spot at the base of the Lenin statue.

I slept that first night shivering through vile dreams, both hands on my passport. In the morning, I stumbled into the white gold of sunrise, and it occurred to me that no one on the planet knew my whereabouts. I could stay here, create a new identity and start my life over. It was a Sunday. Winsome, fearless—what did I have to lose? I wandered in awe of Odessa's diverse architecture, her lanes and boulevards and views of the Black Sea. I walked mile after mile, at times disturbed by the number and condition of beggars and amputees. I changed dollars into coupons, keeping my money hidden at all times. I learned there was no train to the airport, only one bus. A cab would cost me 100,000 Ukrainian coupons. For one coupon, I bought a loaf of bread and two-dozen plums, toting them in my sack. When I bought water I downed the whole bottle, leaving the empty bottle for a beggar.

Blisters throbbed, bleeding through my socks, yet I liked the aimless drift in sunshine, energized by throngs of beachgoers. I worried about not having enough cash to pay for a visa, and tried not to dwell on it as I slummed through outdoor markets and rode crowded busses and trolleys. I learned from a cabbie whose taxi was a converted ambulance that I could find an international phone at the airport. It was noon when I took a bus there, a two-hour wait for a half-hour ride. I'd need to wait two days before the visa issuing office opened. I phoned Gabriella. Our connection lasted about a minute before getting cut. I'd had to shout, but at least she knew I was safe. After walking back to the train station, a three-hour hike, I decided to bathe in the Black Sea.

Though I found the beach surprisingly litter free and ascribed it to a culture that had yet to adopt ridiculous amounts of packaging, it was too crowded for my thoroughly American need for personal space. Naked boys and girls peed at water's edge. Far too many dogs paddled to masters, some of them quite plump for their Speedos. I swam in my underwear, scouring off the road without guilt, and no one even bothered to take a second glance. Then I napped blissfully on hot grayish sand, relieved that none of my belongings had been stolen.

On my way to the train station, I found a length of cardboard to my liking. While sleeping a second night, a cop kicked me in the ribs and asked what the hell I was doing there. Taking my cue from the other drifters, I didn't tell him. I got up and walked away. He didn't care. He just kicked another set of ribs and asked the same question.

On Tuesday, the visa office was supposed to open at eleven, and so I showed up around ten expecting a wait. I sat with two Syrian men, both of them striking in handsome suits. I began speaking to them in Russian, and they looked stunned when they learned where I was from. Neither had ever met an American. I chatted and they listened politely. They didn't smile, but seemed genuinely entertained as I told them my story. Three hours later, a cherubic officer in uniform arrived with a brown-bag lunch and a bottle of vodka. He happily took my fifteen dollars and stamped my passport.

The next morning, I clawed my way on board a local diesel bound for Chisinau. Out of the mob of passengers, some of whom crawled through windows to get in, I was likely the only one who'd bothered to buy a ticket for this short-distance turtle with wooden benches. When my passport was asked for, I thought twice before handing it over. It was returned without comment. I stood most of the way, squeezed between other passengers, all of us sweat-soaked, smelly and miserable. I didn't care. I amused myself by thinking of different ways to tell this story. I'd use hyperbole, an audacious style, starting with: "There I was, alone in the middle of nowhere, Gabriella's tears weighing on my heart...."

John Flynn taught Advanced ESL and American Literature to future Moldovan language instructors at the State University Alec Russo in Balți, Republic of Moldova from 1991-93. He has published six poetry chapbooks, one short story collection, Something Grand, *and a volume of translations* Blackbird Once Wild Now Tame *from the Moldovan poet and historian Nicolae Dabija. In 1998, his book* Moments Between Cities *earned the prize for best poetry volume by a RPC Volunteer. He's been nominated for a Pushcart Prize, and earned awards from HG Roberts Foundation, Virginia Poetry Society, and Worcester County Poetry Association. His* Seven Postcards From a Former Soviet Republic, *based on PC experiences, earned the Erika Mumford Prize from the New England Poetry Club. His first novel,* Heaven Is a City Where Your Language Isn't Spoken *came out in early 2011 from Cervena Barva Press. For a sample of his published work go to www.EditRed.com/ionelajo.*

PEGGY HANSON

Cowards Die a Thousand Deaths

*Seeing local class disciplinary measures can
also be a source of culture shock.*

EIGHTY KIDS PER CLASSROOM DAUNTED ME AT TWENTY-TWO. IT
would daunt me at my current age. In less than six weeks, I'd
lost control of my students, who lost their interest when the
novelty of having a foreign teacher wore off and they couldn't
understand a word she was saying, having never heard a word
of English spoken previously. So what if we were in *Book
Six* according to the national curriculum requirements? They
wanted rote assignments as they'd always had. How strange to
deal with English as a communication tool.

Within six months my students had taught me far more language skills than I would ever teach them. "*Konusmayin!* Don't
talk!" I'd shout in my sleep. "*Oturun!* Sit down!"

When I asked Abdullah Bey, the math teacher, how his
classroom always seemed quiet, he swirled his tea in its tulip-
shaped glass, smiled gently and said, "They know I will beat
them. You must beat Turkish students. They expect it." I
hated the idea. Un-American, right? Yet, I'd been sent out
by President Kennedy himself to do something—teach some

English—and that wasn't going well. Somehow, I had to instill some discipline into my classroom.

About then we got a new principal at Cankiri Lisesi. His name was Veli Soysal, nicknamed "Deli Veli, Crazy Veli" because of his ferocious temper and cruelty. He'd been sent to our little provincial town to bring order—this was his thirtieth or something assignment in a twenty-year career. He was the last resort of every school, and quickly sent on when parents protested. I was terrified just to hear him give the weekly speech with students standing outside the school saluting the flag. I had nightmares featuring his bull-like features. Deli Veli. Deli Veli...

It is always tempting to remove oneself from a threat, and I tried to pretend Veli Bey wasn't there, that we had a normal person in charge, that nothing would happen to all of us just because Deli Veli was in Cankiri. One day I had had it with Orta III, the last year of middle school. Eighth graders. Three to a hard wooden desk, those near the windows freezing, those near the pot-bellied coal stove too hot. Spitballs flew. Chatter, chatter, chatter. My head ached and I had a sore throat.

"The next person who talks out of turn will go to the principal!" I realized the desperation in my voice wouldn't convince anyone. I somehow had to get these kids' attention. Somebody talked. It was a boy near the back who I felt had smirked during part of the lesson.

"You!" I shouted. "To the principal!" The room grew quiet. The boy got up and left. I taught the rest of the lesson. After school I got a message that Veli Bey wanted to see me. Knees shaking, I went to his office. There, black and blue and bleeding stood the boy I had sent earlier. "I want you to see that this delinquent will not bother you again," said the principal. He brought his fists out and hit the boy, then kicked him. I wanted to gather the thin frame into my arms to comfort him.

Instead, I stood frozen with fear and self-loathing. I have no memory of getting out of that room. But Veli wasn't finished. He came to my classroom and dragged his demoralized victim to the front. "This dog dared to insult our foreign teacher! (Bam!) This is what happens to anyone who does that. (Kick.) We are Turks. We do not tolerate this."

Word spread like wildfire. For a few weeks, all my classrooms were quiet. The boy in the back never got back even a smile, to say nothing of a smirk. I'm sure I gave him an A on everything. His face haunted me at night.

Then one day, as I walked the aisles giving dictation, an older student who had failed a number of years made a low-pitched comment as I passed his desk. My Turkish wasn't good enough to understand the words, but the meaning was clear. Without thinking, I turned and slapped his face. (Abdullah Bey said beat them, right?)

Ali was nearly my age and not about to take public humiliation from anyone, especially a woman, an infidel. He rose in a fury to deal with me. The boys in the class jumped to their feet, grabbed Ali, and held him away from me. Voice shaking, finger pointing, I said into shocked silence, "Get out. Do not come to my class again. Get out!"

Ali went. Obviously, I would never send anyone else to Deli Veli. The students had figured this out some time ago. Somehow, we made it to the bell.

My nightmares grew exponentially worse after the Ali incident. I was guilty for going against my own culture in hitting Ali. I was guilty for sending the first student to Deli Veli in the first place. I was even guilty for not sending this student to the principal. I couldn't do it. They might kill each other. It was a grim era of self-doubt. Was I so pliable that this Anatolian town could take me and mold me, tear me away from what I had thought I knew about principles?

I was frightened to death of Ali. Abdullah Bey told me one day in the teacher's lounge that he had been permanently expelled by the principal. Some of the boys from the class had told Veli Bey about the classroom incident. I shuddered at the thought of the two violent personalities confronting one another. I remembered the mask of hate and anger on Ali's face that day in the classroom. Try as I might to forget, I remembered Veli Bey's beating of the other boy in my presence. Home! If I could only go home. But it would be as a lesser person when I did. A person who could hit a student. A person who could cause a student to be hurt by someone who viewed himself as my accomplice.

A few nights later I attended a teachers' party. Deli Veli was there. My heart jumped into my throat. Perhaps I would faint when he came near me. He's coming. Oh, no! My knees hit each other. Veli Bey's face was bewildered, almost kind. Hurt. He came up to me where no one else could hear and said, "Why didn't you tell me?"

It's hard to talk around a heart in one's throat. I mumbled something, probably in English, and moved away. Every day, I expected retribution from Ali. Fear became my constant companion. It was not a question of whether, but of where and how he would get me. It was nearing sunset as I walked home that day, down the cobblestone streets to where the bridge lay over the river. I had bought tomatoes and lamb chops for dinner, which I carried in a typical string bag.

As I started across the bridge, I realized that Ali was coming toward me. No one else around. Just Ali. How perfect for him. I wanted to collapse. You don't collapse when you want to. Undoubtedly, I was in my last moments. This was it. Somehow, I got up the courage to look directly at Ali, as though I were not afraid. At least I would see what came at me.

What came at me was a large grin and a salute from Ali. Relief flowed from head to foot, like a cooling waterfall. I managed a small smile. Bracing my shoulders, I went on across the bridge, determined that having been given another chance at life, I shouldn't waste it.

That night, I decided being a Peace Corps Volunteer wasn't so bad, after all. Not that I'd considered leaving—this was the sixties, after all, and President Kennedy had sent me. Everyone was counting on me. Quitting was not an option.

Like the others in my group, I was on an idealistic mission here in Turkey. At least, that's what people in America thought. Was I a fraud? This didn't feel idealistic. As time progressed, the mission's boundaries had become less clear than they were back in Washington. Was I learning nothing? What was the point?

In the end, I decided I would stay in Cankiri, put one foot ahead of the other and try to teach a little English. That had been the assignment.

I had learned something about my own boundaries, at least.

Peggy Hanson was a Peace Corps volunteer and English teacher in Turkey, T-1, and Yemen. She has been a broadcaster for Voice of America in Washington and India.

✳

Unarmed Man

*Sometimes frustration trumps the little rituals
that maintain the status quo.*

I ARRIVED IN MY VILLAGE THREE MONTHS AFTER JOHN LEFT. JOHN
was the first Peace Corps Volunteer to spend two years in this
town of 7,000, just a few kilometers south of Russia and almost
inside Siberia. John was the first Volunteer to endure this
town's negative 40-degree winters, its admiration for foreigners, and its love of vodka. Although I never met him, I spent
my entire two years in this town competing with John. In the
first months of my service, people called me John out of habit;
that is what they were used to calling the American Volunteer.
Most people, however, when I said, "I am Alex, not John,"
would apologize, introduce themselves, then would strike up a
friendly conversation. Usually these encounters would end in a
handshake, an exchange of telephone numbers or even a shot
of vodka. This story is an exception.

It is my second December in Kazakhstan. There is one local
drunk who, despite the fact that I have lived in this town for
seventeen months and have corrected him on numerous occasions, still calls me John. I run into him twice a week and every

time I see him, he approaches me with his oversized and fetid leather coat hanging off his body, his arms not even through the sleeves—as a child feigns dismemberment after a pretend duel with the Black Knight—and he shouts, "John, hello!"

I hate this man.

My assignment in Kazakhstan is located in a region the State Department might classify as a "hardship post." State pays its Foreign Service officers extra money if they work in areas where living conditions vary substantially from those of the United States. The Peace Corps, on the other hand, sends its Volunteers into exile in Siberia for a couple of dollars each day. We become jaded, I admit, but we also grow. We learn to cope with our situations, to learn from our experiences, and to become active and vested members of our communities instead of mere observers and commentators.

Our encounters are always brief and follow a rigid pattern. As soon as I see him, I dread the next sixty seconds of my life. He spots me and shouts "John, hello! Do you speak English?"

"Yes, I do," I respond.

He then scoots close to me and bumps me with his shoulder as he tries to force out the few English words he knows. "A…A…American. Y…You. J…J…John. Hello. Speak English." The smell of vodka is overwhelming. In my perfect fifth-grade Russian I tell him, once again, that my name is Alex and that it is nice to see him, and I go on my way.

For over a year, the same episode has replayed every few days. It would not have bothered me had he not called me John every single time. John. Every single time. Over a year. I gradually become hostile. I tell him to stop calling me John. I tell him my name is Alex. I tell him he drinks too much and it affects his memory. I tell him to stop bumping me. I even anticipate his bumps and bump back on a few occasions. No matter what I do, he sees me a couple of days later and slaps me with "John, hello!"

It is a Friday morning during this expectedly cold and snowy December.

I am a teacher. School starts at 8:30 A.M. on Friday, and I have six lessons with no break; four of them are with unruly, rude, and inattentive classes that I despise. Friday is my least favorite day, and on most Fridays during this semester, I wake up in a bad mood, dreading the hours that are to come. I leave my house at 8:28. The snow is falling in handfuls and what is already on the ground had been there for months and packed down into a slippery surface that won't be cleared until April. The temperature is about -20 Celsius (-4 Fahrenheit) and the sky is pitch black. Because of our heightened latitude, today there will only be about five hours of light. This day has all the components of a shitty day, except one. But as I stumble across the town square, already late to work, I see that final component walking in my direction.

At first it is merely a silhouette against the light of the street lamp reflecting off the snow, drunkenly trying to find a path in the fresh powder. We move closer to each other, and the silhouette identifies himself by the unencumbered flopping of his jacket sleeves.

"John!" The figure cries, shattering my will to live.

"No," I think, "I'm not in the mood; I can't take this right now."

He, however, is in the mood. He is also transporting at least a liter of vodka within his bloodstream at 8:30 A.M. this morning. I do not respond. I just walk by, thinking I will walk a little faster and get away from him. He pursues me, having yet to bump me with his shoulder. Walking in these difficult conditions, he has an advantage over me. He has lived here all his life and easily adapts to snowy and icy terrain. Me, I fall down.

I try to get away and he is walking beside me, bumping me and calling me John. I can feel myself becoming angry, and I hear myself thinking "I am going to hit this man, and for no reason other than his calling me John." I dash away those thoughts. "No. I'm not hitting anyone. Ignore him." And just as I tell myself to ignore him, he nudges me one more time, takes a few quick steps ahead of me and stops right in my path.

I don't know what prompted his change in behavior that day, why he pursued me, confronted me that morning. Perhaps the difference was that we always saw each other in the afternoons and his intoxication was at a different level in the morning. Perhaps it was that I always acknowledged him and corrected him. We had a ritual, and we broke it that black December morning when I hit him. He stopped in my way, and instead of moving around him, I continued on my path and put a stiff arm out in front of myself. He hit the ice and I stopped. My heart fell into my stomach, and the images of all of our past encounters hit me like a brick in the face. I looked around to see if anyone had witnessed what I just did. It was dark. No one saw, but I was still guilty of hitting an innocent and unarmed man.

Unarmed man—*noun*: a man with no arms.

I helped him up and apologized profusely. He scurried off, eager to distance himself from me, and after a taking few steps he looked back at me and mumbled "Fuck you, Alex."

I stood for a moment and watched him disappear into the fog and the falling snow, unaware of the time, the cold or the awful children that waited for me at school. Finally, he remembered my name!

Alexander Briggs taught English to 5th- through 11th-grade students and served as faculty advisor to comedy troupes, English clubs, basket-ball teams, and break-dancing groups in Kazakhstan, Kaz-17, from 2005-07. Upon returning to the States, he continued working as an educator in a Brooklyn, New York high school. He currently attends Seton Hall University School of Law in Newark, New Jersey, and upon graduation in 2012, intends to use his language skills and inter-national experience to pursue a career in international law.

SHAUN INGALLS

Two Tongues

When learning the subtleties of language really matter.

THE INTIMIDATION AND SELF-DOUBT SET IN WHEN I RECEIVED MY invitation to be a university English language instructor in Kyrgyzstan. It wasn't the job title that scared me. I had recently completed my student teaching in a local junior high, and I was excited to take on the challenge of teaching in a foreign land. Something else raised my anxiety level to a place it had never been before. It was about two-thirds down the page in the section labeled "Languages Spoken: Kyrgyz and Russian," when my stomach wrenched involuntarily and the cold sweat formed rivulets in my armpits.

Two languages. I will be learning two languages. Repeating to myself silently, then out loud. There must be some kind of mistake! I had barely survived high school Spanish. I studied Farsi in college because there were only about ten people in each class and I figured my survival rate would increase as the professor-student ratio dropped. Now I just felt like God was playing some kind of sick joke. I imagine my God is very playful and has a fantastic sense of humor. Not this time. I wasn't laughing.

Training in Kyrgyzstan was exciting. The sink-or-swim conditions proved surprisingly effective. The first few weeks were pretty intense. We learned basic survival words and phrases in both languages. Then we started concentrating on our designated "primary" language. If a Volunteer was going into a remote village, they spent the bulk of their training time learning Kyrgyz. Volunteers in the cities and universities spent their time learning Russian. This is a very simple explanation for a very complex sociopolitical rationale for learning both languages. All told, I spent about three weeks learning Kyrgyz and the rest of the time with Russian. Survival was the name of the game. If you wanted to spend $10 for a ten-minute cab ride, you neglected your studies. If you wanted to be lost on a bus as it rattled its way through the suburbs of Bishkek, you didn't practice your phrases for direction. If you liked being interrogated by police officers for three hours, you never learned how to say, "I'm a Peace Corps Volunteer, and you are in violation of the Geneva Convention!" Needless to say, three months is not much time to learn two languages well. However, we did practice quite a bit and everyone in my group understood the seriousness of our situation. We learned two languages, period. Russian and Kyrgyz. *Dva yazikov. Ekee teel.*

The use of two languages, three if you include English, presented several opportunities for misunderstanding. One of those situations occurred on a cold winter morning in the middle of nowhere. One icy February weekend, I decided to visit a fellow Volunteer. His site was the last stop on a desolate road that led to…somewhere in another country. The busses were unreliable, infrequent, and fully loaded with an assortment of people, beans, potatoes, sheep, chickens, and the occasional Peace Corps Volunteer. I will always remember standing in the frigid morning air, waiting for my only chance to get back to civilization—for lack of a better word. When the bus arrived, it was packed. I was resigned to stand for the two-hour journey. There was the slim chance that several passengers would get off at another town midway, a Dante-esque Purgatory of sorts. That is what I was thinking about while being supported by at least four other passengers in the rear of the bus on this very early, very cold, very crowded, and very hung-over Sunday morning.

When the bus stopped, a sense of dread always followed. Why are we stopping? Is the bus broken? Have the police stopped us? Is there an accident? A sick passenger? Or worse, are we picking up MORE people? Then I saw them, three young men. Three very loud, very drunk men, pushing their way onto the bus—not out of rudeness mind you. The pushing was simply a matter of physics. They were getting on and sheer force was the only way they could displace those of us already standing in the aisle. As they entered the bus, the tallest one looked directly at me and said something. He said it loudly. He said it clearly.

This is what I heard: "*Ya loobloo teebyeh!*"

Now, I knew enough basic Russian to know that it meant *I love you*. In a slurred, and somewhat distorted dialect of drunk Russian, he said that he loved me. He shouted it. Now, I did not recognize this man. In fact, he didn't even resemble anyone I knew. Furthermore, he didn't say those endearing words with the facial expression one would expect. Oh, and the fact that I am a male—and was one at the time—added to the confusion. As he kept repeating this mantra, I could tell he was growing more and more agitated. His friends appeared to tighten their grip on his shoulders and their attempts to calm him intensified. I imagine my subdued grin and obvious bewilderment did not improve his demeanor. He looked like he wanted to kill me. That's when the Volunteer next to me clarified things.

"He doesn't love you, dude. He wants to KILL you! *Oobyoo*, not *loobloo*."

Ah, yes, the distinction was now clear. One simple consonant sound was about to turn our relationship upside down. Now I understood the drunk man's facial expression and all of its subtext. Now I felt the sense of fear and helplessness that he was hoping to instill in me. Oh God! You are a funny son-of-a-bitch!

Needless to say, I survived the experience. The drunk men exited the bus in Purgatory, and I lived to see another day. Kyrgyz and Russian are now forever a part of who I am and what I will always be. The fine line between love and hate has never been more visible than on that incredibly educational bus ride on that freezing February morning. *Kyrgyzstan, ya loobloo teebye*!

Shaun Ingalls served as a University English teacher at Arabaeva Pedagogical Institute in Talas, Kyrgyzstan, K-5, from 1997-99. Following his Peace Corps service, Mr. Ingalls worked as a high school generalist in a Yupik Eskimo village for two years. Since 2002, he has been teaching high school English and theater at the Southeast Career and Technical Academy in Las Vegas, Nevada, where he lives with his beautiful wife and daughter.

LISA SWAIM

*
* *

On the Rails

Hope you get good coupe mates, because it's going to be a long ride.

A HALF-MOON GLOWS THROUGH THE CLOUDS IN AN OTHERWISE dark sky. A pocket moon, which Ukrainians say means you should keep a close watch on your money. An icy cold evening in mid-winter. We're on school holidays, and I am trying to visit a friend in western Ukraine for a long weekend, but either there are no tickets or the agents are holding them back for those who can pay substantial bribes. During these early years of Ukraine's economic crisis, nearly everyone I know attempts to make some money on the side to supplement their official salaries, which are both paltry and sometimes months in coming. Most of the secondary school teachers I work with travel to Poland during their holidays to buy something there that they can resell for significantly more in Vinnytsia's market. I've had no success trying to buy a ticket. One of my teacher friends, Larissa, has taught me how to ask the conductor to take me along. In these strange times, the conductor may choose to take an extra passenger and keep the cash for himself.

If I were wise, I would stay at home. It is rare for a young woman to travel alone, especially at night, but that is when the long distance trains run. I measure my desire to see my friend who is a seven-hour and then a four-hour train ride away against the things that can go wrong. Generally, I trust. I trust in the generosity of Ukrainians, in the safety in numbers (each coupé holds four people), in my limited Ukrainian and slightly better Russian language skills, and in my feminist American "can do" notion that I can take care of myself. I am twenty-four years old.

I stand on the second track, shivering, bundled to my eyes, unable to see to the sides unless I turn my whole body fully—I turn to the right, to the left, to the right again, nervously, to steal glimpses of my fellow passengers. They are ticketed, cold but secure, mostly traveling in pairs or small groups. I see the light down the track, the noise begins, and then the monster rolls in, Soviet, sturdy, a dark green dinosaur exhaling steam, wheels smoking, slowing, and my race has begun. I have five minutes to work the train. I begin at one end: I ask repeatedly, "Do you have a free place?" to each wagon conductor. Each time, a gruff, "*Nyet.*" It's hard not to become discouraged after five or six sharp responses. Finally, it seems I have an interested partner in crime. "Take me, please, to L'viv," I implore. "O.K., I have a place...but with me," he says. I mull it over, trying to determine what he means from his smile. I decide that I'd rather wait for the next train, which was to come in a few hours. I'll have to prepare my strategy for my next race, which will be a precious six-minute attempt.

I spend the next three hours again trying to buy a ticket properly, legally, but there will be no tickets to L'viv tonight. In the train station, there are masses of people waiting, most of them now sleeping. Some of them appear to have been there for days, perhaps refugees from Chechnya. The waiting room has a hopeless air about it. It smells like body odor, stale vodka, cheap sausage from the mostly barren snack bar, urine. I witness a couple of fistfights.

It's late now, just before midnight, and there are fewer people on the track. The lights of the train and the sweet smell of burning brakes draw closer, and I'm off. "*Nyet*" "*Nyet*," "*Nyet*," "*Nyet*," "What?...*Nyet*!," "*Nyet*." Finally, a young woman conductor sizes me up and puts down the steps for me without a word. We haven't yet negotiated a price, but she must think I look to have money. "Get on," the older women lingering on the platform urge kindly before they wave goodbye to their friend already on the train. I take this as a good sign—they seem to think it is a reasonable idea for me to travel this way. I step up as the train begins to move, leaving the older women and my confidence behind.

I stand awkwardly in the corridor, having paid a fair black market price. The young conductor opens the door to a sleeping coupé and asks a question in a low voice. A man's voice answers, loudly, "Is it a boy or a girl?" Another man's voice, laughing, "If it's a girl, young, we'll take her!" The train is from Kiev, a garbled mix of Ukrainian and Russian emanate from the smoky cabin in a drunken slur. They've likely been drinking for the last five hours. Oh, God, she's going to put me in there.

I pull her aside, "Excuse me please, but is there a place with a woman? I'm a little afraid."

"No. They are policemen, and there will only be two," she answers.

I imagine the fact that they are policemen is supposed to be reassuring, but this makes me more nervous. She has me by the arm now—my options are to go in or to be thrown off at the next station—so I go in, under escort, sit down with four drunken but, it turns out, amiable fellows on the lower bunks, am offered vodka, pried at with questions.

"Are you Polish? Romanian? Ukrainian?" (This last asked out of politeness, although they know I am not) until I admit my nationality and my hometown. This sets them off into rounds of "Hello! My name is Sasha!" and "You from Frisco?"

My worry dissipates a little. Two of them are quite kind, but another is already reaching for my hand. The one who knows Frisco stands up, takes my bag and leads me down the hall away from the "drinking company" to his daughter's compartment. "There only girls," he says in English. I am grateful.

He opens a door and says proudly, "There my daughter." I peer in and see a wizened old creature, one hand up, shielding its eyes from the light. I can't tell whether the creature is a man or a woman. Frisco shuts the door again. "Excuse," he says, "I drink."

He opens the first door again, the drinking company, who welcome me back with cheers. He shuts the door, moves down the corridor in the opposite direction. The next door is his daughter's.

He settles me in, introduces me to the daughter as a "poor American" in need of a place to rest, makes my bed haphazardly so that the sheets are twisted, and goes out.

I hear loud voices from the drinking company, especially as the train stops at the stations, but they have been drinking vodka now for six or seven hours, so soon it is quiet and Frisco returns.

"Are you asleep for real?" he asks me, surprising me (an English teacher) with his use of this English idiom.

"No," I mumble.

"May I talk with you?" he asks.

"O.K.," I say.

He launches into a monologue in Russian about how difficult a time it is in Ukraine, and here I am on a train, without a ticket, how I don't know what might happen in this place. I try to determine whether he means Ukraine in general or the drinking coupé. He asks if he may take my hand. I hesitate to offer it and the woman in the bunk below me (a stranger to us both) intercedes by asking him to show his joy at meeting an American in the morning. It's quiet, dark, early morning. I can see his military watch glowing, his hand still stretched toward mine across the aisle, and then he rescinds it. I exhale, relax, feel safe enough among strangers, drift off to sleep. I'll make it by myself to L'viv and then on to Ivano-Frankivsk in the daylight. The trust has not been American hubris this time. American privilege, yes. I can afford to travel and when the time comes, I can afford to leave. I can afford to take a vacation when all around me people are struggling just to get by.

Lisa Swaim served as an English as a Foreign Language teacher at spetz-shkola N 1, a Ukrainian national school, in Vinnytsia, Ukraine, Group 2, from 1993-95. Her group of teachers was the second Peace Corps group in newly independent Ukraine, preceded by a group of business volunteers by some eight months. Since that time, Lisa has been an ESL teacher, coordinator of a study abroad program in Russia, an international student and scholar advisor at a variety of colleges and universities in the United States, and now serves as the Assistant Director of the Center for Global Engagement at Kenyon College, in Gambier, Ohio. She married fellow PC-Ukraine Volunteer John Deever in 2001, whose story appears elsewhere in this volume. They have two children, Alexandra (Sasha), 8, and Jacob, 6, who haven't yet been to see the Ukrainian region of Podillia, where their parents fell in love.

AMBER WEISS-WHITLEY

✦

Stuck

A Volunteer, a car with holes in the floor, and pool of mud.

It was Naruiz, the Kazakh New Year. While I was enjoying the dancing, socializing, and drinking that accompanied the holiday, I had the nagging suspicion that I needed to see if my host mom had ordered a taxi for the following day. Although taxis in Chapaevo weren't like those back home in Ohio, there were regular drivers of varying skill who could be called on for a ride to the city, and my host mom seemed to know all of them. When I walked in, she explained that all the taxis for the next day had been booked.

However, one of her *znakomie*—a friend of a friend of a friend as these things usually worked out—was getting ready to go to the city, and he agreed to take me. He was leaving in twenty minutes. I counted my blessings and rushed to pack.

The car pulled up, a rusted yellow Soviet-issued clunker that appeared to have been manufactured not long after the end of WWII. I swallowed the lump that had formed in my throat as I watched the driver lift the hood to hotwire the vehicle in order to start it. I took a deep breath and got in the car. I was a tough Peace Corps Volunteer, I told myself. Nothing scared me…right? Having successfully started the car, the driver shut the hood and got in, tying his door shut with a length of rope.

The weather for the past week or so had been more interesting than normal, with snow falling each morning only to melt by the afternoon, so the main road had become even more potholed. Although the end of March, Naruiz was the worst day yet, with blizzard-like snow obscuring everything and severely limiting visibility. The roads in the village were a mixture of ice and water and mud churned up more by each passing vehicle. The car rumbled onto the main road, fishtailing along the way.

This didn't seem to concern the driver, so I sat back and tried to relax. The tops of the car doors didn't sit flush, so it was actually snowing inside the car. Through the rusted out holes in the floor, I saw the road rushing by. My feet were cold from the water that had leaked into my boots. The heater in the car also wasn't working. I sighed and leaned back to watch the snow that fell through the crack in the door melt on my arms and legs. I just needed to get back to the city, and these were minor discomforts.

Somehow the vehicle managed not to shake apart for the first leg of the trip. After about an hour of driving, we reached a construction zone where bulldozers and other paving equipment sat languishing. With the road completely blocked, the driver detoured off the road to the grasslands of the steppe, where the still-lingering freeze provided extra traction in the muddy grasses. Ironically, going off-road actually felt safer than traveling on the main road, saving us from the hydroplaning and fishtailing that was not uncommon during spring and fall road trips.

Finally, we reached our last obstacle before the city: the new bridge. With the bridge still under construction, we were again forced to detour off the road. Here, the detour was muddier than anywhere else, and involved going down a steep, unpaved incline off the main road. Everyone was forced to use the same detour; drivers couldn't just travel further out into the steppe to find traction, like they could almost anywhere else. Even worse, part of the detour appeared to be under a small lake about fifty feet wide and thirty feet across, a result of the melting snow and ice.

Stopped right before the detour, we watched quietly as a Jeep in front of us rolled down the incline and bravely plowed straight through the lake. Water sprayed out from the tires of the Jeep as it crossed the lake and reached the other side. I could hear the wheels spinning in the driver's head as he contemplated whether or not his car could make it through the lake. There was no way to go around. I looked over at my fellow passengers with bewildered look, as if to ask: "Is he really going to do this?"

Every instinct I had cried out to say something, anything. Instead I sat there silently, as did the other passengers. Suddenly, the driver floored the gas, hitting the water as fast as he could, and we all instinctively leaned forward as if that would help the car push through the lake. The tension was palpable as the water level reached nearly over the tires. At first, it seemed like we were going to make it. We were ten feet in, then fifteen, and then the car ceased moving forward. The car was too heavy and too short; we were stuck.

Water began filling the car through the holes in the floor and bottom of the door. I looked around frantically, trying to find a way to avoid getting wet while hoping that the water would stop before it hit seat level. I put my feet up on the back of the driver's seat, but not before frigid water had crept through the cracked, fake leather of my boots to soak my toes and socks.

I suddenly remembered the police station on the bridge. There were law officials nearby, I thought to myself, when they saw us, they'd have to come help. Looking over at the station, I spotted three men standing outside in their gray uniforms. They were pointing toward our cab, stomachs heaving up and down, as they laughed at us. I realized that there would be no help from that group.

To my relief, the water stopped seeping into the car just below seat level. Still, there was the question of what next. The driver climbed out of the door and shimmied his way onto the roof of the car, managing to lift the hood and not fall into the lake. Once the hood was up, I could see what looked like leather jackets stuffed around the engine.

Water and smoke started spurting out everywhere as the driver tried to get the engine running again, balanced precariously on one edge and a bumper as the man in the passenger seat floored the gas. After a few minutes of more black smoke and spurting water, the driver gave up, shut the hood, and climbed back into the car where he promptly began to take off his socks and shoes and waded into the water to go find help.

We found little help from bystanders. The police at the station could be seen sometimes peeking out the window to check on us. Other cars, having learned their lesson by seeing our predicament, took a detour on the detour, avoiding the lake by going down another muddy incline. Our driver came back to the car after about ten minutes with a wire contraption that he seemed to have made with some left-over construction materials found on the side of the road and fastened it to the front of the car. Then he waded away again through the lake and went to stand by the bridge, trying to flag down a vehicle that was willing to pull us out of the mud.

By that time, we had been stuck in the lake for about forty-five minutes and my feet were getting very cold and had begun to ache. I wasn't sure how long I could go without warming up. Getting out of the car didn't seem like a good option, since that meant I would have to wade through the lake and get even wetter. However, as my feet continued to ache, this option seemed to look better and better. Another half hour, I decided, and I would get out of the car, wade in the lake, and hitch a ride from a passing vehicle.

A large dump truck came to the rescue before the half hour was up, and our driver hooked the wire contraption to the truck's bumper. Ten minutes later, we were free from the lake.

The truck stopped us not far from the police station, and we all got out as the driver tried to start the car again. After a few attempts it started, and the driver left it running while he began scooping water out of the front and back seats. More water was dripping and oozing on its own through the holes in the floorboards, like water draining from a colander.

I began to laugh. Not a full-bodied fall on the floor laugh, but rather a slightly high-pitched crazy "I can't take any more stress" giggle.

The driver looked over at me angrily as he continued to scoop water out from the back seats. "Something funny?"

"No," I answered and turned away, trying unsuccessfully to mask the convulsions shaking my shoulders.

I wasn't sure what set off the fit, but once I started laughing it was almost impossible to stop. Most of the time I lived and worked in Kazakhstan without conscious awareness of the fact that I was halfway around the world living in a culture that was as foreign to me as I was to it. I had gotten used to living there, used to the rhythms of life and work to the point that most of the time it felt natural.

It took special moments like the one I found myself in to remind me that I was indeed far from home. Yes, we were stranded not twenty feet from a police station where instead of helping the cops watched and laughed; yes, my feet felt like there were icicles inside my socks and I was worried about losing a toe; yes, it had snowed on me from the inside of a car; yes, there were holes in the floor of the car big enough to see through; and yes, like everything else, somehow it managed to work out for the best. Despite the discomforts and the obstacles of the trip, we eventually made it back to Chapevo safely, and it reminded me why I loved this country. I love Kazakhstan.

Amber Weiss-Whitely served as an English teacher in Kazakhstan, Kaz-15, from 2004-06. In addition to teaching English, she organized a teacher training seminar, summer camp, and various English clubs involving students and teachers from multiple schools. She currently resides in Cincinnati, Ohio, where she teaches freshman composition and literature. In her free time, she helps immigrants from the former Soviet Union with acclimation and language fluency.

BONNIE LANDES PURA

A Camel's Revenge

"Trust in Allah, but tie your camel." —*Arabian Proverb*

SOUNDS OF MEN SHOUTING, AND ANIMALS STOMPING, PULLED ME into consciousness early one autumn morning in 1964. It was just after the village council had decided on the most suitable living arrangements for the young single woman (me!) and the move had been made. So it took a second or two for me to realize that I needed to dress more quickly than usual because I was now smack in the middle of the village and could be called upon in an instant, for whatever reason.

The scene from my window overlooking the square was reassuring: indeed, a picture perfect Peace Corps moment. Camels from a neighboring Turkish mountain village were being relieved of their heavy burdens of firewood and one was already being loaded with huge bags of lentils, beans, and other staples for the trip back. A small crowd of village men and children stood by watching, mouths agape. It appeared that a camel had a complaint. Foam followed the petulant mouth of the lead male camel as he swung his head in protest to the heavy weight so soon again. Shouts of the camel master froze into silvery whispers as he bullied the beast into calm.

Snap! "Great, I got it! Now let's hope this picture turns out with the red from the blanket in bold contrast to the color of the camel...maybe I will have it copied to include in my Christmas notes. Oh, what's that spinning in the air? Oh my god!"

In a sudden swoop, the camel twisted, swished and swirled his powerful neck around, grabbed his master's shin and began swinging him in the air, six feet off the ground. Once, twice, three times, four times he circled there until the villagers wrestled camel and man apart. I couldn't believe my eyes.

Medical attention was needed, and it had already been established that the Peace Corps Volunteers had medical supplies! What's more, they had had medical training! At least that was the rumor. "Just how far was the PC medical kit the size of a three-ring notebook and a high school first aid course going to go in this case?" I wondered.

We met on the stairs: the young bringer-of-bad-news halfway up, medicine woman halfway down (yes, me!).

"Stop the bleeding, clean the wound, keep him warm." I could hear my head voice repeating the instructions over and over, mainly to keep my rising panic at bay.

It was two hours before the bleeding could be brought under control; this camel's teeth were three inches long. I had long since exhausted my supply of gauze and bandages and was reluctantly using the immaculate, beautifully embellished scarves the village ladies brought straight from their hope chests, to do their part. It was the fasting month of Ramadan, so the man would take nothing: not even aspirin, which was the strongest painkiller in my medical kit. When the only vehicle in the village, a rickety bus held together by baling wire and a prayer, finally started, it was 4:00 in the afternoon. This entire ordeal had begun at 7:30 in the morning.

Before the bus had pulled out, I made the village head man, whom I had come to know and trust, promise me to "let the doctor know the camel may be rabid as it was foaming at the mouth," but as they bumped off into the darkness, I doubted he would have the courage. In 1964, a villager didn't have much clout with a doctor in a modern Turkish hospital.

A few days later I heard it had taken them three hours to make the forty-kilometer trip to the hospital. A few months after that, I learned that the camel master had recovered from both the camel bite and the thirteen rabies injections to the stomach. And now, forty years later, still living in Turkey, I know that aspirin thins the blood, and camels, under stress of any kind, foam at the mouth.

What an experience that first encounter was for me, and how much I learned about Turkey, camels and human endurance, especially my own!

Bonnie Landes Pura served as a Rural Community Development (RCD) facilitator in two villages in Turkey, T-5, from 1964-66. In her second site she opened a pre-school project aimed at introducing young children to the delights and disciplines of a classroom. During a third year, as a Volunteer Representative, Bonnie assisted women in continuing RCD programs in eastern Turkey. After marrying and raising a family in Turkey, Bonnie returned to southern Ohio in 2009 to care for aging family and is active in the regional Returned Peace Corps Volunteer organization there.

M A R K   L E W A N D O W S K I

✦

Caroline

What happens when we are far away from home,
caught between our values and love?

YOU MIGHT DECIDE THAT THIS IS A LOVE STORY, BUT IT BEGINS IN
the most unlikely place: on the two-mile stretch of road
between Auschwitz and Birkenau, the largest of all Nazi concentration camps, not long before the road became congested
with Orbis tour busses carting day-tripping foreigners to the
camps from Warsaw or Cracow, and with German or Italian
cars that dwarfed the ubiquitous Polski Fiat. It was the summer
of 1990, the sky was cloudless, and I was in Europe for the first
time. Since I was alone, I did my best to befriend fellow travelers, so that I'd have company seeing the sights in any one particular city. In a youth hostel in Cracow I met two American
women and convinced them to accompany me to Auschwitz.
They hadn't thought of including Auschwitz on their itinerary
because they imagined the trip unmanageable, or because of
personal ambivalence, I wasn't sure.

At Auschwitz, we walked in a daze by the displays housed
in the barracks, the panels of graphic exposition, the enlarged
photographs of malnourished children, the rooms illustrating

the typical day for a prisoner, the cases packed with the personal effects confiscated from the prisoners. But not until we visited the barracks dedicated to the Jewish plight in the Holocaust did the full force of Auschwitz hit us. Over a small urn of ashes buried in the floor of the last room in the barracks, an American rabbi offered Kaddish, a prayer for the dead. His keening voice was so heartbreaking that not even the reconstructed gas chamber, the last stop on our walking tour, could elicit the same rending emotions.

When we left Auschwitz, my companions were still crying and hanging on one another. But because we were in a hurry to catch an evening train back to Cracow, we kept up a brisk pace on the road to Birkenau. Fearing where a Polish city bus might take us, we walked the two miles. Occasionally, I heard one of my companions sniffle and wipe a nose. Once the gate of Birkenau was in sight, I quickened my step even more. I walked for a few moments before I realized my companions were not behind me. I looked back and saw them stopped on the side of the road. Busses and Polski Fiats sped past them. One of the women was at least six inches taller than the other. She held her shaking friend, who had her face buried in the taller woman's neck. I turned back to Birkenau. To the right of the gate stood a field where an old man scythed hay. A small girl, in dress and bonnet, skipped down the path he was creating through the tall hay and gathered the fallen stalks in her arms. Behind them was a horse and carriage. Whatever the girl dropped the horse lunged for and slowly chewed. The fence and front tower of the concentration camp cast their shadows across the field. The old man and the girl crossed and re-crossed the lines between light and dark.

I walked back to my companions. The taller woman smiled when I stopped in front of her, but there were fresh tears on her cheeks. Her friend was still sobbing into her neck.

"It's the Kaddish," the taller woman said.

I sighed, slid my foot through the pebbles on the road bank. "Why didn't you tell me you were Jewish?" I asked.

"We were advised not to tell anyone in Poland," she said.

That morning, on the rickety train from Cracow, we had met a Polish actor who spoke fluent English. He was on the way to Auschwitz to visit his mother, a librarian in the camp's archives. After telling us what to see in the camps, he began to defend his countrymen against the anti-Semitism they are notorious for.

"You must understand," he had said, "that Auschwitz was first built for Polish intellectuals and clergymen. They were the first victims of the Holocaust. The Jews came later. The very people most likely to make a stand against the Nazi's plans were dead before Hitler created the Ghettoes. Tell me, he asked, would small communities in your Midwest really put their own lives in danger to save Negroes?"

"Of course," my two companions replied.

"Bah!" the actor said. "Poles are more familiar with your history than you are with ours. Let me tell you something. My family is from Oswiecim, or Auschwitz, as the Nazis named it, and how history remembers it today. My mother remembers the war very well. By 1944 she had to wear a handkerchief across her face, night and day, because of the stench of burning bodies. She had little to eat. Most of what was grown in the region went to the Germans. Could she resist? Could she smuggle food for the starving Jews when she herself was going hungry?

"The penalty for asking about what was happening in the camps, or for even looking at the camps, was instant death. No trial. One false move and you got a bullet in the head. She had children to feed. My grandfather was forced into the German army. His brothers were already dead. The only people left in the town were women, children and old people. Most were worked to near death on their own farms.

"Should they have stood against the German tanks and machine guns with shovels? Do not get me wrong. Many people in my town helped Jews. They smuggled in food, clothing, and news from Cracow. Many of those were eventually caught and murdered. Not all Poles hate Jews."

"Yes," the actor had continued. "You will see skinheads in Poland. On this very train ride you will see anti-Semitic graffiti."

Sure enough, we soon passed electrical boxes with "Jewish WC" painted on them, and more than a few abandoned sheds showed a gallows with the Star of David hanging from it.

"But this is not the norm," the actor said. "Perhaps in America you occasionally see racist graffiti. The Ku Klux Klan still exists, yes? But not all Americans are part of the Ku Klux Klan."

My companions had been wary. Me? My father's parents came from Poland. I was not willing to admit that I came from anti-Semitic stock. My sister was married to a Jew, whom I would later love as a brother. We would celebrate Hanukkah with him, he, Christmas with us. My grandfather, had he been alive, would probably have rejected him. Whether this was because my grandfather was Catholic, or because he was Polish, I couldn't say. A little of both, perhaps.

Back on the road between Auschwitz and Birkenau, I continued to shuffle my feet. My companions were advised not to tell anyone that they were Jewish. Had they taken me as an anti-Semite, just because of my Polish name? Is this why they were hesitant to come to the camps with me? Paranoid, I thought.

"We can skip Birkenau," I said, my head down. "We can just wait for the train in the station."

"No," the smaller woman said, pulling away from her friend. "I'm O.K., really. I was afraid it would affect me this way. But now that I'm here I want to see everything."

She took hold of my arm and we walked to Birkenau's gate.

My companions and I made it back to the Cracow hostel, which was on the grounds of a medieval convent, just moments before the eleven o'clock curfew. The other guests were already asleep. The shorter woman went straight to bed. The taller woman and I sat at the table in the common room and wished we had beer and cigarettes. Five minutes after we sat down, the watchman came in and said that we had to go to sleep. We couldn't understand his Polish, so he had to mimic what he meant. He wasn't happy about this. We nodded, but he wouldn't leave until I opened the door to the men's dorm.

Once he was gone, the taller woman suggested that we find a place more private. If there had ever been a gulf between us created by her faith or my ancestry, it was now gone. Long lost relatives of mine very well might have turned in long lost relatives of hers to the SS for a loaf of bread. What did this matter now? We were just two college students seeking adventure in Europe, two bodies wanting warmth. We could share one night of passion, then part ways, me to Budapest, she to Prague. We would never see each other ever again.

This is what I like to think, at least. Now, when I look back at this moment, I wonder if she just needed comfort after the emotional turmoil she had experienced in the concentration camps. Even though the camps had made me weep, I knew that by the time we were alone, all thoughts of the Holocaust were buried deep inside of me. I just wanted to get into her pants.

We embraced. I grew hard. We locked arms and explored the nooks and crannies of the hostel. But every hallway led to a door. The watchman could pop out of any one of them, anytime. When we knew it was hopeless, we sighed and embraced one last time. She went back to the woman's dorm and winked at me as she opened the door. Frustrated, I slumped back to my own hard bunk.

One year later, I returned to Poland as a Peace Corps Volunteer. I was assigned to a tiny teacher's college in Biala Podlaska, a town of 50,000. During our meeting, the school's director encouraged me to have an affair with one of my students. She pulled a picture from a file.

"Her name is Kasia," the director said. "Isn't she pretty? She's smart as well. Not the smartest in the college, but not the worst."

"I don't understand," I said.

"You should have a personal relationship with her," she said.

"Are you serious?"

"A happy personal life means a happy professional life," she said, her face stern.

My director, like my students, could not understand why an American, a rich American, no doubt, would be willing to spend two years in Poland. My Polish blood made it easier for some to accept my presence. Others thought that the Peace Corps offered a way for Americans to avoid the army. Or maybe I was repaying my government for a loan, or I was slipping out of an entanglement with a pregnant woman back home. Regardless of the conclusions they drew, they would do just about anything to keep me, the only native speaker in the school, in Poland for the duration. This would include the director's offer, as well as her tendency to allow me free rein in the classroom, even while she ruled the other teachers, the secretary, and the students with an iron fist. The director instructed the students to keep me happy, which meant that they were expected to invite me to their houses for dinner, take me to their parties, ensure I wasn't alone during holidays. I soon became friends with most of my students, so I like to think that their attentions became voluntary.

I became very close to Kasia, and today, seven years after leaving Poland, we still write, and when in Europe, I visit her. We never had an affair. Instead, I fixated on Caroline.

Ah, Caroline! Even her name was special. Her real name was Malgosia.

How she acquired the American "Caroline," I never found out. There were seventeen students in the college that first semester, and four were named "Malgosia." Her nickname set her apart from the others, but she didn't need this device. Unlike most of the other students, born in Biala Podlaska or one of its surrounding hamlets, Caroline was from Warsaw. Many Poles hoped to one day live and work in Warsaw, Poland's capital and main city. That's where the good jobs and schools were, and in 1991, when Western consumer goods hadn't yet spread to the provinces, virtually anything could be bought in Warsaw. It also showcased great restaurants, theaters, world-class symphonies and opera. People who did not live in the city looked on its inhabitants with envy. Caroline dressed better than her classmates, wore brighter makeup, and spoke English more fluently. She seemed to know more about Poland and the West than anyone else, and in class, I could always rely on her for answers when the other students were stumped.

Caroline had short, auburn hair, which she tinged purple, in accordance with a Warsaw fashion. Her skin was pale, her breasts large. Her eyes were dark brown, and sparkled behind her expensive glasses. She had sharp cheeks and a pointed nose. Like Hawthorne's Georgiana, she had just one physical flaw: her two front teeth were bent inward, which made her incisors even more pronounced than usual. When she flashed a smile over french fries and beer in Biala Podlaska's one decent restaurant, I often gazed at her across the table and fantasized about taking her back to America with me and having her teeth fixed by a dentist unavailable to her in Poland, even in Warsaw.

Even though I was smitten with Caroline, I never initiated any move toward physical intimacy with her. My director had given me indirect permission to do so that first meeting. Like many Peace Corps Volunteers, I relished the attention laid upon me by the people I had been sent to help. I became uninhibited. I drank and smoked too much and flirted with woman more than I ever would have in the United States. No one in the school or in the town would have looked aghast at an affair I might have with one of my students. I was American, and this gave me privileges.

Why I didn't at least try to have an affair with Caroline that first winter is hard to say. She had a boyfriend, yes, but he lived in Warsaw. I was involved with another Peace Corps Volunteer, but she was stationed on the other side of Poland, near Poznan, seven hours away by train. There were many cold, winter nights when both Caroline and I were alone. Because Caroline was from out of town, she stayed in a miserable dormitory on the outskirts of Biala Podlaska. There was no paved road leading to it, and only occasionally did the building have sufficient heat or hot water. Our college was the only one in town, so with the exception of two of her classmates, the other residents were high school students who lived in places too far to commute from.

Her weekdays were awful. No family, no real connection to the place where she laid her head at night. I imagined that her weekdays were similar to mine. I met her every Wednesday at the restaurant in the center of town, along with other students who were interested in practicing English outside the college. During these meetings, or occasional parties, Caroline and I shared moments. Something unspoken passed from my eyes to hers. When she squeezed past me to go to the bathroom, she lingered longer than necessary behind my chair and brushed the back of my head with her fingertips. When other students invited me to their homes for the holidays, or for the weekends, she remained silent and looked down at whatever she was eating, occasionally cocking her head so she could spot me with one eye. Poles love visitors and proudly proclaim that "a guest in one's home is God in one's home." Considering how much time Caroline and I spent together, how friendly we were to one another, the fact that she never invited me to her home seemed incriminating, first to my other students, and then to me. I believed that she was afraid of what might, or might not, happen.

And maybe I was as well. I never invited her, alone, to my apartment, where there was always heat and hot water, even though I invited other students. I didn't spend significant time alone with her until my last day as a Peace Corps Volunteer in Poland. Part of me saw her as "The One," I now know. The magnitude of this feeling might have frightened me into passivity. Or the knowledge that I would have two whole years to make any serious decision about her made me patient.

Winter progressed. Our mild flirtations with one another continued. At the restaurant, she stopped mentioning her boyfriend.

Midway into the spring semester, I decided to assign each student a novel by a major American writer. Because the college owned no class sets of any one novel, the students and I had to rely on the rag-tag assortment of books collected and donated to the Peace Corps by then First Lady, Barbara Bush. Each student would prepare a paper and oral presentation about their book. On the morning I passed out the novels, I was happy to hand Caroline Saul Bellow's *Herzog*.

"This is the most difficult novel here," I told her. "But you are very capable of understanding it, and appreciating it."

I smiled. She smiled back and took the book.

After my classes that day, I graded papers in the college's office. The secretary wasn't in, and the director had the students for a phonetics class. During their break, one of the other Malgosias came in carrying Isaac Singer's *The Magician of Lublin*. She asked if she was disturbing me and waited at the door.

"Of course not," I said, waving her forward. "Please come in."

Office hours are an alien concept in Poland. Polish professors would rarely meet with a student beyond the classroom, unless it was to administer punishment, or to "ask" the student to run a personal errand. This Malgosia, who went by Margaret, hesitated at the door, which was no surprise.

"What can I do for you?" I asked.

She took a few steps forward, but still kept distance between us.

"It's this book," she said. "I can't read it."

"What do you mean? Of course you can read it. Your English is good and you have two months to finish it."

"Yes," she said. "But it's about Jews."

"Excuse me?"

"It's a Jewish book," she said. "Do you have another book to read?"

"Margaret, the author was born in Poland." I said, my voice beginning to tremble. "He won the Nobel Prize. The novel takes place in Lublin."

"I know this," she said, her voice growing quiet. "But do you have another book to read?"

Rage burned my insides. I wanted to stand, to grab the book and smack her with it. How dare you, I wanted to shout. How can anti-Semitism exist in a country where Auschwitz still stands? After I was done smacking her and yelling at her, I wanted to jam the book down her throat.

Instead, I sat there, glued to my rock-hard chair, and stared at her until she dropped her gaze to the floor. This Malgosia was a decent student. She was pregnant and engaged to be married. Maybe she thought the book too long, or too difficult, and was using this as a sick excuse. My rage began its retreat.

"Fine," I said. "Leave the book. I'll find you another."

She leaned forward and laid the book in front of me.

"Thank you," she said.

Two minutes after she left, in came Caroline, *Herzog* cradled under her arm. She wore a tight sweater and flowing, printed skirt. She hadn't bothered to knock, nor did she inquire if she was disturbing me. She flashed a smile, marched straight up to my desk and plopped down into the chair next to it.

"How are you doing?" she asked, dropping the novel onto the desk.

"Fine," I said. That wasn't the case, however. Deep down I knew what was coming. The rage was beginning its ascent up my throat.

"What can I do for you?" I asked.

"It's this book you assigned," she said.

"Yes?" I said, my voice rising.

"The author is Jewish," she said.

"So what?" I yelled.

She looked into my eyes and tried to hold them as she had many times before over a beer in the restaurant. I felt my eyelids narrow.

"You will read that book," I said, "or you will fail."

She looked away.

"I'm sorry," she said. "But I can't read a book about Jews by a Jew. I can't. Do you have another book?"

I jumped out of my chair, leaned down and brought my lips inches from hers.

"You idiot," I shouted. "You stupid, fucking idiot!"

The force of my breath threw back a wave of her hair and made her blink. She leaned away from me, her eyes wide and frightened, her lips quivering.

I wasn't finished.

"The world would be a better place if someone bulldozed over Poland and all the people in it. Now, get the hell out!"

Her jaw dropped, revealing that imperfect row of teeth that I had dreamt of fixing. She covered her mouth with one hand, grabbed the novel with the other. She stood and walked slowly to the door.

"I'm sorry," she said. "I'll read it. Of course I'll read it."

She looked back over her shoulder. Tears were pooled at the bottom of her eyes.

I returned her look with a glare. She left. I recounted the novels I had assigned, and was relieved that no other student had gotten Phillip Roth or Bernard Malamud. Not that it mattered. Caroline, my princess! Her prejudice and my reaction to it stabbed at my heart. I fell back into my chair. My knees felt like they were filled with water. I considered telling the director about what had happened. She was a vindictive woman, and would gladly expel any student for the slightest reason. But when she was finished with her phonetics class and entered the office, I said nothing.

The next day I scrapped the whole notion of the novels. Instead, I photocopied scores of short stories and force-fed the entire class a multicultural survey of contemporary American fiction. I was sure that every student by then knew what had transpired in my office the day before. I lectured them about America's diversity, how it was impossible to study the country, or its literature without consideration of its minorities. I indicated that we would be studying literature about Jews, and written by Jews, and that if I heard one anti-Semitic remark, or if anyone refused to read one of the stories, said person would fail the course. All knew that even one failed course meant a repeat of the entire first year's program, not just the course itself.

The rest of the semester passed without problem. However, I stopped meeting Caroline and the other students on Wednesdays. I occasionally bumped into her on the street, or at a party, but whatever "moments" we once shared were in the past only. She ended up with the highest grades in the college that first year, but she didn't return in the fall to complete her studies. She transferred to the teacher's college in Warsaw. Some slots had opened up there, and she never really wanted to leave Warsaw to begin with.

By the beginning of my second year teaching, I had nearly forgotten about the incidents of anti-Semitism the year before. I grew closer to a select number of students, who helped turn my second year in Poland into the time of my life. Who knows how anti-Semitic they were. It's possible, knowing my views, that they shielded their prejudices. However, I like to think they were among those the actor had exalted years before.

At the end of June, on the last day of my stay in Poland, Caroline showed up at my door. Friends and students had been shuttling in and out for the past week. I had been drunk every one of those days, and my lungs were raw with the two-packs-a-day cigarette habit I had developed. My eyes were bleary from lack of sleep, and the floor of my apartment was cluttered with boxes, gaping luggage and clothes ruined from two years of hand washing. A year before, I was anxious to get back to the States, but now I dreaded the idea that I might never again see the place I had called home for two years. Caroline's sudden appearance confused me even more. I hadn't seen her since she left Biala Podlaska the summer before.

"My God," I said, when I opened the door. "Caroline?"

"May I come in?" she asked. "Malgosia told me you were leaving, and I just had to come and say good-bye."

"All the way from Warsaw?" I asked.

"You are surprised," she said and smiled.

I invited her in and asked forgiveness for the mess. I made her a cup of tea. This action, along with my cigarette habit, made her exclaim that I had indeed become Polish. We settled in at my table, drank the tea, chain-smoked first my cigarettes then hers. We talked easily, me about my second year in Biala Podlaska, her about the college in Warsaw. She had picked up a British accent there. When I expressed displeasure at this, she laughed and went on for ten minutes about how much she had learned from me, that no teacher in Warsaw's college compared with me. I shook my head and blushed, then poured her some beer.

Caroline and I talked away the afternoon, never once mentioning Saul Bellow, his novel, or the troubles that occurred between us. Whatever animosity I once felt for her was gone. At that moment, with Caroline across from me, I stopped comprehending her words and just watched her mouth move and let the music of her fluency in the language caress my ears. I couldn't remember why I was leaving Poland, why I was about to take off in an airplane into oblivion like so much smoke.

I sat and took in Caroline's beauty and imagined guiding her to my bed, much as I had in Cracow three years earlier with the Jewish woman. I saw myself taking off her glasses, her earrings, her watch, stripping her of all possessions. Touching her smooth hair, soft enough for a child's pillow or a lining for an ambassador's coat, caressing her body, envisioning the skin of her breasts so transparent I would be able to trace the blue veins mapped around her nipples with my fingertips, but milky pale enough to soften the light from a 100-watt bulb. I saw my hand upon hers and our naked bodies entwined like so many millions of bodies before us.

Oftentimes, I think back on this episode: the ruins of my two years in Poland surrounding us, stale cigarette smoke and cheap beer soiling the air Caroline perfumed. I wasn't in love with her, I reasoned. She was no longer the "One." I had no desire to take her to America to fix her teeth. In the physical frailty of her body I was looking for a brief respite, as I had in the Cracow hostel, from my own human weakness. A scapegoat.

There are other nights, however, while I lay in bed, the Louisiana air, dense with hot moisture, pressing against the windows, when I picture Caroline at my door in Biala Podlaska. Then the gates to my heart swing open. There, love is exposed, too hot and bright to touch. To hold it for just one second, I would give up my ideals and all reason. I would face the scorn of my sister and her Jewish husband. I would bury deep my memories of Auschwitz and the people and ghosts I met there. For there is one part of me that insistently wonders if my feelings for Caroline are indicative of a complicity with anti-Semitism, that printed on my genetic make-up is something as awful as Original Sin. And maybe, just maybe, those two Jewish women I once toured Auschwitz with had reason to fear after all.

I cower under the weight of this realization and burrow deeper into my blankets. Not until I close the gates again, the heat and light fading from memory, does Caroline lapse into a dream. Then, I sleep.

Mark Lewandowski served as a Teacher Trainer at a college in Biala Podlaska, Poland, Group 3, from 1991-93. He is the author of the short story collection Halibut Rodeo. *Other stories and essays of his have appeared in many literary journals. Currently, he is an Associate Professor of Creative Writing at Indiana State University in Terre Haute.*

JEREMY BEER

* * *

Fiesta!

Just because the man is barreling down drunkenly on an icy road doesn't mean he can't find Osama Bin Laden on your behalf.

THANKS TO KAZAKHSTAN, I HAVE NOW SEEN A PAIR OF MY OWN pants frozen solid. I have also seen a frozen pigeon and a frozen dog. The windows in my dilapidated Soviet-era apartment, like those poor pants and dogs and pigeons, have also fully surrendered to the Kazakh winter. With an inch-thick sheet of ice covering the razor thin glass, I can no longer open my windows or see the vacant apartment building across the street. A sacrifice I am willing to make, however, as these frosty windows prevent the neighborhood kids from launching fire-crackers into my living room or yelling questions to me about Britney Spears from the street below. There has been a virtual halt in the little known game of "use this mirror to reflect the sun into the American guy's eyes while he makes breakfast."

Things in Kazakhstan seem to get better every day. Middle-aged women on the street with more gold teeth than enamel ones. Drunk old men stumbling around the bazaars. Cars driving seventy miles an hour on the snow-packed sidewalks (think "funny cars" at Three River stadium, but not as funny).

Everything that once seemed strange about this place is beginning to fade into normalcy. Just the other night I was talking
with my friend Sergei, and I got a rare glimpse of how hard
life here has been over the past fifteen years. We were playing chess, and he began to wistfully tell me about the months
he spent as a young man cleaning up Chernobyl in the days
following the meltdown. He was amused by my thinly veiled
horror as he described the tools and methods the Soviets had
employed to smooth over that disaster. Sergei proudly showed
me the Geiger counter the government had issued him as a
health measure. The idea was that once the counter registered
a certain level of exposure to radioactive isotopes, the person
wearing it would be removed from the clean-up site.

This counter would have been equally at home in a Cracker
Jack box as it was in Sergei's hand.

"You're lucky you don't have cancer," I told him.

"How do you know I don't?" he replied.

"Hum…good point." As if to illuminate this argument,
Sergei picked up his $3 guitar and played me some Elvis
Presley songs that I didn't know. Now, I don't mean to suggest
that everybody here is some sort of victim of the Soviet nuclear
program. For all I know they are, but they certainly don't act
like it. People here seem to have more serious problems to
contend with than the abstract thought of nuclear radiation.
Chief on this list of concerns is the lack of available work.
The other day, when I presented my friend Gulnara with the
observation that Russian people are much more willing to talk
to strangers than Americans, her response was a simple one.
Laughing, she said, "It's not that we are nicer people, we just
have more time to talk because nobody here has a job."

Whatever the case may be, people here love to stand around
and talk about politics, the weather, gossip, their favorite
Brazilian soap opera. This all leads to a pretty relaxed pace of

life. So far, my impression is that things here are not too bad, at least for the younger generations. Unfortunately, many of the *babushkas* (grandmothers) who lived their lives under the Soviet system now find themselves without pensions. There are hundreds of *babushki* with no savings, no families, and no possibility of work. The solution to their problems seems to be to sit in the snow and sell sunflower seeds in -40 degree weather. Hour after cold hour, stooped over bowls of sunflower seeds and three-cent single cigarettes. When talking to them, I try and remind myself that life, in many ways, could be much worse.

An important lesson, I suppose, in the context of current events. It seems to me that, at this point, people over here have kind of stopped caring about terrorism, et cetera. After the 9/11 attacks in the U.S., everybody in town was very consoling, and almost fearful of the American response. Then, about one month after the dust in lower Manhattan had cleared, public opinion in Central Asia began to harden. With the initial American response in Afghanistan, I was told more than once to "go home, because Americans are bad." But, in the past few months, people here have generally been more supportive of the United States.

In the short time I've been here, I've been offered more free food than I care to remember. I've been offered sweaters and potatoes. I've even been offered wives (plural). During a recent taxi ride, my large Kazakh driver offered me his Ford Fiesta ("a nice car, no?") and his skills as a driver/assassin to "go hunt for the Osama Bin Laden." I wasn't sure how to interpret this particular offer. Was this guy just speaking as a representative of the global community or did he actually want to drive his Ford Fiesta down to Afghanistan and give it a shot?

While speeding along in this man's car, I also couldn't help but wonder if he was sober enough to find the brake pedal. Sitting in the back seat, squeezed between two very large men,

I resigned myself to siphoning out what little oxygen I could from the heavy cigarette smoke engulfing the car. The thought crossed my mind that this might be the way I die: sitting sandwiched between two very large Kazakh men in the back of a smoky Ford Fiesta. It was only the incongruous waving of the driver's hands (shouldn't those be on the steering wheel?) that brought me out of my self-pitying trance. As he furiously shook a black piece of metal that he had removed from the glove box all around the Fiesta's cramped interior, he began mumbling about "Bruce Wellis" and "Arnol' Shwarzwegger." It was with more than a bit of concern when I realized he was holding a handgun.

Great. Now instead of just being melodramatic, I had a real reason to be afraid. I couldn't really escape, and I didn't really know how to conjugate the verb "to shoot" (as in "please don't shoot me, sir"). In my mind, I very clearly saw a black-and-white picture of my body, face down in some empty field of snow. My hands started getting sweaty. Then the car stopped, and everybody piled out. The driver came around the rear bumper of the Fiesta and put his arm around me. Together we walked down the sidewalk into a half-constructed building. Mental revision of photograph: substitute dead body in empty field with dead body in abandoned building.

I was served some tea, given the 25-cent tour of the abandoned building, and talked to at great length about the ladies' clothing store this man was planning to build in this very location. "Mannequines, just so," he said, cupping his hands around his own large imaginary breasts. After a brief speech on architecture and its importance in modern commerce, our friend even whipped out his hand-drafted plans for the store (which were strangely detailed and impressive).

By the time I had calmed down from the threat of death and gotten into this variety show, it was time to get back into the

Fiesta. We drove a little ways toward my neighborhood, and then I told them I had to go to the store so they might as well just let me out on the street. We skidded twenty feet on the snowy road to a tentative stop, and I took the opportunity to open the car door and hop out. No worse for wear, I thanked them for the tour, and we all exchanged hearty handshakes as if we had just concluded some sort of lucrative business deal. As I walked away, I realized with amazement that my experience in the Peace Corps was really only beginning.

Jeremy Beer served as an Economic and Small Business Development Volunteer in Kazakhstan, from 2001-03. Upon his return to the United States, Jeremy joined the Foreign Service as an Economic Officer, and has served in El Salvador, Germany, Washington, and the U.S. Mission to the United Nations (New York). Jeremy is married to Jessica Phillips Beer (Peace Corps Togo '01-'03) with whom he has a baby boy, Solomon.

JENNIFER MELEANA HEE

Losing Veronica

How does one explain a mental illness in a
country where nobody's heard of it?

I can't see her. On the bus. On the sidewalk. She would never leave
my side. This is wrong, all of it.
    "DESSY! WHERE'S VERONICA?"
    "She saw her friend and got off to talk to him."
    She is gone.

When I met Veronica, she was no longer living at an orphanage in the village Slatino, but with her uncle. I was the new liaison for Orphan Sponsorship International. My job was to make sure she had everything she needed to attend school like a normal sixteen year old—not a child abandoned as a baby by a schizophrenic mother.

We'd meet for pizza—Veronica's generously slathered with mayonnaise and ketchup. Afterward, we'd meandered about town, comparing Bulgarian fashion (pink) to American fashion (not as pink).

    "Let's buy you this cute t-shirt," I'd say.
    "It's too much money."

"No, it's not. And it's so unique and pink!"

We'd go back and forth. I always ended up getting her the shirt. She deserved it. She was thankful, frugal, and adorable. Three qualities you always look for in a favorite orphan.

Nine hours. How hopeless and incompetent I feel when I ask her simple questions and she stares at me with blank, heavy eyes. Eight hours. She eats nothing but vitamin C tablets. Throws them up. Six hours. There are killer mosquitoes on the bus, she says, help me. Five hours. She tries and tries to exit the bus. I sit her down. Time to shrink and collapse. Four hours. She sees people we know in stranger's faces. Two hours. I don't know her anymore. She thinks I am trying to deceive her. I promise I am taking her home, faster, I promise, stay with me, it's Jenn, remember? She can't breathe, won't listen, cries, throws up, is so not O.K.

To each other, we become someone else entirely.

Veronica was one of the few ethnic Bulgarian children who lived at the orphanage. Most of the kids—as in all Bulgarian orphanages—were of Romani, or gypsy, descent. Since the Roma minority is destitute, still suffering the effects of a history of persecution, families leave their children to be raised by the government. The municipality becomes mother and father, offering bread but not shoulders. Orphanages are decrepit motels where abandoned children raise themselves.

At Slatino, Veronica created structure, listened to her own rules. She would not prostitute herself to older village men, drink, smoke, or act out with no one to act out for. Veronica survived by telling herself she was better than this life. That she would finish school and not end up pregnant. Her best and only friend was a girl named Veli. For all the weekends I spent with Veronica and Veli—baking "Heavenly Pieces of Oatmeal and Chocolate Chip Happiness" cookies, laughing and listening to pop-folk *chalga* hits, Britney Spears and JLo, talking about boys and math homework—I would never have written their unfathomable sixteen years of life into the character sketches of these sweet, open, and trusting girls.

Veronica turned to me—"I can't breathe."
"What's the matter?"
"The diabetics."
"Which diabetics?"
"The ones on the bus."
"How do you know the people on the bus have diabetes?"
"Their smell—I can't breathe from their smell."
"I don't have any idea what you're talking about. Stop being crazy."

Veronica always wanted to know too much about my life—such as why I would leave Hawaii to come to Bulgaria. I'd say it was complicated, which meant, *girl, I can't even explain it to myself.* She wanted my advice on everything from drinking, to boyfriends, to piercing.

My answer to all three: in moderation.

Over the summer, one of our American sponsors came to Bulgaria. He wanted to take Dessy, the girl he sponsored to the seaside. I wanted to invite Veronica. Besides enjoying her company, I knew she was different—she could make it, survive impossible odds—she just needed mentors, positive experiences. She needed to know we believed in her.

We had to.

"Veronica—Why did you order food if you're not going to eat it?"
"We have to take it back."
"Where?"
"Home."

"*We're on the seaside!!!*"

"*We have to! The orphans are hungry.*"

"*What are you talking about? We're eight hours away from home—ice cream will MELT. We. Cannot. Take. This. Food. To. The. Orphans.*"

"*But we have to!!!*"

"*When we get home, we can buy them other food. It'll be fine. Everything will be fine.*"

Our first two days on the seaside were wonderful. We were one big happy Orphan Sponsorship family, the four of us spread out on the sand in Sozopol, eating too-salty corn on the cob, the girls renting paddleboats. We all loved the sun, our freedom.

On day three, I began to notice that Veronica had personality quirks I had not picked up on before. She cleaned an awful lot and folded and re-folded her clothes obsessively. *Girl just loves to fold*, I thought.

She tells me about a boy she has a crush on. I offer her my extremely insightful views on love. She laughs. She seems better. More relaxed. She points to a boy we pass and says he looked like Ivan—her crush. We keep going. Suddenly she stops. She thinks she really sees Ivan. Walking along this random street on the seaside. She begins to approach him, but suddenly realizes it isn't Ivan after all.

We shrug off the failed crush sighting, and get back on the bus to go home.

The girls sit in the back, and I sit in the front.

We arrive at our resort. I get off the bus. The sponsor gets off. Dessy gets off. Veronica does not.

My heart tears and tumbles out of my mouth.

I never get it back quite right.

She was gone. I made the call.

"Hi, Veronica's uncle. I lost your child."

We knew she wouldn't run away.

"*Losho. Mnogo, mnogo losho,*" he repeated, the severity of the situation realized in the simplest of words.

I went to the police.

Dessy called. Veronica had wandered back to a street vendor we had stopped at earlier. She was thrilled when I found her. She couldn't explain what happened. She was disoriented, wouldn't detach herself from my hip.

I knew I had to get her home.

We had to wait until the next morning for a bus. All night Veronica mopped, scrubbed, shook me awake and had to call Veli. Veli could help, Veli was on the seaside looking for her, mopped, scrubbed, where was Veli?, saw snakes on the ground, couldn't we?

What she saw, we couldn't.

"I'm just so confused."

"I know."

I got her home. She was immediately hospitalized. Doctors changed her medications, her diagnosis, her prognosis. She was schizophrenic. She was just depressed. She was very, very depressed. What was she?

Even though I know her breakdown wasn't our fault, none of us feel any resolution. What triggered her to become so ill? She had survived sixteen years of intolerable challenges and came out bright, beautiful, and strong.

I took Veli to see Veronica at the hospital. Veli couldn't understand why she wasn't "like Veronica" anymore. Later, Veli asked me, if I took her on an excursion one day, would this happen to her too?

I tried to explain mental illness; I couldn't explain.

When you leave a country, you can't tie up every loose thread. You have to leave what's done, undone. You are not leaving a job. You are leaving a life. You are leaving children you spent years with. They were little when you met, you remember when you couldn't understand one another, but you'd smile, and they'd smile, and there was always a way to say *I think you're wonderful.*

It's easy to cut the fraying edges, hem neatly the distance between what happened there and your life here. It is so far away; there's nothing you can do now. You tell yourself that; it must be true. I miss Veronica. But it's too much to think about her—the future she doesn't have. I can't zoom in and watch her in their small bloc apartment, her drugged dull eyes on the television, her hours a blank hum. I can't zoom out, see the rest of her life: her uncle dying, her adult years spent in another institution, this time psychiatric, her personality the whim of chemical concoctions. The Veronica I knew was potential bursting.

Is she a case study? Is she the girl who seemed stronger than all the rest, but was merely the confluence of genetics, a ticking etymological time bomb, an age of onset, the logical sum of her environment?

She is somewhere between the girl I knew and a dead girl.

Every time I saw Veli or Dessy since I lost Veronica, we tried to understand what happened together.

I'm still trying.

Epilogue: In June 2006, the local government closed the Slatino orphanage and the children were relocated to other orphanages in Bulgaria. This was heartbreaking, considering the children, having raised each other, were scattered, with no means to even communicate with one another. Veronica is still not in school, still medicated heavily, watching the world through her television. Her final diagnosis was schizophrenia, which her uncle chose not to tell her, as she is terrified of this illness and instead believes she suffers from depression. Veli was transferred to an orphanage in Sofia after Slatino closed. Shortly thereafter she got pregnant, had a baby, and is no longer attending school.

Jennifer Meleana Hee served as a Peace Corps Volunteer in Bulgaria, B-16, from 2004-07. She is currently a freelance writer (emphasis on the free!) and veganish cook living in Seattle with her completely unassimilated Bulgarian street dog. She can be reached at hee@post.harvard.edu.

JOHN KRAUKSOPF

Bakhshesh and the
Western Psyche

There is always another way to do things.

PEOPLE FROM WESTERN CULTURES ARE ALMOST ALWAYS DISCOM-
fited with cultural customs involving *"bakhshesh,"* a word
technically translated as "gift." However, with modern usage
in certain situations, it could also be accurately translated as
"tip" or even "bribe." I had a great deal of trouble with this
concept for the first two years I lived in Iran. Intellectually, I
understood, but viscerally I resisted. The concept is not really
foreign to my own culture, but the range of situations where
it is applied is different. We tip taxi drivers, waiters, and hair-
dressers without feeling unfairly treated. However, "tipping"
someone in a government office to speed up the issuance of
a permit sets off deep feelings of indignation in us. We pay
commissions and finder's fees, even hire third-party expediters,
without feeling ripped off. Yet we feel the *bakhshesh* expected
for various services in a country like Iran is a sign of incurable
corruption and decadence.

I had managed to live for almost all of my original twenty-
one-month assignment in Iran without once violating my

strong American sense of values regarding the payment of *bakhshesh*, and I was perversely proud of this fact as if I had triumphed in some kind of an elaborate game. However, in my last few hours prior to departure from the country, I simultaneously lost the game and gained substantive insight into the place for *bakhshesh* in the Iranian culture. Moreover, I gained confidence in my own ability to function within these cultural concepts. The odd part about the experience for me was that, when it was all over, my culturally American fear of feeling corrupted, abused and ripped-off was not justified.

The incident began when my homeward trip to the United States was drastically rearranged by the Six-Day War of June 1967. I had planned to travel through Iraq, Lebanon and Jordan, but this route suddenly became impossible. I decided to go, instead, through the Soviet Union. Advance arrangement of the complete trip through the official Intourist travel agency in Tehran was required, and this typically took a month or more. I believe I hold the all-time speed record for Russian travel approval by getting my itinerary confirmed and the required paperwork completed in only eight days. The travel agent got the approval by cable from Moscow on Thursday. He managed to issue the Russian air tickets, train tickets, hotel coupons, meal coupons, and tour coupons by the close of business that day. No business was conducted on the Friday Sabbath, but the agent plowed through the Russian visa issuance process on Saturday.

Unfortunately, he wasn't able to get the steamship tickets issued for the trip across the Caspian Sea from Bandar Pahlavi to Baku without the Russian visas in hand. By the time he actually had the visas, the steamship office in Tehran had closed and would not be open again until Monday, the day of the weekly sailing from the Caspian port 250 miles to the north-west of Tehran. My travel agent told me not to worry about this one incomplete detail as I held confirmed reservations, and I could buy the tickets at the shipping company's office at the port on Monday. The ship sailed at 4:00 P.M., so I arranged to get to the port before noon in order to have plenty of time to take care of this business.

After two years in Iran, I had become accustomed to the inescapable delays in getting things done. Peace Corps Volunteers wryly referred to the pace of life in our adopted country in terms of "one-thing days" and "two-thing days." A "three-thing day" was a rare anomaly and a cause for celebration. However, I seemed to be on a roll because of the success I had had in speedily making all of the Russian trip arrangements in Tehran, and I had grown a little careless. My four-hour allowance for steamship ticket purchase turned out to be not nearly enough.

Arriving at the customs shed for exit formalities, I was asked for my steamship tickets. I told the inspector that I had reservations, and I would be purchasing the tickets here. He stopped processing my papers and informed me that the ticket office had closed for lunch and the Iranian version of a *siesta*. It wouldn't be open again until 4:00 P.M. I pointed out that the ship sailed at 4:00 P.M. The inspector nodded that he understood and suggested that I wait for the next Monday's sailing. He could do nothing to help me get the tickets, but without them, he could not continue with the exit formalities. I began some strident and noisy (but culturally appropriate) protests that attracted several other officials from their posts in the largely empty customs building, but produced no action on the solution to my problem. The consensus of all concerned, as well as those who were just kibitzing, was that I would have to wait until the following Monday's sailing. I backed off a little and went into consultation with my Peace Corps companion on the trip and some friends who had accompanied us to bid farewell.

Our strategy session was not getting anywhere when the porter who had brought our baggage in from the taxi deferentially approached me and said that he had overheard my problem and was sure he could help me. In Iran, there is almost always a "way" around this kind of problem. At that moment, I sensed this modest worker would be my guide to discover such a "way."

He signaled me to follow him, and he led me through the customs building and out onto the quay. I left my friends with the bags and trailed after the shuffling steps of the porter's sandals, which were made from discarded tires. About 150 meters past the point where the Russian ship was moored, we stopped in front of the last of several staff houses inside the port compound. The porter said this was the house of the director of the port, and surely this man could help me. The porter rang the bell, and the port director himself, dressed in his pajamas, opened the door. The porter mumbled a few obsequious apologies for disturbing the port director's rest, but noted that I had an urgent problem and then retreated backwards down the porch steps, leaving me to articulate my problem.

The director invited me into a room where he had an impressive desk and a couple of Western-style office chairs along with a picture of the Shah and several other symbols of his authority. From the handy ever-present *samovar*, he personally served the customarily scalding-hot tea in small *estecans* (straight-sided glasses) perched in elegant engraved brass holders. The tea was accompanied by a brass plate piled with lump sugar so I could sweeten the beverage to the socially required degree. We spoke for many minutes about many things. He, too, opined that I would have to wait until the following Monday to make my trip to Baku.

He did, however, keep talking. I recalled my two years of service for the Ministry of Education in Khuzistan Province.

I spoke of the many kindnesses shown to me by the many friends I had made in my adopted country. I noted that having my leave-taking colored and having all my plans for the trip to the Soviet Union destroyed by a trivial problem such as how to get the tickets seemed unnecessary. I knew that there had to be a solution. Surely someone with the power and authority of the director of the Bandar Pahlavi port could help me. He observed that, although he was the director of the port, he had no knowledge of something as mundane as issuing tickets. I pointed out that one aspect of his job was to promote commerce and trade with the Soviet Union. It would truly be unfortunate to have all the arrangements that his Russian colleagues had made for the two Americans go to waste.

Finally, my host reached into the drawer of his big desk and pulled out some ticket stock. He said that he had never written a ticket before, and he wasn't sure he would be able to do it right. However, he wanted to help me since I had done so much for his country. After fumbling for some time with a tariff book, he asked me for 240 tomans (about $32 at the time) for the tickets. I said that I did not have any more Iranian currency, but I had U.S. dollars to pay for the tickets. The recently brightening mood of our conversation darkened abruptly. The director then placed the ticket stock back in the drawer and resignedly said that I would have to wait and go on next Monday's departure.

The director conceded that he did have the authority to issue tickets in an emergency, but noted that he was not a bank. Although he was the director of an international port in a country where black-market dollars were prized, he professed to have no knowledge of what the exchange rate for dollars might be. He wouldn't be able to verify a rate until 4:00 P.M when the national bank downtown reopened after the *siesta*, and that would be too late for this week's sailing.

We seemed to be back at square one, but the director did keep the conversation open. Again I recalled my dedicated service, the wonderful Iranians I had met, how sad I would feel if I couldn't make the journey I had so carefully planned, and how some of the Iranian administrators I had worked with seemed to be clever enough to overcame apparently impossible obstacles. I got out two $20 bills, new, crisp and straight from the safe at Peace Corps headquarters in Tehran and began folding and unfolding them with one hand.

After a time, my host stated that he truly liked me and trusted me. Therefore, he would believe me if I insisted that these two strange green pieces of paper were really worth as much as 240 tomans. As he retrieved the ticket stock from the drawer, I laid the two twenties on the edge of his desk where they remained until I left the house. No mention was made of any change from the $40. With many warm words of gratitude and farewell, I left the director to resume his nap. With an enormous sense of relief, I emerged from almost an hour in the dusky room into the bright sunshine and salt air of the quay.

Eager to get back to the customs shed and report my triumph to my waiting companions, I sprang down the porch steps only to be called up short by my erstwhile guide, the porter, an accomplice whom I had completely forgotten by this time. He had been patiently squatting by some cargo crates, waiting for me to emerge with my problem solved. The porter was quite certain I would be so grateful to the person who had shown me the "way" to solve my problem that I would make sure this person was properly compensated. He told me as much.

I had in my pocket a set of one example of each denomination of Iranian paper money intended as a souvenir. I chose a ten-toman bill (worth $1.30 U.S. and about 1.5 times the daily wage of a laborer at that time) and passed it to him. At first, he protested that his help had been worth much more than ten tomans to me. Knowing from two years' experience that this amount was generous in the cultural context and that only foreigners would have gotten that kind of an aggressive reaction to the amount of *bakhshesh* offered, I scolded the porter for being greedy and told him he had been lucky to get the ten tomans already given to him. This signaled clearly to him that, although an obvious foreigner, I knew what I was doing.

My guide instantly returned to his culturally correct obsequious demeanor, showered me with thanks, and returned to the customs shed to take charge of our bags which would now make the 4:00 P.M. sailing.

John Krauskopf taught English in boys' secondary schools in Ahwaz, the provincial capital of Khuzistan Province in Iran, Group 6, from 1965-68. In 1969, he returned to Iran for the in-country portion of that year's Peace Corps training where he supervised a teacher-training summer school. After ten years of involvement in international student exchange with Experiment for International Living, he spent more than two decades as the foreign student adviser and director of the English as a Second Language Institute in Millbrae, California, before retiring. He is now writing a book about his international experiences. Earlier this year John was appointed corporate secretary of the Western Railway Museum in Solano County, California. He authored the article "Christmas on the Mekong" that appeared in the November 2004 issue of Peace Corps Writers *as part of the ongoing series "War and Peace Corps."*

PART FIVE

SUSTAINABLE PEACE

MARTIN B. TRACY

The Power of Tradition—
The Peril of Exclusion

The most valuable changes in the course of a service are
sustainable. The ones the Volunteer makes in the country…
and the ones the country makes in the Volunteer.

ON AN EARLY SUMMER MORNING IN 1966, A FEW MILES FROM THE
outskirts of the ancient town of Kirşehir, Turkey, the sun rising
rapidly in the blue Central Anatolian sky, our friend Gunaydin,
a local government official responsible for rural water management, steps from the yellow Land Rover, strides purposefully
across the steppe, peers into the valley below, and points a long
finger at the village slumbering below. Perhaps for a millennium, he explains to my wife and me, the source of potable
water for this village has sprung from the earth two kilometers
away. The life-giving liquid has always been transported from
the spring to the village by women, and, according to the villagers, always should be, for it is clearly Allah's wish for there
to be a distance between the water and the village. The burden
borne by women in their daily task is viewed as a negligible
earthly sacrifice expected of religious devotion amid the promise of physical and spiritual pleasures in the afterlife.

Guynadin noted that such religious attitudes, as well as local
culture and history, create significant barriers to changing the

ebb and flow of village traditions. These obstacles hinder government efforts to ease access to water and relieve women of this
arduous chore. Trying to be helpful, the government had come
to the villagers with plans to build a pipeline in keeping with
national goals of modernizing rural infrastructures. However,
the leadership in the village, i.e., the male elders, rejected the
idea out of hand as an affront to Allah and tradition. In response
to having its logical, rational, and just plan for a pipeline so
arbitrarily dismissed, the government decided that the villagers
were clearly too backward to know what was good for them.
Moreover, since the effectiveness of the water management
agency would be evaluated on the number of construction
projects in rural areas, it had little choice but to move forward
with the pipeline. Thus, the government brought in the military
to force the villagers to construct the pipeline at gunpoint. Of
course, the military left when construction was finished and,
shortly afterwards, the pipeline was dismantled by the villagers.

What went wrong, according to Guynadin, was the failure
to engage the village community in decisions about what they
needed or how to meet the needs. His government agency's
intentions to modernize rural communities "for their own
good" ignored the wishes of the community within their religious, traditional, and historical contexts. Moreover, excluding
the community in the decision-making process lost an opportunity to establish village recognition and ownership of the
problem and acceptance of responsibility for dealing with it.
Of course, developing a foundation built around community
assessment and problem solving is time consuming and takes
resources and expertise that the government felt were less
expedient than taking quick and decisive action to construct.
However, such a short-term approach actually made the project much less likely to succeed because the community leaders and stakeholders had no ownership or self-recognition of
either the problem or the solution.

Guynadin challenged us to recall the lessons of Central Anatolian antiquity, which our Peace Corps instructors had covered in our training program at Robert College in Istanbul, stressing the importance of understanding something of the history of the rise of the Turkish peoples in Anatolia. We were taught that knowledge of the historical context of the people, towns, and villages where we would be living was critical to our appreciation of the culture and traditions that would so profoundly impact our capacity to work effectively in our community. This sound advice was reiterated by our friend who wanted us to consider how little the traditions of the village had been impacted over centuries of foreign domination. His point was that the comings and goings of ordinary events and activities of daily life change little even under conditions of great duress and foreign domination. In the case of the village in question, he surmised, this characteristic of village life extended to traditional means of conveying water.

Guynadin did not know the precise age of the village, but it most certainly dated at least back to the ninth century A.D. with the arrival of the nomadic Turkic tribes from Central Asia, followed by the Seljuk Turks spreading the message of Islam westward from their empire in Iran and Mesopotamia. The coming of the Seljuks culminated in the defeat of the Byzantines by Alp Arslan in 1071, paving the way for the emergence of the Ottoman Empire in 1299. Significantly, however, since that time, daily life among the generations of the stable number of families inhabiting the village has altered little. Nor have their means of livelihood or cultural traditions substantively changed. Under such time-honored conditions, cultural or social change of any kind is not just incremental or gradual; it is glacial.

A visitor in the thirteenth century would have observed life in the village that looks much like it did in the mid-1960s. As then, he would have walked through the narrow streets of the village and seen the cobblers at their daily task, sitting in their flimsy lean-to's, impervious to the harsh hot summers and cold winters using their punch, nails, and hammers to repair footwear. As their ancestors had done for hundreds of years, the cobblers worked, along with their friends, neighbors, and relatives, acquiescent to their fate, pausing periodically to enjoy a hot, sweet tea served in a tulip-shaped glass along with a bite of oven fresh bread or a *taze* (fresh) *simit*—a large ring shaped bread covered with sesame seeds. He would have seen the village men tending their sheep as it has been done for millennia. He would have observed little difference in the way farmers prepared the soil for planting or harvesting their fields of wheat or their crops of beans and chickpeas. He would have had his daily morning constitutional squatting over an open hole in the floor washing himself, using only his left hand. He would have drunk water that had been carried from the spring by the village women and eaten food prepared using water from the same source.

By showing us an example of how the government had failed to bring about change in tradition and culture, Guynadin had given his young, well-meaning, and idealistic Peace Corps friends from rural America a valuable lesson not only about the inherent difficulty of transferring processes of change from one culture to another, but the quandaries involved in transferring seemingly rational ideas from modern government to rural communities. Returning from the village to his rambling house near Kirşehir, we sat on the porch and watched a stork fly in and out of its enormous nest on top of the chimney. We took the lemon water offered us to wash our hands and remove the dust from our faces and sipped the hot sweetened tea his wife had served with a dish of baklava.

The experience with Guynadin made a deep impression upon us. We gave serious thought to the notion that sustainable change is more about process than quick results. In other words, it is the manner in which ideas are planted and nurtured within the community that will determine the success or failure of an initiative. Moreover, it is critical that the community be involved in the decision-making process from assessment to implementation, evaluation, and reassessment.

As it happened, in the fall of 1966, we had an opportunity to experiment with this approach to village development, as we were relocated from the relatively urban town of Kirşehir to the smaller, rural Cappadocian community of Urgüp. This came about when the teaching jobs we held in Kirşehir were filled by native teachers and we were asked to go to a rural area where the Turkish teachers of English did not particularly like to live. While, as in Kirşehir, our primary job was to teach English as a second language in the high school, in Urgüp we had a number of opportunities to be involved in community projects. In particular, we became engaged in initiatives to promote tourism in what was then a fledging enterprise, although it has now become a major activity since Urgüp is the gateway to Cappadocia, including sites at Göreme, Nevşehir, Avanos, Zelva, Čavuşin, and Učhisar.

These are magical places where in the shadows of the fairy chimneys—mushroomlike towers of tuff precariously balancing basalt balls of volcanic rock—homes and monasteries were dug into the volcanic cones, towers, caves, and walls. The isolation and unique beauty of the area provided early Christian monks with the perfect place to establish self-supporting, protected communities. The dug-out caves were ideal places from the sixth to the thirteenth centuries to paint their mysterious iconoclastic geometrical patterns followed by images of Christ and saints. When the Christian communities were replaced by the Muslim Seljuk Turks, the paintings were covered over, but many have since been restored and are a major tourist attraction.

However, when we were there in the mid-1960s, the pace of life was similar to that of the village near Kirşehir to which Guynadin had introduced us. Like it, life in the rural communities in Cappadocia was structured around tradition and resistive to the social disruption brought about by changes that threatened that tradition, including education and tourism. As in the 1960s, a visitor to the region in the eleventh or twelfth centuries would have seen the men in the villages riding on the backs of their donkeys down the dusty valley roads maneuvering around the fairy chimneys heading toward the pigeon holes housed in the volcanic walls to gather the guano to fertilize their gardens of cabbages, onions, tomatoes, peppers, and melons, as well as their orchards of apricots and apples. The visitor would have heard the donkeys' braying that periodically interrupted the silence of the night and the morning clucking and crowing of the free range chickens scratching in the dirt.

In this setting, we took a deliberate and slow approach to introducing new ideas by first making friends in the community and participating in the local traditional life. After getting to know some families through our students, fellow teachers, and administrators, we would take part in such daily rituals as the evening stroll. My wife would put on a coat and scarf, regardless of the weather, and hold hands with her women friends as they walked through the town engaging in conversation about children and other family related topics. I would also walk with my male friends, several steps in front of our wives. We would link arms and speak of local economic issues, local and national politics, and how the weather was impacting the crops.

After classes in the high school, we would often go our separate ways. My wife, who taught in a girls' vocational college, would spend quality time with married women in their homes discussing topics ranging from homemaking, raising children, and coping with husbands to methods of family planning. Many of my late afternoons and early evenings were spent in a coffeehouse with the men, playing backgammon and *bezique*, sipping hot tea. In sharing a meal in a local restaurant, despite the Islamic taboo against consumption of alcohol, I might have a beer or drink a fine dry wine that was a product of locally grown grapes processed by the Kavaklidere winery. But not so for my wife, as custom frowned on women drinking.

On occasion we were invited into modest homes where we sat on an earthen floor around great copper plates eating rice pilaf, garbanzo beans, stuffed green peppers, and garlic yogurt from communal plates and bowls, with our legs folded, as best we could, in a yoga position atop closely woven Turkish kilims decorated with geometric symbols reflecting their values, dreams, and culture. It is in such traditional settings that we established a bond of trust and camaraderie that led to opportunities to modify traditional approaches to dealing with tourists as a source of revenue and business. I was able to reinforce relationships with businessmen in the community by offering local merchants English classes in the evenings.

The interaction with these men led to discussions concerning the growing number of tourists from Scandinavia and Germany, who came to Cappadocia not only to explore the marvelous moonscape and early Christian cave dwellings, but also to see the newly discovered underground cities near the village of Derinkuyu. It is not known precisely when the underground communities south of Goreme were constructed or even why. But it is now known that these immense labyrinths, connected by miles of tunnels, descended ten stories into the earth and held up to 20,000 people. They may have been built by the Byzantine emperors and the local inhabitants to escape the pillages of the marauding Huns in the fifth century A.D. When the danger had passed, upon leaving the subterranean refuge, our villagers would have returned to their routine lives and customs.

While many tourists began their visit to Cappadocia in Ürgüp to see these wonders, they would typically come in groups by bus, see the sites, and depart, buying mostly trinkets and the occasional copper plate from the local shops. While there were several restaurants in town, their simple décor and rustic ambiance were not all that appealing to tourists, and the restaurants got little business from them. One obvious problem was that the restaurants did not have menus, and a foreigner who did not speak Turkish had great difficulty in knowing what or how to order. This was despite the fact that they offered good, wholesome, and tasty typical Turkish fare of vegetables and lamb.

Over a period of several months, my wife and I had many occasions at the coffeehouses or in restaurants to engage the owners, the mayor, the high school principal, and local businessmen in conversations about tourism. These informal discussions served the role of brainstorming sessions that led to a number of ideas about improving ways of securing more of the tourists' money for the local businesses, especially the restaurants. The first proposal was to have menus written in both Turkish and English which my wife and I were glad to provide. This was followed by the suggestion that restaurants could improve their appeal by offering tourists a pre-packaged box lunch that could be taken with them on their treks around the area since, at that time, the nearby villages provided virtually no access to food and drink.

Both of these seemingly small initiatives made a significant difference in the volume of business, while adding to our credibility and trust among the town's businessmen and politicians. The "social capital" that resulted from this activity, along with our respected position as teachers, served us well in many ways, enabling us to be more effective agents of incremental change. One indication that we had established ourselves as members of the community was an event that happened a few months before our departure in 1967. I had been invited to attend an all-male dinner in honor of a Turkish physician from Ankara who was a native of Urgüp and was home for a visit with family and friends. During the meal, the *raki* (a strong distilled alcoholic beverage aromatized with anise-seed mixed with water) flowed freely, making for a festive occasion. However, when it came time for the good doctor to make a toast he began blandly enough, but then proceeded to berate all Americans as spies who, looking directly at me, were not to be trusted. Coming to my rescue, my school and business friends ridiculed the doctor's assertions and told him that I was one of "us." The toast abruptly ended with the sudden sounds of the music of the *bağlama* and *zuma*. We all stood, linked arms, and broke into a Turkish folk dance, followed, of course, by more *raki* and more toasts to prosperity, family, and the Turkish way of life.

When we left Turkey for graduate studies in the fall of 1967 at the University of Illinois at Champaign/Urbana, we continued our interest in community development in rural areas in the U.S., as well as in emerging economies around the world. Our Peace Corps experience and graduate education has led to a lifetime of looking for effective ways of bringing about change without making enemies, as Woodrow Wilson once observed. For us, the lessons of the ill-fated water pipeline in the Turkish village near Kirşehir and the lack of business and entrepreneurial know-how to meet the needs of tourists in Urgüp have been that sustainable change of tradition and "the way that things have always been done" in a community must be a product of a process in which the community itself is intrinsically involved. Moreover, how that is achieved is locality specific, i.e., the process of effective change is profoundly dependent on local culture, tradition, and resources.

With regards to proven good practices, our experience has been that there are always model programs in or near targeted communities from which valuable lessons can be drawn and shared. Good practices help all those involved in establishing or improving projects how to identify barriers to sustainable initiatives and how to overcome them. They provide a model of a successful process; introduce innovative ideas; and, yes, typically give a basis for a pragmatic approach to problem-solving.

The failure of the village water pipeline project and the modest success of early tourism in Cappadocia are constant reminders of our formative years in the Peace Corps in Turkey and the difficulty of altering deeply engrained traditions with or without the cooperation of a community. We remain forever indebted to the Peace Corps and the Turkish people of Kirşehir and Urgüp, especially Guynadin for his willingness to share his own administrative frustrations with two eager, but naïve, foreigners in great need of all the advice they could get. The experience set in motion a lifelong process of inquiry and uncertainty mixed with optimism and, occasionally, success.

Martin B. Tracy, Ph.D., has conducted research on social security and policy issues in an international context and on community-based social services in economically developing nations. He has held professional positions with the U.S. Social Security Administration's Office of International Policy and the International Social Security Association, and is a consultant with the International Labour Organization. His academic positions have been with the University of Iowa, Southern Illinois University, and the University of Kentucky. He was a Fulbright Senior Specialist in Social Work at the University of Bucharest, Romania, in Fall 2004.

Acknowledgments

THIS WORK IS ONLY POSSIBLE BECAUSE OF THE LOVE AND SUPPORT of those around me, as well as those who saw something in me and gave me the opportunities to prove myself and build the breadth of experience I have today. I am indebted to all of them.

All those involved with the project deserve acknowledgement. Jane Albritton, who in envisioning this project back in 2007, took a chance on me while I was still serving out my last year of service in Kazakhstan and invited me to be the editor of this volume after seeing a blog I kept online. Without her endless patience, electing to continue working with me despite the countless delays and obstacles my own life threw in the way, I would have never have had the pleasure to be a part of this process, and for that, I am grateful. In addition, I must acknowledge Susan Brady's tireless efforts as Production Director and Chris Richardson's brilliant design work; their contributions were crucial to the final production of this volume. Finally, I wish to thank all of the contributors of stories who took the time to write and share their personal experiences with the world.

Though it's only been three years since I've left the Peace Corps, I suspect that my time in Kazakhstan will continue to be one of the most formative experiences of my life. My involvement and desire to be a part of the project would not have been possible had I not had the opportunity to be inspired by the amazing people that were a part of my life during and after my Peace Corps service.

First, thanks go out to my ever patient family, who (in their Chinese ways) supported my decision to join and stay in the Peace Corps. My mother, Julie Chen, who faithfully accompanied me to Peace Corps information sessions despite her underlying worry about me being abroad for two years, eventually relented and allowed me to go, though I later realized she had taken out a life insurance policy on me during my service. My father, David Chen, was also supportive, and he believed in my judgment and reassured my mother, despite his underlying suspicion that the Peace Corps was a front for the CIA. Parents show their love in so many ways. I owe a debt of gratitude to my sister, Jennifer Chen, who took care of the home and my family while I went off on my adventure. In addition, the rest of my family, all of the aunts, uncles, cousins, and grandparents who gave me messages of support and approval.

Second, my love of the Peace Corps would not have been possible without the people in Kazakhstan who accepted my service, and treated me as one of their own. The hardworking foreign language teachers and students at ВКГУ who made me look forward to going to work every day were crucial, especially Olessya Bogun, Irina Suprunova Teijeiro, Avian Ussenova, Assel Beysembinova, Aray Saniyazova, Yelena Chzan, Marina Basova, and Saule Slyambekovna. Dinara Matkarimova deserves particular recognition for her unyielding support of my work as my counterpart, and always took every effort to ensure that I was both comfortable and happy, even when it meant challenging administrative bureaucracy.

Malika Kazybayeva, one of my most intelligent, talented, and outspoken students, reached out to me within the first few months of my service to become one of my closest local friends. Her family, who always welcomed me to their home, taught me how having a joyful, supportive household contributed to a person's success.

Dana Kaerbayeva was one of the most fearless women that I've ever met and whose unwavering support of my work as well as my cooking kept me going throughout my service. Dana will forever be the known to me as the woman who saved my life, after she and her family protected me while I was being tailed by local thugs and government agents. Those incidents aside, Dana's family deserves credit for their continued, famous Kazakh hospitality.

The Kim family in Almaty, Ira, Gosha, Mila, and Stella, took me in as their own son and will forever remain my family.

I also wish to thank the tireless local staff at the Peace Corps, Kazakhstan office, who went the extra mile to support and inspire me, especially Ufilmalik (Ufie) Turguzhanova, Dr. Victor Britcov, and Galina Petrova. Additionally, the American staff, particularly Linda Schmitz and Barbara Vik also deserves recognition for their support during my service.

Special thanks go to Kris Besch and John Sasser, two country directors that I have had the pleasure to work under. Their level of professionalism and dedication to volunteers and local staff was unparalleled, something that I can only hope to emulate in the future.

Other volunteers that I met during service and who kept me going in good times and bad were also crucial to the development of this book. Samuel Robinson, a Kaz-18, who but for the Peace Corps, I would have never had been friends with, provided me with such new insight and perspectives on life and friendship that it still influences my actions today. Heather Murphy also weathered many storms with me, both in Kazakhstan and in the United States, and she remains one of the most intelligent, empathetic, (and possibly "хитрый") women I have ever met. Daniel Ach, my first guide to Ust-Kamenogorsk and my inspiration for befriending future newcomers. My dearest friends from the Kaz-17s and others from the East Kazakhstan region who toughed out their service with me and were never-ending sources of laughter and friendship, in no particular order: Ashli Gold, Jack and Amy Simms, Amanda Weber, Margaret Burke, Dorothy Seidel Hooke, Michael Hancock, Meghan Mcgee, Andrew VanLew, Yen Le, Kristin Ruger, Tom Dalcher, Hilary Murphy, Mary McWhirter, and Alex Briggs.

Last, other people who provided me with important levels of personal support during these past few years of book writing also deserve recognition. Sarah Connelly, who worked with me on a multitude of issues since my return from Kazakhstan was incredibly important to my self-development and understanding of myself. Nancy Stuart, my ever-patient law school professor, saw my strengths and extended me the opportunities to use them.

Finally, Tara Roberts must be acknowledged for her patience, love, support, and (minimal) complaint when I elected to work on this book instead of spending time with her. She was invaluable in giving me feedback on the introduction and several other parts of this volume.

It is not fair to simply say that without all of these people in my life I would not have produced this volume—it's that without all of these people in my life I would not be the person I am today. I will pay it forward.

Story Acknowledgments

"September 12th" by Dara Ross published with permission from the author. Copyright © 2011 by Dara Ross.

"Peace Corps Expectations" by Diana J. LaViolette published with permission from the author. Copyright © 2011 by Diana J. LaViolette.

About the Editor

Jay Chen served as a University English teacher at East Kazakhstan State University in Ust-Kamenogorsk, Kazakhstan, from 2005 to 2008 as a member of Kaz-17. Prior to the Peace Corps, Jay received dual degrees from the University of California, Berkeley, in Political Science and Legal Studies. Sometime in his junior year, Jay realized that there was probably much more to life than making money or going on directly to graduate school, and he began to explore the Peace Corps as an option. Coupled with three years of experience tutoring other students in writing, Jay started the year-long application process and was off in a plane to Kazakhstan within a month of his graduation.

During his three years of service, Jay taught university-level English, Academic Reading and Writing, American Culture, and Mandarin Chinese to students training to be foreign language teachers and translators. During this time, Jay introduced his students to the works of J.D. Salinger and George Orwell, established the university's first English academic writing course, the first English student-run newspaper, and helped the students establish a Student Community Service Corps on campus.

In 2007, Jay extended his service for another year to complete the construction and programming of an Academic Resource Center and Technological Training Facility for the Foreign

Languages Department. Jay also worked on women's development programs in local villages surrounding Ust-Kamenogorsk.

Jay endured -40 degree Siberian winters, developed a taste for horse meat, was tailed by gangsters and government intelligence agents, was charmed by local women and their respective families, and developed a love and respect for the cultures of Central Asia.

Following his service, Jay returned to San Francisco and attended University of California, Hastings College of the Law, where he served as Co-President of the Hastings Public Interest Law Foundation and worked with local non-profit law firms on numerous international human rights legal issues, including applications for asylum and legal status for survivors of human trafficking and domestic violence. In addition to serving on the Pro Bono Committee, Jay encouraged and mentored several other law students to use their skills to contribute to the public interest. He was named the 2009 Sidney Weinstock Public Interest Fellow, as well as recognized as an Outstanding Pro Bono Volunteer by both UC Hastings and the San Francisco Bar Association.

He also spent time in Shanghai, China, working on foreign direct investment and corporate labor matters. In May 2011, Jay received his Juris Doctor from University of California, Hastings, with a concentration in International Law and continues to this day to speak about the work of the Peace Corps as part of the Third Goal. Jay is currently pursuing a career in Washington D.C. in international development.